U.S.A. IMMIGRATION GUIDE

Fifth Edition

Ramon Carrion
Attorney at Law

SPHINX® PUBLISHING
AN IMPRINT OF SOURCEBOOKS, INC.®
NAPERVILLE, ILLINOIS
www.SphinxLegal.com

Fifth Edition, 2004

Published by: **Sphinx® Publishing, An Imprint of Sourcebooks, Inc.®**

Naperville Office
P.O. Box 4410
Naperville, Illinois 60567-4410
630-961-3900
Fax: 630-961-2168
www.sourcebooks.com
www.SphinxLegal.com

This publication is designed to provide accurate and authoritative information in regard to the subject matter covered. It is sold with the understanding that the publisher is not engaged in rendering legal, accounting, or other professional service. If legal advice or other expert assistance is required, the services of a competent professional person should be sought.

From a Declaration of Principles Jointly Adopted by a Committee of the American Bar Association and a Committee of Publishers and Associations

This product is not a substitute for legal advice.

Disclaimer required by Texas statutes.

Library of Congress Cataloging-in-Publication Data
Carrion, Ramon.
  U.S.A. immigration guide / by Ramon Carrion.-- 5th ed.
    p. cm.
  Includes index.
  ISBN 1-57248-392-X (alk. paper)
  1. Emigration and immigration law--United States--Popular works. 2. Visas--United States--Popular works. I. Title: USA immigration guide. II. Title.

KF4819.6 .C37 2004
342.7308'2--dc22

                    2004024493

Printed and bound in the United States of America.
VHG Paperback — 10 9 8 7 6 5 4 3 2 1

Dedication

To the memory of my beloved father, Ramon, and to my mother, Leonor, who were the first and most important "immigrants" in my life. They not only had the vision of a new life in the United States, but also the courage to implement that vision. In the spirit of my parents' dreams and motivations, this book is also dedicated to all of you who aspire to participate in the American dream.

Acknowledgment

I wish to express my sincere gratitude to Steve Rushing for his insightful and yet very human cartoons; Virginia Kohl for the excellent editing work that she did on the manuscript; my assistant, Paula Harshberger, for her patience and originality in solving many of the format challenges that this book presented; my daughter Andrea M. Carrion for her assistance in making the editorial changes; and finally, to Mark Warda, for his encouragement to write this book in the first place.

CONTENTS

Historical Context
Legal Context
U.S. Consulates Abroad
United States Citizenship and Immigration Services
Inspection, Exclusion, and Removal (Deportation)
General Grounds for Exclusion
Distinction between Immigrant and Nonimmigrant Visas
The Problem of Intent
Unauthorized Employment

Numerical Limitation or Quota System
Family-Sponsored Immigrants
Employment-Based Immigrants
The Labor Certification Process
Special Problems
Child Status Protection Act

Using Self-Help
Law Books

Before using a self-help law book, you should realize the advantages and disadvantages of doing your own legal work and understand the challenges and diligence that this requires.

The Growing Trend

Rest assured that you won't be the first or only person handling your own legal matter. For example, in some states, more than seventy-five percent of the people in divorces and other cases represent themselves. Because of the high cost of legal services, this is a major trend and many courts are struggling to make it easier for people to represent themselves. However, some courts are not happy with people who do not use attorneys and refuse to help them in any way. For some, the attitude is, "Go to the law library and figure it out for yourself."

We write and publish self-help law books to give people an alternative to the often complicated and confusing legal books found in most law libraries. We have made the explanations of the law as simple and easy to understand as possible. Of course, unlike an attorney advising an individual client, we cannot cover every conceivable possibility.

Cost/Value Analysis

Whenever you shop for a product or service, you are faced with various levels of quality and price. In deciding what product or service to buy, you make a cost/value analysis on the basis of your willingness to pay and the quality you desire.

When buying a car, you decide whether you want transportation, comfort, status, or sex appeal. Accordingly, you decide among such choices as a Neon, a Lincoln, a Rolls Royce, or a Porsche. Before making a decision, you usually weigh the merits of each option against the cost.

When you get a headache, you can take a pain reliever (such as aspirin) or visit a medical specialist for a neurological examination. Given this choice, most people, of course, take a pain reliever, since it costs only pennies; whereas a medical examination costs hundreds of dollars and takes a lot of time. This is usually a logical choice because it is rare to need anything more than a pain reliever for a headache. But in some cases, a headache may indicate a brain tumor and failing to see a specialist right away can result in complications. Should everyone with a headache go to a specialist? Of course not, but people treating their own illnesses must realize that they are betting on the basis of their cost/value analysis of the situation. They are taking the most logical option.

The same cost/value analysis must be made when deciding to do one's own legal work. Many legal situations are very straight forward, requiring a simple form and no complicated analysis. Anyone with a little intelligence and a book of instructions can handle the matter without outside help.

But there is always the chance that complications are involved that only an attorney would notice. To simplify the law into a book like this, several legal cases often must be condensed into a single sentence or paragraph. Otherwise, the book would be several hundred pages long and too complicated for most people. However, this simplification necessarily leaves out many details and nuances that would apply to special or unusual situations. Also, there are many ways to interpret most legal questions. Your case may come before a judge who disagrees with the analysis of our authors.

Therefore, in deciding to use a self-help law book and to do your own legal work, you must realize that you are making a cost/value analysis. You have decided that the money you will save in doing it yourself outweighs the chance that your case will not turn out to your satisfaction. Most people handling their own simple legal matters never have a problem, but occasionally people find that it ended up costing them more to have an attorney straighten out the situation than it would have if they had hired an attorney in the beginning. Keep this in mind while handling your case, and be sure to consult an attorney if you feel you might need further guidance.

Local Rules

The next thing to remember is that a book which covers the law for the entire nation, or even for an entire state, cannot possibly include every procedural difference of every jurisdiction. Whenever possible, we provide the exact form needed; however, in some areas, each county, or even each judge, may require unique forms and procedures. In our state books, our forms usually cover the majority of counties in the state, or provide examples of the type of form which will be required. In our national books, our forms are sometimes even more general in nature but are designed to give a good idea of the type of form that will be needed in most locations. Nonetheless, keep in mind that your state, county, or judge may have a requirement, or use a form, that is not included in this book.

You should not necessarily expect to be able to get all of the information and resources you need solely from within the pages of this book. This book will serve as your guide, giving you specific information whenever possible and helping you to find out what else you will need to know. This is just like if you decided to build your own backyard deck. You might purchase a book on how to build decks. However, such a book would not include the building codes and permit requirements of every city, town, county, and township in the nation; nor would it include the lumber, nails, saws, hammers, and other materials and tools you would need to actually build the deck. You would use the book as your guide, and then do some work and research involving such matters as whether you need a permit of some kind, what type and grade of wood are available in your area, whether to use hand tools or power tools, and how to use those tools.

Before using the forms in a book like this, you should check with your court clerk to see if there are any local rules of which you should be aware, or local forms you will need to use. Often, such forms will require the same information as the forms in the book but are merely laid out differently or use slightly different language. They will sometimes require additional information.

Changes in the Law

Besides being subject to local rules and practices, the law is subject to change at any time. The courts and the legislatures of all fifty states are constantly revising the laws. It is possible that while you are reading this book, some aspect of the law is being changed.

In most cases, the change will be of minimal significance. A form will be redesigned, additional information will be required, or a waiting period will be extended. As a result, you might need to revise a form, file an extra form, or wait out a longer time period; these types of changes will not usually affect the outcome of your case. On the other hand, sometimes a major part of the law is changed, the entire law in a particular area is rewritten, or a case that was the basis of a central legal point is overruled. In such instances, your entire ability to pursue your case may be impaired.

Again, you should weigh the value of your case against the cost of an attorney and make a decision as to what you believe is in your best interest.

PREFACE

I am sure the reader has heard the expression, "The gift of youth is wasted on the young." The premise of this book is that knowledge of the law is often wasted on the lawyers. We lawyers frequently complain that if our clients had done (or not done) this, that or the other, we could have done a better job resolving their legal problems. Of course, the reason our clients did not do what they should have done was because they did not know what the law required in the first place. The knowledge that our clients needed was not available to them at the time they were making their decisions.

Typically, clients take what they believe is reasonably responsible action and then seek out the lawyer for advice or reinforcement after the fact. Since the client has already pursued a given course of action, the legal consultant frequently can only comment on the appropriateness of the client's action. Of course, this is an unfortunate legal irony because lay people, even knowledgeable business people, are not always familiar with technical legal requirements applicable to a specific situation.

In the complex field of immigration and *visa law* (we'll call it *visa law* in this book) an early mistake can frustrate or, at the least, complicate plans to move individuals and/or their businesses to the United States. We will try to address this situation by explaining in practical terms the philosophy and logic of the

United States immigration regimen. In short, this book attempts to be a practical handbook that explains to the foreign person how U.S. immigration functions.

This book was *originally* a collection of useful information that I have over the years customarily conveyed to foreign persons during my initial office interviews with them. It was apparent to me that most foreign persons (*aliens*), regardless of their country of origin, were asking the same types of questions. The client wanted to understand the system in order to understand the need to reveal and submit certain types of information. In order to provide a thoroughly useful service to the client, I had to explain much of the background of the law, as well as the philosophy and "mind set" of the U.S. immigration and consular authorities. By thoroughly informing the client, I was able to obtain the proper information that enabled me to provide useful advice in the planning of the client's entry into the United States.

This educational process also assisted clients in learning some of the most important and immediate business, legal norms, and customs that they would encounter in the United States. As I began to write this compendium, it grew into this book. I hope will provide readers with some of the insights that I feel are essential in successfully fulfilling their immigration motivations, both long and short term.

This book attempts to explain the law in a manner that will be understandable to the lay public, especially to foreign persons, whatever their occupations and/or stations in life may be. The book will discuss those features of the law that seem to be permanent and that are likely to apply to most persons seeking entry to the United States. It will not attempt to be the definitive scholarly or technical work in this area, for even as I write, the government is drafting administrative rules and regulations that will implement and further interpret the law.

The book is also written for the lay person, that is, for someone who has not been trained as a lawyer. For lawyers there are several excellent resources that are available, especially through the auspices of the *American Immigration Lawyers Association (AILA)*. These other sources and authors can provide the professional with the depth of knowledge and detail that is purposefully not found in this book.

This book will cover the major provisions of the U.S. visa law as it would apply to a foreign person who is contemplating a move to the United States, whether that move be permanent or temporary. The book will not cover many technical provisions of the law that apply to a person already within the United States.

As further described in this preface, the purpose of the book is to educate the foreign person with respect to the policy and philosophy of the United States immigration regimen on concerns regarding obtaining an appropriate visa for entry into the U.S.A. I do not encourage a lay person to attempt to obtain a visa, other than the visitor's visa *(B-1/B-2),* to the United States without professional assistance. Consultation with a trained professional legal consultant is greatly encouraged.

This publication will be especially helpful to business persons and investors, as well as their advisors, to whom immigration concerns may be secondary to other strategic business planning. It will also be useful to other foreign persons, whether they are students or immediate relatives of U.S. citizens or permanent resident aliens. It is not the author's purpose to encourage nor discourage immigration or the transfer of capital to the United States. Rather, the book is offered in the context of certain political, economic, and sociological factors over which the author has no control or ability to affect. These factors can be summarized as follows.

1. **The relative ease of international transportation and communication.** This phenomenon has created the illusion that political and national boundaries are of less importance now, than in the past. The mass media, as a result of technological advances during the past few decades, has projected the United States culture and way of life to the most remote parts of the world. Thus, many persons in foreign countries may be already familiar with certain cultural characteristics of the United States and may want to participate in our life style.

2. **The interdependence of national economies.** As a result of some of the technological advances already mentioned, the community of nations' business and commerce is more interrelated and interdependent. This often requires the transfer of business personnel to the United States. This, of course, is often a bilateral process with many expansive U.S. firms transferring their U.S. employees to other parts of the world as well. The world economy often pays little heed to national boundaries.

Companies and individuals are often substantially affected by the events or predictions of financial centers far removed from their home offices.

There is a growing body of opinion that there is one global economy and financial market, with three regional centers: Tokyo, New York, and London. These centers are so interrelated that the cause and effect sequence as to their individual influence on the world economy is academic. Each center is so closely dependent upon and influential of the others, that their combined effect on the world's economy is a constant force.

3. **The relative strength and adaptability of the U.S. economy.** This reality makes the United States an attractive market for foreign investment, both on a large and small scale. The *entrepreneurial spirit* reacts much the same way to this fact, whether it is that of a large multinational firm or of a smaller business whose owners are very often also its key employees.

4. **The political stability of the United States.** This is perhaps the most salient characteristic of the U.S. political system. Regardless of the level of hyperbole and passion that may be engendered by various political currents, the U.S. has a history of generally resolving its controversies peaceably.

   The United States has a history of relative tolerance for immigrants from foreign countries—especially for those immigrants who share an affinity for the capitalist ideology. There are pockets of ethnic communities throughout the U.S. where a foreign person of a particular ethnic background can feel secure and find the familiar cultural characteristics of home. The United States is a geographically diverse country with regions resembling those of other countries. Furthermore, various geographic areas of the United States offer pleasant climates, as well as attractive and modern urban, suburban and agricultural areas. There is someplace for everyone.

5. **The United States nurtures personal freedoms.** In the United States, personal and political freedoms such as the right of free speech, right of assembly, freedom of the press, freedom of physical movement, etc., are jealously protected. U.S. residents have the right to succeed and enjoy the fruits of their labors and are expected to bear the risk of failure as well.

As a result of these factors, there is a tremendous worldwide demand for both permanent and temporary visas to the United States.

There are counter-currents, however, to a liberal immigration policy. These are illustrated by the following.

1. **The increase in overall U.S. population and its effect.** This worldwide phenomenon and its local effects has caused U.S. political leaders to take the position that further population growth is generally negative. Indeed, the increasing population places strains on public services in general as well as on the natural environment.

2. **Differences in the ethnic and cultural make up of current immigrants.** This is a more subtly expressed objection, but many Americans seem to resent the changing ethnic makeup of their communities. Statistics verify that the largest percentage of immigration to the United States during the last twenty years or so have come from Asia and Latin America.

3. **The social cost of the presence of large numbers of illegal aliens.** Americans resent their government's inability to deter the thousands of foreign persons who enter the country illegally and then remain permanently or for extended periods of time. Insofar as most of these illegal immigrants are poor and uneducated, they require the expenditures of public funds to provide for them. In addition to certain welfare costs, statistics reflect that a relatively high percentage of jailed inmates are illegal aliens. The proliferation of fraudulent immigration documents and the perceived abuse of the asylum procedures has further eroded the traditional welcoming mentality of the U.S. people and many of their political leaders.

4. **The political rationalization of immigration as the cause of various social ills.** Since non U.S. citizens are not permitted to vote, it has become politically irresistible to blame immigration for many of the country's ills. It has become expedient for many U.S. politicians to take up the issue of immigration as a political rallying point for the furtherance of their own campaigns and careers.

Some of these motivations have resulted in an increase in the control of the quality, quantity, and character of inward migration. However, the convergence of these two drives causes many personal and business problems. Many of them can be avoided or minimized through proper planning.

This, then, is the setting for the writing of this book. The author's intention is to explain the major visa considerations that a prospective immigrant or temporary visitor must understand in order to logically and intelligently plan an entry into the United States. This work may be criticized by certain members of the immigration legal community as being too simplistic and not providing enough detail on certain intricacies of the administrative and legal processes involved in the procurement of visas for foreign persons. I accept such anticipated criticism by stating that I do not intend this book to replace the services of competent professional guidance. Indeed, the book recognizes that professional assistance, not just in the field of law, but also in the disciplines of accounting, marketing, finance, etc., is very often critical in making successful long-term decisions respecting business/visa matters.

The reader is forewarned, however, that the U.S. immigration system is extremely dynamic and legally complex. The governmental agencies do not give individual advice. There are a vast number of unlicensed, incompetent, and unscrupulous individuals who hold themselves out as immigration advisers, consultants, or notarios. These persons are capable of doing great harm to unsuspecting and trusting foreign persons and their U.S. citizen or permanent resident counterparts. This is one area of the law, wherein except for a few cases that present simple and uncomplicated fact patterns, a person is advised to seek professional assistance (i.e., an experienced immigration lawyer). The consequences of bad advice are often very unfortunate and irreversible.

The purpose of the book is to prepare and educate individuals (and/or their employees) so they and/or their professional consultants may comply with the requirements of the United States immigration regimen. It is my purpose to describe the methodology and bureaucratic psychology of the U.S. immigration regimen. An understanding of these institutions will help enable a person or company to adapt to the overall situation as it otherwise applies to him or her.

Some may criticize the inclusion of more detail than the average person is willing to know. My response is, with all due respect, this book is not written for the average person. It is written for that special person who, in search of economic and personal improvement, desires to expand personal and business activities beyond the borders of home by transferring some or all of those activities into the most dynamic society on this planet: the United States of America.

Ramon Carrion

Publisher's Note

In the past several years, the governmental agencies responsible for immigration benefits and enforcement have gone through major reorganizations and name changes. The *Immigration and Naturalization Service* (INS) that operated under the Department of Justice, was the governmental agency over most immigrations issues. It no longer exists. After the events of September 11, 2001, the government consolidated most activities relating to homeland security (which includes immigration matters) into the *Department of Homeland Security* (DHS).

Under the DHS, twenty-two previously miscellaneous domestic agencies became coordinated into one department to protect the nation against threats by providing a better-coordinated defense of the homeland. Divisions of the DHS analyze threats and intelligence, guard the nation's borders and airports, protect critical infrastructure, and coordinate the response to future emergencies.

As part of its formation, bureaus were created that took over the functions of the INS. Those bureaus include the *Bureau of Citizenship and Immigration Services* (the agency most commonly associated with immigration matters), the *Bureau of Immigration Customs and Enforcement*, and the *Bureau of Customs and Border Protection*. During the transition the bureaus have been referred to by a variety of names and acronyms. Initially they were often referred to by BCIS, BICE, and BCBP respectively.

Changes within governmental agencies (especially those dealing with immigration) are continual. In late 2003, the bureaus replaced the "Bureau of" with "United States" thus changing their names to *United States Citizenship and Immigration Services*, *United States Immigration Customs and Enforcement*, and *United States Customs and Border Protection*. With this designation change, new acronyms are being used: USCIS, ICE, and CBP respectively. (While this publication uses the new designations, you are likely to still find the previous names used or a combination of the old and new designations being used by other sources.)

INTRODUCTION

The last two years have witnessed an almost revolutionary reassessment of U.S. immigration policy by the United States government. The immediate impetus for this reassessment was the terrorist attack of September 11, 2001 on our country. The majority of the perpetrators involved in the attack had entered the United States on either student or tourist visas. This fact fed a public perception that the attacks were facilitated by a lax visa system coupled with complacent immigration and border officers who failed to detect the threat caused by the entry to the United States of the terror perpetrators. History will provide a better conclusion as to the true causes of our nation's inability to have detected the attackers in time to have avoided the death and destruction that was wrought on our nation on the fateful day. Nonetheless, the country's leaders, detecting the sense of public outrage and fear, undertook a series of changes to our country's immigration regimen.

Some of the changes were formal and jurisprudential, while other equally important changes resulted from a hardening or a realignment of bureaucratic attitudes. In both cases, these had been preceded by a series of adaptations and conscious changes that were effected by the government post 9/11.

One of the most dramatic and immediate changes was the abolition of the *Immigration and Naturalization Service* (INS) and the transfer of its jurisdictional authority to a newly created executive cabinet level department known as the *Department of Homeland Security* (DHS). The functions of the INS have been transferred to three separate bureaus within the DHS.

One of these independent bureaus is the *United States Citizenship and Immigration Services* (USCIS) to which was assigned authority for the adjudication of immigration benefits. This bureau adjudicates immigration benefits that are requested either at the petition of qualified U.S. sponsors or in some cases by qualified aliens who requested certain non immigrant benefits.

The *United States Immigration and Customs Enforcement* (ICE) undertook the responsibility of investigating violations of and enforcing the immigration regimen as to non U.S. citizens already residing in the United States. It encompasses not only the normal investigative functions of law enforcement, but also all authority for the removal of aliens from the United States.

The third agency, the *United States Customs and Border Protection* (CBP) assumed the authority of the former Border Patrol and was charged with the responsibility of protecting the borders of our country from unauthorized penetration. This organization combines the functions of customs and immigration inspections at the nation's borders, airports, and seaports. This is the officer that the alien will likely encounter upon entry to the United States.

The three bureaus all fall under the Department of Homeland Security as illustrated below.

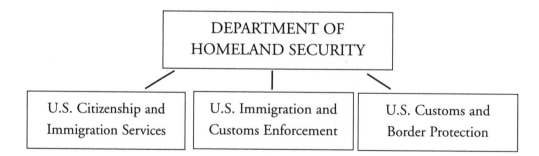

The idea behind creating three separate agencies of government was to eliminate the sometimes ambiguous attitude by the former INS that had been charged with the responsibilities for both adjudicating immigration benefits and enforcing sanctions against immigration violators. It seemed that no one was happy with this past arrangement. The benefits-community often complained of the high-handed manner the INS often treated both aliens and U.S. sponsors in their quest to obtain a specific immigration benefit for an alien. The law enforcement community complained of the seeming inability of the INS to enforce the immigration law and to remove immigration law violators. Indeed, given the high stakes involved in both of these responsibilities it seems, at least in retrospect, that the co-mingling of these responsibilities were doomed to failure, at least eventually.

The new arrangement under the common bureaucratic umbrella of the DHS seems to address this ambiguity. It remains to be seen whether each agency will be able to maintain its operational independence and jurisdictional integrity—and function effectively.

Another change is the change in attitude of the government bureaucracy. It is harder to gauge or quantify, but it is as important as any change in the text of the law or regulation. In short, no government official wants to be the one whose signature approved the visa application of the next terrorist or notorious criminal. The trauma to the nation of the terrorist attacks of September 11, 2001, has had a devastating impact on the immigration system. A fear exists that the terrorist enemy is a skillful and cunning adversary who will seek access to the country through the normal channels of immigration and commerce and thus, increased security measures and attitudes will be necessary to thwart this threat. This security concern results in delay and increased scrutiny in the processing of almost <u>all</u> applications for immigration benefits.

We have specifically chosen, in this edition, not to include USCIS forms for two reasons. First, the forms are often changed either as to the data required or as to the filing requirements. In the past, many foreign persons, as well as their U.S. sponsors, have been prejudiced by following what were obsolete instructions on official forms. Second, the forms are available on the Internet from the USCIS site and thus are immediately available together with the current instructions and filing costs. The website is **http://uscis.gov**.

We have, however, included some government policy memoranda that address certain important issues. These memoranda not only provide specific answers to questions, but also provide excellent insight into the government's philosophical approach to immigration policy.

At the time of the writing of this book, there were several *bills* (proposed laws) pending before the U.S. Congress that would implement changes to the U.S. immigration law regimen. While there is no useful purpose served in discussing the merits of proposals that may never be enacted as law, it is important to discuss why there are still attempts by the Congress to further modify the U.S. immigration law regimen.

The Developing Culture of *No*

One of the principal complaints as to the former INS (sometimes referred to as the *legacy INS)* was the built-in bureaucratic conflict of interest in having the same agency adjudicate benefits applications while at the same time enforcing, through deportation, violators of the immigration regimen. This dichotomy was only exacerbated by the complex and sometimes contradictory nature of the immigration law and statutes. This dual and conflicted role was supposed to be cured by splitting the INS into three separate and independent bureaus under the supervision of the Department of Homeland Security.

Reality has, at the time of the writing of this edition, tempered most of the expectations of the immigrant community as to the benefits expected from the reorganization of the immigration regimen. Adjudications delays have increased to record levels . More importantly, there has been no noticeable improvement in the bureaucratic mind-set or attitude of the USCIS adjudicators. It appears that the mission of the DHS to protect the security of the nation has taken precedence over the mission of the USCIS—to concentrate on providing service to its customers—U.S. family and employment sponsors and their immigrant beneficiaries.

This emphasis on security can be most clearly seen with the *Memorandum of Understanding* that has been signed by the DHS and the Department of State. This interdepartment agreement provides, among other things, that even though visa adjudication is still within the province of the Consular Offices of the Department of State, the actual issuance of visas will be governed by DHS policy decisions. Its personnel will have ultimate authority to veto or approve issuance of individual visas. This process can only create further delays in the visa issuance process at the U.S. consulates abroad.

So far the most tangible result of the transfer to the respective bureaus of the DHS of immigration adjudication and enforcement has been to bestow to the USCIS yet another rationale for delay, obfuscation, and intransigence—the need for additional security. This writer believes that it will take a considerable amount of time for this negative culture to dissipate. It will require a new generation of USCIS adjudicators who have not grown up in the enforcement branch of the immigration regimen as well as courageous political and administrative leadership.

In any event, this reality should generate a degree of caution in the mind of any person who seeks to receive or sponsor an immigration benefit. The growing complexity of the legal and administrative regimen coupled with the reticence of its adjudicators to approve petitions and applications means that most persons should seek professional assistance in accessing the immigration regimen. This is almost contradictory given that most of the governmental forms can be found on the Internet. The problem is that the law's complexities are often not immediately apparent (even to governmental adjudicators) and the consequences of mistakes can often be irreversible. Caution should be the password.

For the reader, this means that frequent changes in the immigration regimen are a reality. Before any specific steps are taken along the path of immigration, it would be wise to consult with an experienced immigration counselor. (This suggestion to consult with a competent immigration law professional is a recurring theme in this book. I apologize in advance for occasional redundant statements along this line.)

I | OVERVIEW OF THE VISA SYSTEM

Every time foreigners come to the border of the United States seeking entry, even if only for a holiday visit, they confront the formidable *immigration* regimen of the United States. The term *immigration* (in the context of this book) means every entry or attempted entry into the territory of the United States.

The immigration system of the United States is the product of unique historical and political forces that produce some seemingly incongruous policies. Immigration has created a procedural system that is so complex and obscure that it almost creates the opportunity for a foreign person to unintentionally violate the law and then provides almost no methodology for a foreign person to correct the violation.

It is a system that requires the foreign person to know in advance of any filing or application what the applicable law is, since the immigration system often does not provide an applicant an opportunity to modify his or her approach in order to comply with the law. For this reason, it is imperative that foreign persons and their advisors understand the special meaning given to many terms that are routinely used in business and in normal conversation.

Historical Context

The United States was founded by immigrants, that is, by people who were not originally from the nation. History reveals that during the first 150 years, the motivating force for immigration to the United States was privation and persecution abroad. People came to the United States to escape negative forces in their home countries. They came to this country fully expecting to experience personal sacrifice in exchange for political, economic, and religious freedom. Until the end of the 19th Century there was basically no control or limitation on immigration to the United States.

However, since 1882, a series of general immigration statutes have been enacted in response to the type and numbers of people who had previously entered. From that year forward, the United States embarked on a series of restrictions on immigration. Thus, specific national origins quotas were imposed from time to time that were ethnically and racially discriminatory. Quantitative restrictions were introduced into the immigration regimen in 1921 with the passage of the first quota system applicable to designated nationalities.

Immigration has come to the United States in waves of specific nationalities to escape adverse conditions such as drought, famine, depression, religious persecution, etc. in their countries of origin. While that is still the case today for many persons, many others now seek to come to the United States for temporary periods of time in order to accomplish specific business, cultural, or other personal goals. These include education, tourism, business investments, and entrepreneurial exploitation. While the deprivation of the crowded steamship has been replaced by the comfort of the jet airliner, the administrative problem at the immigration counter has not changed very much.

Legal Context

The Constitution of the United States, the organic document that established the unique political existence of this nation, is almost silent on the entire question of immigration. There is only a fleeting mention of this subject in that document. It does not contain a political or philosophical articulation of a policy or system of immigration. In very concise language, the Constitution simply authorizes the U.S. Congress to make the laws concerning immigration. There is no statement of policy or principle manifested in the Constitution concerning the subject of immigration.

McCarran-Walter Act

The *McCarran-Walter Act* molded the basic structure of the immigration law as we know it today. With its passage in 1952, a new phenomenon began to emerge. The U.S. immigration system began to partake of a more democratic character as the law attempted to apply admissions policies without direct regard to national and racial origins. The last trace of racial or ethnic discrimination was removed with the abolition of the separate quota for Western Hemisphere aliens in 1978.

Immigration Act

When the McCarran-Walter Act was repealed by the *Immigration Act of 1990*, the immigration policy of the U.S. again experienced some substantive changes. As a result of the Act, the law now emphasizes the policy of attracting immigrants who possess desirable occupational skills or economic resources. The law still provides for the unification of families and close relatives of U.S. citizens and, to a lesser extent, of permanent residents. The law, now for the first time, established a category for the issuance of permanent visas to investors who establish or invest in new job creating enterprises. There have also been some substantial changes with respect to the issuance of temporary visas to the United States. One reality is constant and indisputable: there is a higher demand for visas, permanent and temporary, to the United States than there is supply and/or perceived need. With this general background, let us look more closely at the United States visa system.

Illegal Immigration Reform and Immigrant Responsibility Act

In 1996, the *Illegal Immigration Reform and Immigrant Responsibility Act* (IIRAIRA) was signed into law. This law, while designed to stem the flow of illegal immigration to the United States, also harbored some mean-spirited provisions that can be dangerous to both U.S. citizens and foreign persons alike. This law contains certain retroactive provisions that render persons deportable, who in some cases, have been long-term, abiding citizens of the United States. It also makes deportable dependents such as spouses and children of foreign persons who may have inadvertently exceeded or violated their status.

Visa System

The United States federal government has jurisdiction over all visa and immigration matters. The individual state and local governments have only a limited role in this field, such as the initial processing of *labor certification applications*. As an illustration of this point, I would emphasize that the quality and strength of the alien's connection with state and local governmental and business institutions are of very limited help in qualifying for a long-term visa. This elementary fact is very often overlooked by foreign persons who do not understand the nature of the federal system of government in the United States.

In fact, the programs and policies of a state concerning a particular subject can be different from those of the federal government on the same subject. Unfortunately, if the subject matter in question is one that the Constitution of the United States assigns to the federal government, then the federal law takes precedence over the state law. This is the reality with matters concerning United States immigration policy.

Failure to fulfill the detailed requirements of the United States visa system can often result in a denial or delay in the issuance of a visa petition, even if the local or state authorities welcome individuals and their investments. In short, neither the *U.S. Citizenship and Immigration Services (USCIS)*, nor the U.S. consul abroad, depends upon the recommendations of the local or state government or of the local Chambers of Commerce, community service organizations, etc. The alien entering the United States must comply with the formal requirements of a federal bureaucratic system that is largely insulated from *outside* interests.

U.S. Consulates Abroad

Outside of the United States, aliens deal almost exclusively with the United States consulate or embassy in their home country. The U.S. consul has, within the confines of the law, almost complete discretion as to whom and under what circumstances a visa to the United States will be granted. Furthermore, there is no appeal from a denial of a visa by the U.S. consul other than for interpretations of law. This means that an alien should have a complete understanding of the law and should be thoroughly prepared and documented to comply with the law before the alien first approaches the U.S. consul on any visa question.

The U.S. Department of State, acting through its U.S. consulates abroad, does not view itself as a counseling agency for individuals who seek to immigrate to the United States.

NOTE: *Read this paragraph again and accept it as a fundamental principal in dealing with the host country United States consulate with respect to visa matters.*

In addition, the local U.S. consul abroad probably has an in-depth understanding of political and economic conditions of that country. It is able to apply that knowledge and experience in adjudicating the intentions and motivations of individual applications of host country citizens who seek visas to the United States.

United States Citizenship and Immigration Services

An alien who is already in the United States and who seeks an immigration benefit will deal with the *U.S. Citizenship and Immigration Services* (USCIS). This agency is a bureau within the *Department of Homeland Security* and operates through various regional and subregional offices throughout the United States. A list of the current offices can be found on the website of the USCIS at **http://uscis.gov**.

Once aliens are already in the United States, they enjoy *slightly* more procedural rights than would be the case if they were outside the United States.

Certain visa petitions such as the *Form I-129* (used for the *L-1* Visa) must be filed within the United States at a regional office of the USCIS. Other visa petitions, such as for the *B-1* Visa, must be filed abroad at the local U.S. consulate. Some visa applications may be filed either in the United States or the U.S. consulate abroad. Often the choice of where to file a petition can be either a strategic or tactical decision depending upon many factors, including the prevailing and often divergent attitudes of these two U.S. agencies. There are four *Regional Service Centers* within the United States to which individual petitions are sent for adjudication.

There is a trend toward centralizing this approach to ensure uniformity and efficiency. As a result of this trend, it is clear that the USCIS is developing a cadre of officers who are knowledgeable about current business practices as well as current legal and social trends in the United States. This is often lacking in certain U.S. consular posts abroad since often the adjudicating officers have received little training and are rotated frequently. The regional service centers are essentially *think tanks,* to which access from the public, including even immigration attorneys, is limited. The philosophy of utilizing these regional service centers is to ensure that visa petitions will be adjudicated in an objective manner.

Regardless of how foreign persons may have entered the United States, after their entry they are under the jurisdiction of the USCIS.

Inspection, Exclusion, and Removal (Deportation)

Every independent nation has complete discretion as to whom it will admit within its borders. When aliens appear at the U.S. border or other port of entry, they are subject to the power of inspection and deportation by the immigration inspector. The purpose of the inspection is to determine whether or not the foreign person is admissible to the United States. Inspectors of the *U.S. Customs and Boarder Protection* (CBP) have the right to examine the alien's passport and visa to ensure that the physical person in front of them is the person identified in the travel documents.

Additionally, the officer is authorized, by interrogation and physical inspection of luggage and of the person, to determine whether the person is entitled to enter the United States in the visa category requested and for how long a duration. Lately, the duration of stay under particular visa categories has been established by regulation, so that in most instances the immigration inspector is bound by the term established in the applicable regulation or operating instruction. Normally, the actual inspection time takes only a few minutes unless the inspecting officer suspects an irregularity.

Upon inspection and in accordance with law, U.S. immigration officers may exclude an alien from entering the United States, if they find the alien ineligible to enter the U.S. This power to exclude is the primary obstacle to an alien entering the United States. It should be noted that many foreign persons complain of rudeness on the part of the CBP inspectors at the ports of entry. Unfortunately, one's experience with the inspection process depends upon many factors, not the least of which is the inspector's personality.

Inspectors often view themselves as police officials trying to prevent illegal entry into the United States, rather than as good will emissaries of the United States. This unfortunate attitude is reinforced by the strong demands for visas to the United States and by continuous attempts by certain aliens to circumvent the law and attempt to enter the United States illegally. I can only warn alien readers of this fact, so that they will not be overly intimidated by the occasional unfriendly reception they may receive at the point of entry. If the foreign person reads this book and understands how the immigration system functions, he or she will get through the border with the least amount of upset and inconvenience.

One of the most controversial changes wrought by *IIRAIRA* is the power given to immigration inspectors to exclude a person from entry to the U.S. on an expedited basis and without appeal of any kind whatsoever. In effect, the inspector becomes judge and executioner. Even a person with a valid visa may be excluded or admitted provisionally on parole or under a process called *deferred inspection* at the border, if the immigration official determines or suspects that the alien is not entitled to use the visa in his or her passport. Indeed, the law provides that a person who attempts to enter the United States with a visa that is inappropriate for the alien's intended or perceived purpose can be summarily removed on the basis of fraud and become permanently ineligible to enter the United States.

"I BELIEVE YOU ARE WHO YOU SAY YOU ARE LORD BELLYWOO, BUT
REGULATIONS REQUIRE ME TO INSPECT YOUR HAIRPIECE."

General Grounds for Exclusion

IIRAIRA enacted broad and profound changes with respect to the grounds for the *removal* of aliens to the United States. (*Removal* is the term for the official removal of aliens who have *either* already entered the United States or who seek admission at a *port of entry.* This book deals with the concept of removal as excludability from entry and not with the concept of removal as applicable to a person who has already entered the United States and is being removed for violations of law or regulation after lawful admissibility.)

Among the many changes created by *IIRAIRA* is the power of expedited removal given to the immigration inspector coupled with the elimination of all appeals from the inspector's decision. Aliens encounter the concept of exclusion or *removal* when they appear at the U.S. consulate and apply for a visa and, again, when at the border attempting to enter the United States. Thus, an alien might have the visa petition denied by the U.S. consular office because the consular office believes that one or more grounds of exclusion may apply to the particular alien. Decisions made by consular officers are difficult to reverse since they are granted broad discretion in interpreting the factual circumstances surrounding any particular alien petitioner.

If aliens already have a visa in their possession, the inspector at the border may deny them entry to the United States on the basis that one or more of the following grounds of ineligibility for admission might apply. With respect to certain of the grounds for inadmissibility, the law provides *waivers* or *exemptions* that may permit a foreign person to enter the United States even though one or more grounds for inadmissibility may apply. When the term waiver is used in the context of inadmissibility, it refers to an exception or a pardon of the grounds for inadmissibility.

Health-Related Grounds These primary grounds would apply to any foreign person found by the *Department of Health and Human Services* to have a communicable disease of public health significance. This would include, for instance, any person who has been diagnosed as HIV positive. This category of inadmissibility would also apply to any other form of communicable disease such as tuberculosis.

In addition, the law now requires that a foreign person seeking admission as an immigrant (permanent resident) provide documentation of having received vaccination against a myriad of vaccine-preventable diseases such as, mumps, measles, rubella, polio, tetanus, influenza type B, hepatitis B, and any other vaccination against vaccine-preventable diseases recommended by the Advisory Committee for Immunization Practices. There are waivers available for this requirement if it can be documented that it would be medically dangerous for the person to receive the vaccination or if there is proof that the person was previously vaccinated.

This ground of inadmissibility would apply to any foreign person determined by the Department of Health and Human Services to have a physical or mental disorder or to manifest any behavior that could or that has in the past posed a threat to others. The determination that a particular person has a physical or mental disorder will be made on a case-by-case basis.

If the Department of Health and Human Services determines that the alien is a drug abuser or a drug addict, the alien could be rendered inadmissible from entry. This ground of inadmissibility is separate from the provision that would bar any person from entering the United States who has been convicted of any criminal offense involving drug use. Apparently, experimentation alone will not render a foreign person inadmissible, but it is not clear what conduct would be included in the exception of mere *experimentation*.

The law also provides grounds for discretionary relief against inadmissibility if the foreign person has necessary family ties and otherwise proves mitigating circumstances that would waive this ground of inadmissibility and permit the alien to enter the United States in spite of being found to be a drug abuser or addict. The purpose for the waiver provision is to keep families together and to prevent a hardship where a proper family environment would mitigate any danger to the public. The law also provides that grounds for exclusion on this basis may be waived if a bond is provided.

Criminal Grounds

There are essentially six grounds of inadmissibility on the basis of criminal conduct.

1. Conviction or admission of a crime of moral turpitude or a crime involving a *drug offense*. It is important to understand the concept of crimes of moral turpitude. This designation refers to those crimes that are indicative of bad moral character, such as crimes of theft, assault and battery, murder, rape, and the like. There are limited waivers (dispensations) to exclusion for persons convicted of any of these offenses. A waiver is available for conviction of minor offenses (those defined as

offenses for which the sentence imposed is less than six months). A waiver is possible if the crime was committed by an alien who was under the age of eighteen at the time of the crime, and the crime was committed more than five years before the date of application for the visa. Another exception applies to crimes for which the maximum possible penalty does not exceed one year, and, if the alien was actually convicted of the crime, where the alien was not in fact sentenced to a term of imprisonment in excess of six months.

2.   Conviction of two or more crimes if the combined custodial sentence imposed is for *five years or longer* regardless of whether or not the crime arose from a single stream of events or whether or not the crimes were of moral turpitude.

3.   When the consular or immigration officer knows or has reason to believe that the alien is or was a *drug trafficker* or was a person who aided, abetted, or conspired in drug trafficking.

4.   Any alien who was involved in *prostitution* or is coming to the United States to engage in any other unlawful commercialized vice.

5.   Aliens involved in serious criminal activity who have asserted immunity from prosecution and departed. This would apply, for instance, to persons who committed crimes or committed acts that could have been crimes, but who asserted *diplomatic immunity*.

6.   Aliens who have been convicted of *aggravated felonies* as that term is defined by law. Generally, aggravated felonies are crimes the government has identified as being so serious as to warrant the alien's removal from the United States. The definition of *aggravated felonies*, however, is so broad as to encompass many offenses which many persons consider to be minor offenses. The other problem with the law is that the government attempts to apply it to persons who committed the aggravated felony many years ago, even before the law was enacted. This has resulted in some very harsh consequences in individual cases.

Warning: As a result of the aggravated felony law, any person who has ever been convicted of any crime anywhere in the United States should consult a qualified immigration attorney before undertaking a trip outside of the United States.

Waivers of excludability on the above grounds may be available under section 212(h) of the *Immigration and Nationality Act* for non-drug-related crimes, for prostitution or for conviction of a single offense of possession of thirty grams or less of marijuana. The waiver is available upon the passage either of fifteen years from the disqualifying event coupled with proof of the alien's rehabilitation, or in the event of extreme hardship to designated U.S. citizens or permanent resident relatives, i.e., spouse, parent, son, or daughter.

This waiver is not available to aliens who have already been admitted to the U.S. as permanent residents if since the date of their admissions they have been convicted of an aggravated felony or the alien has not resided continuously in the U.S. for at least seven years before the date removal proceedings are begun. No court has jurisdiction to review a decision of the USCIS to grant or deny this waiver.

Security and Related Grounds

This category of inadmissibility would apply to the following.

1.   Any person who, in the opinion of the U.S. consular officer, entered the United States to engage in *prejudicial and unlawful activities* that would include espionage, sabotage, and violation or evasion of laws concerning the prohibition of export from the United States of goods, technology, or other sensitive information. (There is a waiver possible for anyone who violates the provision concerning the export of technology, if the person seeks to reenter the United States solely as a nonimmigrant.)

2.   Anyone who is engaged in *terrorist activity* and who is an active member of the PLO. Terrorist activity is defined to encompass active support for terrorist organizations through a variety of activities, including fundraising. The Secretary of State can also designate the organizations that are considered to be *terrorist organizations*.

     Terrorist activity in this case is defined to apply immediately to a person who is an officer, official, representative, or spokesman of the Palestinian Liberation Organization. Terrorist activity also includes, hijacking or sabotage of any vehicle or conveyance that includes aircraft and seagoing vessels; killing, detaining, or threatening to kill or injure another individual in order to compel a third person to act or abstain from acting as an explicit condition for the release of the individual; as well as a violent attack upon an internationally protected person.

To engage in terrorist activity also is defined to include—

> *an act that the actor knows or reasonably should know affords material support to any individual, organization, or government in conducting a terrorist activity at any time, including any of the following acts:*
>
> > *providing any type of material support, including a safe house, transportation, communications, funds, false identification, weapons, explosives, training through any individual the actor knows or has reason to believe has committed, or plans to commit, an act of terrorist activity, or anyone who solicits funds or other things of value for terrorist activities or terrorist organizations.*

3. Anyone whose entry would have a foreign policy consequence seriously adverse to the interests of the United States. This is a general exclusionary right given the U.S. Consulate. Exceptions to exclusion on these grounds are made for foreign government officials and politicians in cases in which their exclusion would be based upon speech or association that would have been lawful in the United States.

4. Other individuals who are not foreign government officials who intend to engage in speech or association that also would be lawful in the U.S. This is also subject to veto by personal determination of the Secretary of State based upon a compelling U.S. foreign policy interest.

5. An alien who seeks to apply for immigrant status and who was a member or is actively a member of a *communist* or *totalitarian party.* An exception to excludability on this basis is available for those persons who were members of the Communist party on an involuntary basis or who were members when they were under the age of sixteen. An additional exception to excludability is available to persons whose membership terminated two years before the visa application was made. If the totalitarian party still controls the alien's country, then an exception can be made for former Communist party members only if their membership terminated at least five years previous to application for entry.

6. Waivers or exceptions to these grounds of excludability are available for any of the above aliens who are immediate and dependent family relatives of U.S. citizens, if they are otherwise not a threat to U.S. security.

7. Anyone who participated in the *NAZI persecution* of World War II or in *genocide*. There is an exception to this exclusionary grounds for those persons who are seeking to enter the United States only as diplomatic representatives.

8. This category of inadmissibility applies to persons who are or are likely to become a *public charge,* meaning they cannot support themselves. In determining whether an alien is excludable as likely to become a public charge, the government official must take into account the alien's age, health, family status, assets, resources, and financial status as well as an *Affidavit of Support.*

    The Affidavit of Support. The law now requires every alien seeking admission as a family-sponsored immigrant or, in certain cases, as an employment-based alien, to provide a legally enforceable financial guarantee by a U.S. sponsor. The sponsor must document sufficient income to provide the alien with an income level that is 125% of the poverty level as established every year by the Director of the Office of Management and Budget (OMB).

    NOTE: *The key word here is document. The income is documented by Federal Income Tax returns as well as a letter from a current employer or, in the case of a self-employed person, by a letter from a qualified accountant or other reliable financial expert.*

    If the U.S. sponsor does not have sufficient income to meet this requirement, the law allows the use of assets that are readily convertible to cash to substitute for income. In this case, the assets must have a value that is five times the amount of income being substituted. The sponsored aliens can contribute the value of their assets for this purpose.

    Example: Suppose that a U.S. citizen husband is petitioning for his foreign wife and her two children. The U.S. citizen husband also has a child who lives with him. Thus, in their household there will be a total of five persons. Let us also assume that for the year in question, the Director of the OMB has determined that a family of five requires the sum of $27,000.00 per year in order to meet the 125% requirement. If the U.S. citizen husband only has income of $25,000.00 he can make up the deficit of $2,000.00 with assets (perhaps a bank savings account or equity in a home) that have a value of at least $10,000.00 ($2,000.00 x 5 = $10,000.00).

The law also provides that the U.S. sponsor shall remain liable to the government for any means-based economic benefits that the alien receives until the alien either becomes a citizen or has worked a total of forty qualifying quarters of time. This is the equivalent of ten years of employment. A divorce will not terminate the financial and legal obligation of a sponsoring U.S. spouse. The law allows the federal and state governments, as well as the sponsored alien, the right to file a legal claim against the U.S. sponsor in order to enforce this provision. The *Affidavit of Support* now creates consequences for the sponsor and alien that require some analysis based upon the particular personal and financial circumstances of the parties.

Protection of the U.S. Labor Market

This category of *inadmissibility* applies to persons who are entering the United States seeking to engage in gainful employment. Anyone who seeks to enter the United States to work and who does not have a *Labor Certification* from the United States Department of Labor is *inadmissible*. (Refer to page 45 for a discussion of employment-based permanent residency visa preferences that require a labor certification.)

Professional athletes are permitted to move from team to team after admission to the U.S. if the new team is in the same sport as the previous team. In addition, the league in which the teams play has a combined total revenue of at least $10,000,000.00.

Physicians

Also excludable under this designation would be those physicians who are unqualified to practice medicine in the United States. In order for physicians to enter the United States, they must have passed an English proficiency test and must have taken one of two national medical exams.

Uncertified Foreign Health-Care Workers

Any person seeking to immigrate as a permanent resident for the purpose of performing labor as a healthcare worker, other than as a physician, is inadmissible unless the alien presents a certificate from the Commission on Graduates of

Foreign Nursing Schools or from an equivalent independent credentialing organization that confirms: 1) the alien's education, training, license, and experience is equivalent to that of a similar U.S. worker; 2) the alien is sufficiently competent in the English language; and, 3) the alien has passed any test that is recognized by a majority of States as predicting success on the profession's licensing and certification examination. The validity of these tests is to be determined solely by the Secretary of Health and Human Services and are not subject to further administrative or judicial review.

Illegal Entry into the United States

This category includes: an alien present in the U.S. without being admitted or paroled or who arrives in the U.S. at any time or place other than as designated by the USCIS is inadmissible. There is an exception for certain *battered women and children* as long as they can establish that their illegal presence is caused by the battery or extreme mental cruelty. The concept of battered women and children is discussed on page 61 of this book.

In addition, any alien who without reasonable cause fails to attend a removal proceeding and who then seeks admission to the United States within five years of the alien's departure or removal is inadmissible.

Persons guilty of material misrepresentation of any petition or other document with respect to a visa. This provision bars foreign persons from entering the United States who seek or have sought to obtain a visa, documentation, entry or other immigration benefit by committing fraud or otherwise willfully misrepresenting material facts. There is a waiver for this exclusion ground for those persons who are immediate relatives of United States citizens or of permanent resident aliens or for cases where the fraud occurred at least ten years before entry. These grounds of waiver of excludability apply only to persons seeking to enter the United States as immigrants.

Any alien who falsely represents or has falsely represented himself or herself to be a citizen of the United States for any purpose or benefit under the immigration law or under any other federal or state is also inadmissible.

Any alien who was admitted as a nonimmigrant and who has obtained any governmental benefits for which the alien was ineligible, through fraud or misrepresentation, under federal law is excludable for a period of five years from the date of the alien's departure from the United States.

Also included are stowaways and smugglers of aliens. Waivers of excludability are available to aliens guilty of smuggling their immediate family members. (This section, however, would not apply to anyone engaged in the smuggling of a person into the United States for profit.)

Finally, violators include student visa abusers. An alien who obtains a student visa *(F-1)* and who violates a term or condition of such status by either attending a public school for longer than permitted or by transferring to a public school from a private school shall be excludable until the alien has been outside the U.S. for a continuous period of five years after the date of the violation. Presumably this exclusion grounds would apply even to a child and even if the violation were attributable solely to his or her parents or guardians.

Entering without Proper Documents

Grounds of inadmissibility apply to aliens who do not have a valid visa or entry document or who do not have the required documents in support of their immigration status upon entry. There are general waiver provisions applicable to those grounds for exclusion.

Persons Ineligible for Citizenship

This category of exclusion applies to persons who are ineligible for citizenship because of violating U.S. military service requirements and who are draft evaders.

Aliens Previously Removed

Any alien who has been ordered removed and who again seeks admission within five years of the date of removal at the point of entry (or within twenty years in the case of a second or subsequent removal or at any time in the case of an alien convicted of an aggravated felony) is inadmissible.

Any other alien who is removed from the U.S. after entry is barred from entering the U.S. for a period of ten years from the date of the departure or removal (or for a period of twenty years in the case of second or subsequent removal or at any time in the case of an alien convicted of an aggravated felony).

Bar to Entry Based upon Prior Unlawful Presence. Any alien (other than an alien lawfully admitted for permanent residence) who was unlawfully present in the United States for a period of more than 180 days but less than one year, voluntarily departed the United States prior to the commencement of removal proceedings is barred from reentering the U.S. for a period of three years from the date of such alien's departure or removal.

Any alien who has been unlawfully present in the United States for one year or more, is barred from entering the United States for a period of ten years from the date of such alien's departure or removal from the United States.

The term *unlawfully present* generally means the overstay by a foreign person of the time authorized by the USCIS. As such, is usually noted on the *Arrival-Departure Record (Form I-94)*, for a person to remain in the United States. It also includes the time after the USCIS or the immigration court has determined that a person has violated the conditions of admission. It is important to bear in mind that the definition of unlawful presence is a dynamic one and as of the date of the publication of this book, the USCIS was interpreting this term to include the time that a foreign person is required to remain in the U.S. while in formal removal proceedings.

The bar may be waived by the USCIS in its sole discretion if the alien can establish that its imposition would create an extreme hardship on a U.S. citizen or permanent resident spouse or child.

In addition, the bars to reentry based upon unlawful presence do not apply to any period of time in which an alien:

✪ was under the age of eighteen years;

✪ had a bona fide asylum application pending;

✪ was the beneficiary of a family unity protection application; or,

✪ was a battered woman or child.

The time when an alien who has been lawfully admitted to the U.S. has pending a nonfrivolous bona fide application to change or extend status is not counted as unlawful presence for a maximum period of 120 days—provided the alien has not worked without authorization.

An alien who has been unlawfully present in the U.S. for an aggregate period of one year or who has been previously removed from the U.S. and who then seeks to enter the United States at a place other than a lawful entry point is permanently inadmissible. This permanent bar can be waived by the USCIS if the alien's attempted reentry is at least ten years after the date of the alien's last departure from the U.S., if prior to the alien's reembarcation at a place outside the U.S., the USCIS has consented to the alien's reapplication for admission.

Loss of Nonimmigrant Visa

In addition to the described penalty to persons who accumulate time in *unlawful status*, there is also a penalty for merely overstaying the duration of stay, that is defined in the person's arrival-departure record (*Form I-94*) (this is *out of status* compared with *unlawful status*). A person who overstays the defined period of time as stated in the *Form I-94* is deemed be out of status and suffers the immediate voidance of the nonimmigrant visa on which the stay was premised—even if the overstay was for as short a period of one day.

Thus, a person who enters the United States on a nonimmigrant visa, say a *B-1/B-2* and is admitted as visitor *(B-2)* for a period of six months, will lose the visa as soon as he or she is present in the United States in excess of one day of the defined date of required departure. This is the case. Even though the visa as contained in the passport will not have any markings on it and will, to all outward appearances, seem to remain in full force and effect. Thus, upon a subsequent reentry to the United States a person who was previously out of status will be deemed inadmissable for not possessing a proper travel document or visa. If the person is removed from the United States on that basis then he or she will now be subject a five year bar against reentry (for attempted entry without out a proper visa).

NOTE: *The person described will also be deemed to be in unlawful status (in addition to being out of status) after having accumulated a period of 180 days in the United States.*

Polygamy

It is against the public policy of the United States for a person to have more than one spouse.

Alien Guardians Accompanying Helpless Aliens

An alien who is accompanying another alien who is inadmissible and who is certified to be helpless from sickness, mental or physical disability, or infancy and whose protection or guardianship is determined to be required by the inadmissible alien is inadmissible.

International Child Abductors

This ground applies to an alien who may be involved in a domestic (family) dispute involving child custody. During these emotional controversies, aliens may be tempted to simply remove themselves and their children from the United States to their country of origin and avoid the possibility of the United States citizen acquiring child custody rights. Under U.S. and international law, such conduct is improper and amounts to *domestic abduction*. An alien who is found to be an international child abductor is excludable without relief. There are no waivers available for such a person.

Unlawful Voters

Any alien who has voted in violation of any federal, state, or local constitutional provision, statute, ordinance, or regulation is excludable.

Former Citizens who Renounced Citizenship to Avoid Taxation

Any alien who is a former citizen of the U.S. who officially renounced U.S. citizenship and who is determined by the Attorney General to have renounced U.S. citizenship for the purpose of avoiding taxation by the U.S. is excludable.

NOTE: *If any of the above categories of inadmissibility apply, the alien who is considering making a visa application to the United States should consult a qualified U.S. immigration attorney before submitting the application. These categories can also be grounds for deportation in the event the alien enters the country by misrepresentation or omission of information.*

Distinction between Immigrant and Nonimmigrant Visas

There are generally two types of visas available to foreign persons seeking to enter the United States: a *permanent residency* or *immigrant visa* (also known as a *green card*) and a *nonimmigrant visa* or *temporary visa.*

There is only one type of permanent residency visa, and once that is obtained, there are no special subclassifications or conditions attached to that visa—except as to the two-year condition placed on aliens who have obtained *conditional residence* based upon either an employment creation petition or a spousal petition based upon marriage to a U.S. citizen. The permanent residency card (*Form I-551*) is also called the *green card*—even though the card is no longer green in color. Regardless of how a person obtained a green card—whether as a result of marriage to a U.S. citizen, as a result of a labor certification, or by other family relationship to a U.S. citizen—the resulting permanent residency visa consequences are the same in every case. Permanent residency visas enable foreign persons to live and work wherever they choose without distinction as to how the permanent residency visa was obtained.

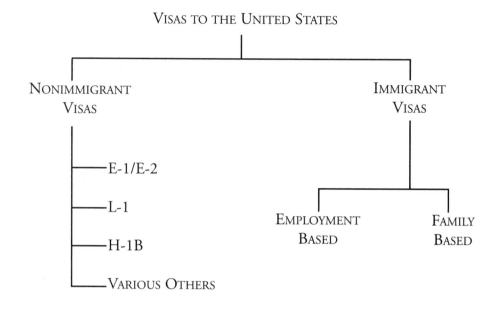

There are, however, many different types of temporary visas. Each visa has its own set of qualifications and conditions, both as to their duration and as to the activities the alien may lawfully undertake in the United States in accordance with the visa. (The previous diagram illustrates this fundamental, but very important point.)

Chapter 2 of this book will discuss the permanent visas and Chapter 3 will discuss some of the most important temporary visas. Which category of visa (permanent or temporary) is the most appropriate for a foreign person depends upon many factors deserving of study and consideration, not the least of which is the alien's own intention.

The Problem of Intent

Probably the most important concept to be understood by any foreign person is the importance attached by the immigration authorities to the alien's *intention* as to duration of stay and purpose in the U.S.

Example: A permanent residency visa is given only to a qualified person who intends to remain living in the United States permanently. A temporary (nonimmigrant) visa is issued only to a qualified person who intends to stay in the United States for a temporary period and then depart. In the latter case, if the alien's immediate intention is to remain permanently in the United States, then the only type of visa he or she can qualify is the immigrant visa.

Looking at it in reverse, the alien would not be qualified for a temporary visa if an immediate intention to remain in the United States permanently is had, even though he or she might be otherwise qualified to obtain that temporary visa.

There are exceptions to this rule, but in general, an alien who meets the objective qualifications for a nonimmigrant visa will be denied that visa or entry to the United States under that visa if the U.S. consul abroad or the USCIS examining officer at the border feels that the alien's true intention is to remain in the U.S. permanently. Furthermore, all aliens entering the United States are presumed to be immigrants (and thus excludable) unless they can demonstrate that they have a valid nonimmigrant visa in their possession and are entitled to enter the United States under that visa.

In the event the immigration border inspector determines that a foreign person is not entitled to enter the United States, that foreign person can be denied the right to enter and be required to return to his or her country of origin. In some limited cases, however, the immigration officer may permit the foreign person to enter the United States on *parole* and then schedule a formal hearing at the local office of the USCIS to determine whether or not the person should be *removed* or *admitted* to the United States.

Thus, instead of a *welcome*, there is a *keep out* attitude framed in the law. This has two possible practical consequences.

1. U.S. consular officers in the foreign country will only grant a nonimmigrant visa if they are satisfied that the person will return to his or her home country. If U.S. consuls are not so convinced, then they may deny issuance of the visa, regardless of whether the alien meets the other objective qualifications for the issuance of the visa.

2. Aliens may be *excluded* or *removed* at the border if the immigration officer is convinced that their intentions for entering the U.S. are different from those required by the visas in their passports or they are otherwise not entitled to enter the United States. (This policy should be thoroughly understood by those wanting to enter the United States.)

The question of intent is oftentimes an elusive concept to understand unless one looks at it from the point of view of the U.S. consular officer. In adjudicating a visa application, the consular officer asks him or herself whether the foreign person has been persuasive in establishing that the purpose of the entry to the United States is consistent with the type of visa sought. Here are some problem examples that have occurred in my practice as well as that of other immigration lawyer colleagues.

✪ A family, including school-age children, applies for a visitor visas with the stated purpose of entering the U.S. for a visit during the normal school year of the foreign country. The consular officer feels that a vacation that interrupts the children's school year is not normal and therefore the family (the parents) may harbor an intention to remain in the United States.

✪ Similar facts as above, but the family members are issued visitor visas by the U.S. consular officer and are admitted to the United States as visitors for a period of six months. Several months after admission the family applies for an extension of stay for an additional six months. Except for unusual circumstances, the application for extension of stay will be denied because, among other things, it would be a violation of visitor visa status for the parents to place the children into schools— especially public schools.

✪ A single young adult from a third world country applies for a visitor visa and is denied. He is highly trained and educated, but the consular officer is simply not convinced that this person will not return to his home country. The consular officer has the benefit of experience to substantiate his or her suspicion.

✪ A citizen of a third world nation that is experiencing economic, political, or social upheaval and who is the parent of a U.S. citizen is denied a visitor visa. Statistically, a significant percentage of such persons do not return to the country of origin. This can result even if the foreign person has significant assets abroad and may be beyond the normal working age.

✪ A foreign person seeking to invest in a U.S. business enterprise is denied entry because the consular officer in unconvinced that the true purpose of the stated entry is investment as opposed to permanent immigration.

✪ Another foreign person similar to the one described in the above example is allowed entry to the U.S. on visitor status. Within a short period of time, he acts in a manner inconsistent with the visa status in which he was admitted by initiating a job search. When the above facts come to the attention of the immigration authorities the result was a denial of the application for the new visa status sought because the entry to the United States was for a purpose other than that which the visa status authorized.

✪ A foreign person who holds *lawful permanent residency (LPR)* status spends the majority of her time abroad over a multiyear period of time and merely *visits* the U.S. for brief occasional periods. She is denied reentry when the customs and immigration officer determines that the she has effectively abandoned her LPR status.

Another set of points to remember in analyzing these questions of intent is as follows.

✪ The foreign applicant always has the *burden of proof,* whether at the U.S. visa consulate abroad or at the U.S. *point of entry* (POE). Pure logic is not the order of the day here, rather, normally persuasive circumstances.

✪ If the evidence that is submitted in order to persuade the adjudicator is not immediately *self-explanatory,* it is probably worthless. As an example, if an applicant submits a copy of a bank statement as evidence of his or her financial ability and the account balance is insignificant, it is generally a waste of time to attempt to present additional evidence (or explanations) to explain or justify this fact. Either present *clear and favorable evidence* or submit nothing at all.

✪ *First impressions* are very important. How foreign applicants dress, how they speak and conduct themselves, and how they organize their applications are all very important. U.S. immigration adjudicators usually favorably reward candor and honesty and penalize deception and ambiguity.

✪ Consular officers are probably not experts in the field of business or any other specific occupation. Therefore any evidence presented should be direct and easy to grasp. Consular officers, however, are very bright and will grasp the point that the evidence attempts to show and, conversely, will discern an intention on the part of the applicant to confuse rather than to elucidate.

NOTE: *Foreign persons must accept that their intentions will be under scrutiny by the U.S. immigration and consular authorities when they apply for any type of visa.*

Unauthorized Employment

The United States government is attempting to stifle illegal immigration by enforcing its laws against unauthorized employment by aliens. It seeks to accomplish this goal by imposing civil and criminal penalties on United States employers who hire aliens who are not legally authorized to work. This law renders it difficult for aliens who are not authorized to work to engage in meaningful employment since it exposes their employers to legal sanctions. The employer, thus, becomes part of the enforcement apparatus as a result of self-interest in avoiding the civil and criminal sanctions imposed by the law. The employer is required to file a *Form I-9*. It establishes the documentation that the alien presented to the employer to verify the alien's authorization to work. In addition to the employer sanctions, aliens are still subject to removal if they are found to be engaged in unauthorized employment.

The law provides for the grant of work authorization to certain aliens in the United States who might not otherwise be eligible to work. Thus, aliens for whom an immigrant visa is immediately available, such as immediate relatives of U.S. citizens, may obtain work authorization. In most cases, an identity card, known as an *EAD (Employment Authorization Document)* with a photograph of the alien is issued as documentation of this status.

2 PERMANENT IMMIGRANT VISAS

The United States establishes two general categories of persons who may immigrate permanently to the United States. One of these categories is composed of persons who are subject to an annual worldwide numerical limit. The other category is composed of those persons who may immigrate at any time regardless of the worldwide demand for immigrant visas. The first group of persons is subject to a system of categories or *preferences* that determines the priority of immigration classifications based on the annual quota. The annual quota is 675,000 persons. This is known as the preference system for permanent visas.

There is another group of persons who are not subject to the preference system and who, when qualified, may enter the United States regardless of the annual numerical quota system. This classification is known as *nonpreference* immigrants. This category includes *refugees* (who have their own quota) *immediate relatives* of United States citizens, and *children* born to a permanent resident during a temporary visit outside the United States. Most persons entering the United States as nonpreference immigrants are immediate relatives of United States citizens. In this book, we will characterize immigrant visas by the terms *preference visas* and *nonpreference visas*. Preference visas are discussed in this chapter. Nonpreference visas are discussed in Chapter 3.

The United States preference system for immigrant visas is sometimes called a *numbers game.* That is because the law establishes the total number of foreign persons who will be admitted annually to the United States as permanent residents. In order to understand the system of immigrant visas, it is important to understand how the numbers game works.

Of the total annual quota of immigrant visas, every nation is limited to an annual maximum number of permanent visas for family-sponsored and employment-related permanent residency visas that cannot exceed seven percent of the total annual number of available visas. (Dependent areas such as St. Kitts, Nevis, etc. are limited to two percent of the yearly quota.)

Generally, the birth place of the alien determines the country that will be charged for immigration and visa purposes. There are, however, special rules that allow the immigrant authorities the right to charge the aliens' spouse's or child's home country with the immigration number rather than the principal alien's country in order to provide for a family unity.

One way to visualize the worldwide numerical limitations quota is to imagine a long line of persons attempting to enter the Unites States. In order to get to the immigration counter to have one's visa application considered on its merits, each person has to take a number and wait in line. In our metaphor, the number on the line is the *priority date.* That is the date the alien's visa petition or application was accepted as complete. When the alien's priority date is reached, his or her immigrant petition will be considered on its merits. It is this waiting period that we refer to when we speak of the backlog or delay in the annual numerical limitations quota. For instance, a three-year backlog for persons coming to perform labor means that only persons who filed petitions or labor certifications three years earlier would be eligible for admission to the United States. In addition, persons from certain countries may have an even longer waiting list because their home countries may have already exceeded their annual limitation.

Of course, not everyone who desires to immigrate to the United States is eligible to receive a permanent residency visa. The law establishes certain categories *(preferences)* of persons who may enter the United States by way of this annual worldwide limitations quota and establishes other categories of persons who may enter without regard to the numerical limitations quota. Entry to the United States is based upon qualitative and quantitative restrictions, all of which are scrupulously regulated by the immigration authorities.

Numerical Limitation or Quota System

As stated in the beginning of this chapter, most foreign persons seeking to enter the United States as permanent residents or immigrants are subject to a world-wide annual quota of 700,000 persons, unless they are also in one of those special categories previously discussed in the last chapter.

The law establishes four preferences of family-sponsored immigrants and five preferences of employment-related immigrants. The following table illustrates this system.

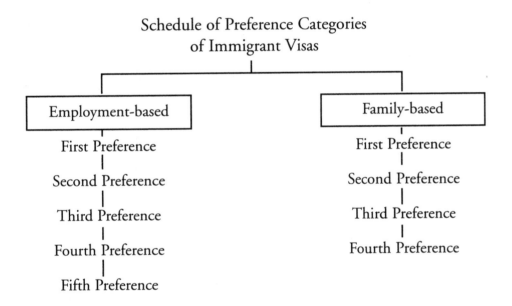

Schedule of Preference Categories
of Immigrant Visas

The annual numerical limitation or quota for family-sponsored immigration is 480,000. Of this number, the law establishes that a minimum of 226,000 visas is reserved for distribution among the four preference categories which will be discussed below. The annual limitation or quota for employment related visas is 140,000. These numbers are subject to change depending upon the political vagaries of the U.S. Congress. The following sections discuss the principal qualifications and conditions of each of these preferences.

Family-Sponsored Immigrants

The law establishes four preferences for persons who are eligible for permanent immigrant visas to the U.S. based upon family relationships. The total number of visas under this category is 480,000 visas. These annual numerical limitations represent the total number of visas issued to all immigrants based upon family relationships, including immediate relatives of United States citizens.

NOTE: *Immediate relatives of U.S. citizens are not counted under the family-sponsored preference category.*

The number of family-sponsored preference visas is set at a minimum of 226,000. So, in fact, the total number of family-sponsored preference visas could rise above the 226,000 minimum if a large number of immediate relative petitions were filed in any given year. (The formula for determining the exact number of family-sponsored preference visas is somewhat complex, but for purposes of this book, it is sufficient to know that the total number of family-sponsored preference visas is now considerably higher than it was previously.)

First Preference   *Unmarried sons and daughter of U.S. citizens.* The first preference comprises persons who are the unmarried sons and daughters of U.S. citizens. This preference is allotted 23,000 visas annually and includes adult, divorced sons and daughters of U.S. citizens. An unmarried son or daughter is defined differently under the law than a *child*, since a child is defined as an unmarried person under the age of twenty-one years. A child (as opposed to a son or daughter) of a U.S. citizen is under the age of twenty-one years, is unmarried, and is entitled to enter the U.S. without regard to the numerical limitations formula.

The first family-based preference is a category of limited application and of limited demand and, as a result, is not backlogged on the worldwide quota. In the language of the immigration system, this preference is considered *current*. Anyone who qualifies may make an immediate application for an immigrant visa.

Second Preference   *Spouse and unmarried sons and daughters of lawful permanent resident aliens.* This preference pertains to spouses and unmarried sons and daughters of lawful permanent resident aliens. This preference is different from the first preference because it benefits certain relatives of permanent residents as opposed to U.S. citizens. Please note that the term *unmarried son or daughter* is different from the definition of child and in order to comply under this preference, the son or daughter must be unmarried at the time of the application for the visa, though the person may be of any age.

This preference is allotted a minimum total of 114,200 visas. This preference is subdivided so that at least seventy-seven percent of such visas are to be allocated to spouses and children of permanent residents. The other twenty-three percent of the total number of visas under this preference is allocated to the unmarried sons or daughters of permanent residents. A divorced son or daughter of a permanent resident will qualify under this preference.

If a permanent resident alien of the United States marries a foreign person, the U.S. residents' foreign spouses does not receive permanent resident status (and thus will not be permitted to enter the United States) until his or her priority date is current. In a typical situation, after the marriage takes place, the permanent resident spouse would file an immigration petition for the foreign spouse. The foreign spouse would have to remain abroad until his or her priority date became current. If the foreign spouse were already in the United States, there is no assurance that the USCIS would permit the spouse to remain in the U.S. until the priority date became current.

On the contrary, if an alien beneficiary remains in the United States in *unlawful status* for a time period in excess of 180 days of the original expiration date of status as determined in *Form I-94*, then the foreign person will not be able to *adjust* his or her status in the U.S. He or she will be required to depart the U.S. in order to process the grant of permanent residency. The departure from the U.S. will then trigger either the three- or the ten-year bar against reentry to the U.S. The only waiver to the three- or ten-year bar is for situations in which the U.S. or permanent resident spouse or child can establish, in the sole discretion of the USCIS, that it would be an *extreme hardship* to the U.S. citizen or permanent resident to enforce the bars.

In December, 2001, Congress enacted a law that made it possible for foreign persons already resident in the U.S. who were beneficiaries of petitions for permanent residency filed before April 30, 2001 to apply to adjust to permanent residency within the United States after paying a civil penalty of $1,000.00. Thus, by law, all these persons could avoid the three- or ten-year bar because they were permitted to apply for permanent residence from within the United States (after paying the $1,000.00 penalty).

The section of law that permits this procedure is known as Section 245 (i). It contains a cut-off date when a foreign person's petition must have been filed in order for the foreign person to apply for *Adjustment of Status*. (This procedure is described in more detail later in this book.)

This law expired on April 30th of 2001. Persons (and their spouses and children) who were the beneficiaries of petitions for permanent residency that were filed on or before that date may still be eligible to apply for *Adjustment of Status*. That is because the benefits of the law remain with the foreign person regardless of the fact that they may be eligible for permanent residency through a different sponsor.

Example: Assume that a foreign person was the beneficiary of a petition filed on his or her behalf by a U.S. citizen sibling on or before April 30th, 2001. Sometime in 2004, the foreign person then becomes the beneficiary of petition for permanent residency filed on his or her behalf by an employer. At the time the U.S. employer files its petition on behalf of the foreign person worker, the foreign person and his or her immediate family members will also be eligible to apply for *Adjustment of Status* to lawful permanent residency. This is because the foreign person had been *grandfathered* by the prior petition of the sibling to the benefits of Section 245(i).

Third Preference *Married sons and daughters of United States citizens.* This preference provides for a total of 23,400 visas, plus any visas that have not been used by the first two family-sponsored preference groups. The third preference benefits qualified persons who are the married sons or daughters of U.S. citizens. As with the family-sponsored second preference, a divorced person qualifies as a beneficiary of this category. This preference, as of the writing of this book, was also backlogged and is expected to remain so in the foreseeable future.

Fourth Preference *Brothers and sisters of United States citizens.* The fourth preference provides for a total of 65,000 visas or twenty-four percent of the worldwide annual quota plus any visas that have not been utilized by the first three family-sponsored preference groups and benefits qualified persons who are the siblings (brothers and sisters) of United States citizens. The United States citizen petitioner must be at least twenty-one years of age in order to file a petition on behalf of the sibling. Half brothers and half sisters are entitled to the benefits of this preference, as long as the sibling relationship was created before both of the siblings were twenty-one years of age.

As a result of the relatively wide spread eligibility standard of this visa, there is a long waiting list for this visa preference. In the language of immigration law it is heavily *oversubscribed*. In fact, the actual waiting list for a new petitioner based upon the current rate of advancement of this preference is probably more than fifteen years. This is because advancement of the priority date does not coincide with the normal advancement of the calendar. Over the last few years, the priority date for this preference has advanced at a rate of approximately one week per actual calendar month.

Many United States citizens, in order to benefit their brothers and sisters, might almost routinely file an immigrant visa petition for their foreign siblings, on the basis that at some unspecified future time their brothers or sisters may wish to immigrate permanently to the United States. This action can result in an unfortunate trap, since the foreign sibling may be unable to obtain a temporary nonimmigrant visa to the United States as a result of the filing of the family-sponsored fourth preference petition by the sibling in the United States. This is because the filing of the immigrant visa petition establishes that the foreign person has an intention to reside in the United States on a permanent basis. Of course, this intention conflicts with the temporary intent required for any one of the various nonimmigrant visas, even the *B-2* visitor visa.

When the foreign sibling is a business person who may need to come to the United States on temporary business and does not already have a *B-1/B-2* visa, it is probably better to avoid filing the fourth preference petition unless the foreign person already has a valid *B-1/B-2* visa in his or her passport. Otherwise the foreign sibling may have (as a condition to obtaining his *B-1/B-2* visa) to convince the U.S. consul in the home country that he or she intends to return to the foreign country after each visit to the United States and presently has the intent of visiting the United States only on a temporary basis. This is especially true in the case of persons who are nationals of developing countries or of countries from which there is a history of visa fraud.

While it may seem logical that foreign persons who have a fourth preference petition filed on their behalf, which has at least a seven or eight year waiting period if not considerably more, would still have an intent to return to their home country after a short visit to the United States, the United States consular authorities may require some special proof or documentation before granting a temporary visa to the foreign person.

NOTE: *It is important to bear in mind that all of the family-based beneficiaries (foreign persons for whose benefit the petition was filed) are subject to the three- and ten-year bars against reentry to the United States if they are unlawfully present in the United States for a period of 180 days or more.*

Employment-Based Immigrants

While the family-sponsored preferences provide for family unity and are premised upon familial relationships, the following employment-based preferences—with the exception of the *employment creation* visa—are intended to benefit qualified U.S. employers who need certain qualified workers. Unless a foreign person is fortunate to have an immediate relative who is either a citizen or permanent resident of the United States, or unless the foreigner qualifies as a refugee or an asylee, the employment-based preferences are the only avenues of obtaining a permanent residency visa.

The law establishes five main categories of employment-based immigrants. The total number of employment-based immigrant visas is 140,000 annually, plus any unused family-sponsored immigrant visas during the previous fiscal year. The table illustrating the employment-based categories follows on the next page.

IMMIGRANT VISAS

<u>Employment-Based</u>
✪EB First Preference
├── Nobel Prize winner, chairperson of Mercedes Benz
├── Researchers, scientists, AIDS vaccine scientist
└── International executives

✪EB Second Preference
└── Masters plus degree professionals

✪EB Third Preference
├── Professional with Baccalaureate Degree
├── Two-year training or experience
└── General or unskilled labor

✪EB Fourth Preference
├── Certain juveniles
├── Ministers of religion
└── Retired former employees of U.S. Government abroad

✪EB Fifth Preference
└── Employment creation investors

First Preference   *Priority workers.* There are 40,000 visas annually available under this category. This preference category encompasses three subcategories of immigrants:

- ✪ persons of extraordinary ability in the arts and sciences, in the field of education, business, or athletics;

- ✪ outstanding professors and researchers; and,

- ✪ multinational executives or managers who will work in the United States for the same multinational employer for whom they were employed abroad for one out of the last three years in an executive or managerial capacity.

The most distinguishing characteristic of this visa preference aside from its high level of achievement is the fact that a labor certification from the U.S. Department of Labor is not required as a prerequisite to obtaining this visa. In fact, the alien does not need to be *sponsored* by a U.S. employer. Qualified employment-based first preference immigrant may petition themselves.

Aliens of extraordinary ability. The high level of achievement that is required by this preference category is demonstrated by sustained national or international acclaim that must be extensively documented. The alien must be seeking to enter the United States to continue work in the field of endeavor that is the subject of the acclaim. In addition, the alien's presence and activities must be of benefit to the United States. These requirements must be established with documentary evidence of a highly reliable nature.

The required high level of achievement can be demonstrated by receipt of a major internationally recognized award such as the Nobel Prize or the Academy Award for motion pictures. Alternatively, the alien must provide at least three of the following types of evidence:

- ✪ receipt of a lesser national or international prize or award for excellence in the particular field of endeavor;

- ✪ membership in associations that require outstanding achievements of their members, as judged by nationally or internationally recognized experts in the particular field;

- ✪ published material in professional journals, major trade publications, or the major media about the alien's accomplishments in the field of endeavor. (These items must include title, date, author, and must be translated into English.);

- ✪ participated on a panel or individually as a judge of the work of others in the same or allied field of endeavor;

- ✪ original scientific, scholarly, or artistic contributions of major significance in the field of endeavor;

- ✪ authorship of scholarly articles in the field, in professional journals, or other major media (national newspapers, magazines, etc.);

- ✪ display of his or her work at artistic exhibitions in more than one country;

✪   performance in a lead, starring, or critical role for organizations or establishments with distinguished reputations;

✪   commanding a high salary or other significantly high remuneration for services in relation to others;

✪   commercial success in the performing arts, as shown by box office receipts; or record, cassette, compact disk, or video sales; or,

✪   other comparable evidence if the above types of evidence do not readily apply to the alien's occupation.

NOTE: *The listing of evidence is part of the regulatory scheme designed to explain the intention of the statute as well as to provide a comprehensible system of documentation. Therefore, a petitioner should not be discouraged if the technological medium that is being used (DVD's, MP3, etc.) is not specifically mentioned. The examples given only attempt to define the larger category of the industry.*

The USCIS has ruled that notwithstanding the furnishing of the minimum amount of documentation requested by the foreign person, there is no assurance that the petition will be approved unless from the totality of the evidence, the USCIS is convinced that the foreign person has satisfied the qualitative condition of *extraordinary ability*.

NOTE: *There is absolutely no substitute in this area for the assistance of an experienced and competent immigration attorney in the preparation of the documentation required to fulfill the requirements of this visa preference.*

Outstanding professor or researcher. Aliens qualify as an outstanding professor or researcher if they have received international acclaim in a particular academic field; have had at least three years of experience in teaching or research in the field; and, seek to enter the United States for a tenured or tenure-track teaching or research position. The position can be for a university or other educational institution or for a private employer so long as the employer has at least three other persons employed in full-time research.

Evidence that the professor/researcher is recognized internationally requires at least two of the following:

✪ receipt of major international prizes or awards for outstanding achievement in the academic field;

✪ membership in academic associations requiring outstanding achievement;

✪ published materials and professional publications written by others about the alien's work;

✪ participation on a panel, or as an individual judging work of others;

✪ original scientific/scholarly research contribution; or,

✪ authorship of scholarly books or articles.

Multinational executive or manager. In order to qualify as a multinational executive or manager under this preference, aliens, during the three years preceding the application, must have been employed for at least one year by the same multinational firm or other business entity that employs them in the United States. Furthermore, the alien must seek to continue rendering services to the same employer in a managerial or executive capacity. The definition of *executive* and *manager* is identical with the definition of those terms under the *L-1* visa rules.

This preference category represents an excellent planning opportunity for individuals who also qualify for the *L-1* nonimmigrant visa (discussed in more detail later in this book). There is no specific requirement as to the size of the petitioning company or its gross business volume, but the company (employer) must have been in business in the United States for at least one year prior to the filing of the immigrant visa petition (*Form I-140*).

The law establishes the definition of the terms *managerial capacity* and *executive capacity* and they are identical for both this immigrant visa category as well as the nonimmigrant *L-1* intracompany transferee visa (Chapter 3). In order to be qualified as a manager, a person must:

✪ manage a corporation, department, subdivision, or function;

✪ supervise and control the work of other supervisory, professional, or managerial employees, or else manage an *essential function;*

✪ have the authority to make personnel decisions as to hiring and termination, or else function at a *senior level*; or,

✪ exercise discretion over the day to day operations of the activity or function for which he or she has authority.

NOTE: *First-line supervisors are excluded from the statutory definition of a manager unless the employees supervised are professional.*

Thus, a manager includes persons who manage a function as well as other people. The term *executive capacity* is also redefined as follows:

✪ the person must manage an organization, major component, or function;

✪ has the authority to establish goals and policies;

✪ has wide latitude and discretionary decision making authority; or,

✪ receives only general supervision from higher executives, board of directors, or stockholders.

The above definitions encompass executives who also perform tasks necessary to produce the product or provide the service offered by the organization if the executive is also a professional, such as an engineer or architect. This subcategory would permit an owner of a business enterprise to immigrate to the United States so long as he or she could otherwise satisfy the substantive eligibility requirements described above.

In a situation in which the prospective employee was also an owner of the enterprise that would hire him or her, the USCIS will scrutinize the petition very closely to discourage fraud. A specific job offer is not required for issuance of this visa, even though it is contemplated that the alien is coming to perform valuable services for a business entity. This subcategory is very advantageous and is therefore closely scrutinized by the USCIS in order to ensure that it is not abused.

This category represents an important alternative to the *Employment Creation Visa*. Proper planning by a qualified investor can result in issuance of a permanent residency visa without the necessity of investing one million dollars in a new enterprise that creates a large number of jobs.

Second Preference

Aliens of exceptional ability. This preference benefits aliens who have:

- ✪ advanced degrees or their equivalent in professional fields or

- ✪ exceptional ability in the sciences, arts, or business.

In order to establish the first status described, the alien must submit the official academic record showing a United States advanced degree or a foreign equivalent degree; an official academic record showing that the alien has a United States baccalaureate degree or a foreign equivalent degree; and, evidence in the form of letters from current or former employers stating that the alien has at least five years of progressive, post-baccalaureate experience in the specialty.

In order to establish exceptional ability in the sciences, arts, or business, the alien must document at least three of the following:

- ✪ an official academic record showing that the alien has a degree, diploma, certificate, or similar award from a college, university, school, or other institution of learning relating to the area of exceptional ability;

- ✪ evidence in the form of letter(s) from current or former employer(s) showing that the alien has at least ten years of full-time experience in the occupation;

- ✪ a license to practice the profession or certification for a particular profession or occupation;

- ✪ evidence that the alien has commanded a salary or other remuneration for services that demonstrate exceptional ability;

- ✪ evidence of membership in a professional association; or,

- ✪ evidence of recognition for achievements and significant contributions to the industry or field by peers, governmental entities or professional or business organizations.

The USCIS has indicated that it will consider comparable evidence that is appropriate to the alien's application *in the event the alien cannot provide the type of documentation listed above.*

The law allows a person to have the equivalent of an advanced degree if that person has at least five years progressive experience in the profession beyond the bachelor's degree. Persons who have exceptional ability in business, however, will still be required to obtain a labor certification. It is important to note that the possession of a degree, diploma, certificate, or similar award from a college, university, school, or other institution is not sufficient evidence of exceptional ability by itself. Thus, there must be something beyond the basic qualification in a field of endeavor in order for a person to qualify as having exceptional ability.

The National Interest Waiver. For this preference category, a job offer and labor certification from the Department of Labor is required unless the USCIS waives that requirement in the national interest. Since the labor certification requirement is such a difficult and expensive process, the alien or the employer should consider whether or not a case can be made that the particular job benefits the national interest.

A series of administrative law decisions has defined the government's policy with respect to establishing the requirements for the *national interest waiver* of the labor certification. The range of cases and decisions indicates that the government requires a fairly direct benefit to the community-at-large before it will agree that a job is in the national interest. A job, for instance, that consists of basic research in attempting to find a cure for the AIDS virus will satisfy this requirement. A job that results in the rescue of a company from bankruptcy and that saves dozens of other jobs will also meet this burden.

As a matter of strategy, it is imperative to identify an issue of substantial national interest and then demonstrate how the job in question benefits that national interest in order to prevail on this issue. It is normally necessary to obtain the written opinion of an objective expert in order to prove that a particular job satisfies the national interest. I do not recommend that a person attempt to obtain the national interest waiver without the assistance of a competent and experienced immigration law consultant.

Third Preference

Skilled and unskilled workers. This preference is a general category that includes all other aliens who attempt to obtain permanent residency in the United States based upon an offer of employment. This category also has 40,000 visas annually plus any of the unused visas from the first two employment-based preferences. A job offer from an employer, as well as a labor certification from the U.S. Department of Labor are required. The subject of labor certification is discussed later on in this chapter. The employment-based third preference contains three sub-categories:

✪ skilled workers, defined as aliens capable of performing a job requiring at least two years of training or experience;

✪ professionals with a bachelor's degree (only); and,

✪ other workers, also referred to as unskilled workers, who are capable of filling positions requiring less than two years of training or experience.

The first two subcategories share 30,000 of the 40,000 visas allotted to the third preference. Only 10,000 of the 40,000 annual visas in the third preference are available to unskilled workers. The present immigration law is geared toward bringing in skilled workers for the economy and is skewed against bringing in unskilled workers.

The segregation of the unskilled workers from the other two above mentioned skilled and professional categories will prevent these from becoming as heavily oversubscribed and backlogged as is the category for unskilled workers.

This preference is based on job availability and often the inquiry is a detailed analysis of the requirements of the job that forms the basis for the visa petition. It is important to bear in mind that in these types of petitions, the foreign worker bears the burden of proving that he or she is qualified either by training, education, or experience to perform the job and the employer must prove that it is financially able to pay the wage for the job. All of the important terminology has special administrative and legal definitions that must be objectively satisfied to the satisfaction of the government by both the alien and the U.S. employer.

Fourth Preference

Special immigrants. This preference category is allocated 10,000 visas annually plus any left over visas from the higher employment-based categories.

Ministers of religion. In order to qualify for this category, the religious worker must have been a member of and working for the religious organization for at least two years and be seeking to enter the United States as a minister of religion. This visa preference has an expiration date that is usually extended. It is necessary to verify that this particular category is still available at the time of application.

Certain juveniles. A third sub-group of special immigrants is aliens who have been declared dependent on a juvenile court and for whom a court has decided that it is not in their best interest to be returned to their homeland. The natural parents of such aliens are unable to derive any immigration benefits simply because their child has gained special immigrant status.

Fifth Preference

Investors/employment creation. This employment-based preference category contains 10,000 visas per year for foreign persons who invest a minimum amount of capital in a new enterprise that creates employment. The 10,000 annual visas are a fixed number and does not benefit from any unused visas in any of the other employment-based preferences. The amount of the required investment ranges from a low of $500,000.00 for *targeted employment areas* up to a high of $3,000,000.00 for an enterprise located in a region deemed to be of low unemployment. The alien must have invested the capital after November 29, 1990 or be in the active process of investing the capital.

The standard investment must be of $1,000,000.00 and must create at least ten full time jobs for U.S. citizens, permanent resident aliens, or other immigrants lawfully authorized to be employed in the United States. This group of ten workers provided for by the law cannot include the investor or the investor's immediate family.

Targeted employment areas. The law encourages investment in areas of high unemployment or other areas known as *targeted employment areas* and those areas are defined as rural areas or areas having an unemployment rate at least 1$^{1}/_{2}$ times the national average. A total of ten jobs still need be created and the required investment is reduced to $500,000.00. A total of 3,000 of the 10,000 annual visas in this preference category are reserved for this level of investment. A *rural* area is defined as an area outside of metropolitan statistical area or a municipality with a population of less than 21,000 people.

In order to implement the application of the $500,000.00 amount, it is necessary for the individual states to designate, subject to federal government approval, the state authority that will determine the geographic areas or political subdivisions that are identified as rural or targeted employment areas.

The administrative regulations published by the USCIS provide that a qualified investment includes the purchase of an existing business so long as the enterprise's net worth, after the completion of the sale, is at least 140% of the value of the enterprise prior to the date of the acquisition or that there is a forty percent increase in the level of employment. This requirement will preclude an investor from merely purchasing an ongoing business without causing any substantive improvement in the capital or employment levels of the enterprise.

In addition, the regulations provide for the purchase and overhaul of a troubled or undercapitalized business enterprise by a foreign person so long as the acquisition will save jobs. A troubled business is defined as one that has been in existence for at least two years and has experienced a twenty percent diminution of its net worth during the last two years. In any event, a total of $1,000,000.00 (or $500,000.00 if applicable) must be invested and ten jobs must have been created or preserved.

The ability to reorganize an existing business in compliance with this visa category feature is very interesting because business consultants agree that in most instances it is preferable to purchase an ongoing business enterprise rather than for a person to attempt the development of a business from the beginning—especially in the case of a foreign person. Since there is a highly developed industry in the United States for the acquisition and sale of existing commercial enterprises, it is advisable for a prospective foreign investor to utilize the services of these professionals in the identification of a suitable acquisition. (The occupations of business brokers and mergers and acquisitions consultants is explained in more depth in Chapter 5 of this book.)

This visa requires that the investor manage the business personally and does not anticipate that the investor be merely a passive financier. There is an exception to this rule in the case of a limited partner of a limited partnership formed in accordance with the requirements of a certain uniform limited partnership law. The provision for the limited partner is contradictory to the requirement that the investor directly manage and/or supervise the investment. This is because the limited partnership act referred to, by its very terms, defines the limited partner as a passive investor. Since a limited partnership interest is a security and will support an employment creation investor visa, one wonders why the regulations do not also permit other types of securities or passive investment arrangements to warrant a permanent visa as long as the requisite level of employment is created.

The law provides a number of measures to discourage fraud by immigrant investors by providing for fines of up to $250,000.00 and jail for up to five years. In addition, the law makes the grant of permanent residence to immigrant investors conditional and has established a two-year trial period. During this two-year period, by rule and regulation, the USCIS will determine whether the enterprise was in fact established, whether or not the capital was in fact invested, and whether the alien did sustain the enterprise. During a ninety-day period prior to the end of the two-year period, the investor must file an additional petition with the USCIS requesting that the conditional status of residence be removed.

Under this preference category, only a very few such petitions have been approved. In the beginning of the program in the early 90's, the then INS approved many investment schemes that clearly were bogus or even fraudulent. As a consequence the since adopted approach is almost totally opposed to common business sense. In short, the government now requires that the alien prove the following:

- ✪ that the alien was involved in the initial development of the enterprise. The elements of proof for this requirement are ambiguous at best since very few foreign investors who enjoy the liquidity of a million dollars of capital are naive enough to invest this sum in a scheme that they alone developed;

- ✪ that the alien not premise the investment on the obtainment of permanent residency. This requirement is so laughable that it hardly merits comment, except to say that most banks would not countenance lending such a sum to a key person if that person could not give assurances that he or she would be a resident in the community or at least the state in which the enterprise was functioning;

- ✪ that the alien is not guaranteed a redemption of his or her investment by the syndicator or general partner of the business enterprise in which the alien has invested;

- ✪ that the alien establish by documents and accounting records the legitimacy of the capital which has been invested. This requirement is open-ended in that there is no logical manner of ruling out that the investment capital is not tainted. This provision obviously favors aliens coming from developed countries which have a strong and stable tax collection and reporting mechanism. If there are other investors (U.S. or otherwise) in the enterprise the legality of those funds must also be documented; and,

✪ that any promissory notes which are used by the investor to complete the investment must be *perfected* (this is a term used almost exclusively in U.S. jurisprudence) so as to guarantee that the holder of the note has complete recourse against the alien investor.

The list is not exclusive. What is clear, is that the promotion of investment in the U.S. is not a strong consideration and that the government has adopted a most pedantic and disruptive attitude towards this preference. In short, since the agency feels insecure with this preference category, it has adopted the most simplistic approach possible. Indeed, the government has gone so far as to revoke visa petitions that had been previously approved.

Conditional grant of visa. This visa will be issued initially for a period of two years after which time, if the investment is still in place, the visa will be permanent and no longer subject to the investor's continued personal involvement in the enterprise. In order to remove the two-year condition and grant the alien permanent residence, the alien must file a *Form I-829* together with appropriate documentation.

The petition for removal of conditions must be accompanied by the following evidence:

✪ documentary evidence that a commercial enterprise was established by the alien;

✪ evidence that the alien invested or was actively in the process of investing the requisite capital;

✪ evidence that the alien has, in good faith, substantially met the required capital investment and continuously maintained his or her capital investment over the two years of conditional residence; and,

✪ evidence that the alien created or can be expected to create within a reasonable time ten full-time jobs for qualifying employees. In the case of a *troubled business* as defined above, the alien entrepreneur must submit evidence that the commercial enterprise maintained the number of existing employees at no less than the pre-investment level for the period following his or her admission as a conditional permanent resident.

If the alien investor fails to file *Form I-829* within the ninety-day period immediately preceding the second anniversary of the date the alien obtained lawful permanent residence on a conditional basis, then the alien's permanent resident status shall be terminated and removal proceedings will be started.

If an entrepreneur dies during the prescribed two-year period of conditional permanent residence, the spouse and children of the entrepreneur will be eligible for removal of conditions if it can be demonstrated that all the conditions of the investment have been met.

This immigrant visa category is quite appropriate for the acquisition of hotel/motel properties, especially in resort or tourist areas where the real estate (*propiedad inmueble*) can be expected to retain its value. It is the author's personal view that foreign persons should favor the more conservative approach to investment in the United States until they have developed insight into the economy and business customs of the location in which they are investing. Real estate enterprises, including hotels and motels, and other franchised enterprises are good candidates for this level of investment so long as they are sufficiently labor intensive to satisfy the above described job creation requirements.

Remember that by becoming permanent residents of the United States, foreign persons become United States taxpayers and thus, subject their worldwide income to taxation. Proper pre-investment planning is absolutely essential in order to avoid fiscal disasters, and a foreign investor should consult a number of consultants, both abroad as well as in the United States to assist in the various phases of the investment. (In this regard, the reader is invited to peruse the section on taxation starting on page 173 of this book.)

The Labor Certification Process

As explained previously, the second, third, and fourth employment-based preferences require as a precondition, the prospective employer receive a *labor certification* from the U.S. Department of Labor. The labor certification is a finding that there are not enough qualified workers in the U.S. location where the foreign person will perform the job or services and that the employment of the alien will not adversely affect the U.S. labor market. In practical terms, this means that an employer will offer a position to a foreign person and will employ that foreign person if the Department of Labor approves the employment.

It is difficult to obtain a labor certification from the Department of Labor. First, the processing time for the labor certification, which is a prerequisite to filing the second and third employment-based visa petitions, can be one year or more in length. In addition to the job certification delay, the alien must still wait for the *priority date* to become current for the visa itself. The prospective employee receives his or her priority date on the day that his or her labor certification request (*Form ETA 750*) is accepted for processing by the U.S. Department of Labor.

The prospective employee cannot file the immigrant visa petition until the labor certification has been issued. At times there have been *backlogs* or delays in the time within which an employer could file the petition. Thus, this additional delay, if any, must be added to the normal processing time for the application for labor certification.

The application for job certification is filed on a form known as *Form ETA 750* which is comprised of two parts, A and B. Part A is completed by the employer and lists the employer's requirements, while Part B is completed by the employee and lists the employee's qualifications.

The process is initiated when the employer offers the alien a job and then files an application for a labor certification with the U.S. Department of Labor. The form is filed with the local state labor office which then processes and transmits the form, together with its recommendations, to the regional U.S. Department of Labor office.

Requirements

In order to obtain a labor certification, the employer must prove to the Department of Labor that:

- ✪ the job being offered to the alien is available and is otherwise open to persons in the United States;

- ✪ there are no unreasonable or unnecessary conditions placed on the position; and,

- ✪ the wage offered is at least the prevailing wage in the community.

In the United States, a job requirement that a person must speak a particular foreign language is considered *prima facie* unreasonable and can only be overcome by proof that knowledge of a foreign language is essential to the proper performance of the job. The employer must also prove that it has made a reasonable effort to fill that position with U.S. citizens or permanent residents. The employer is required to advertise the position in a newspaper of general circulation, (sometimes in a professional or trade journal), and must post in the place of employment information concerning the availability of that position.

In order to fully appreciate the philosophy of the Department of Labor and the USCIS with respect to the issuance of labor certifications, the following quotation from the *Federal Register* concerning the employment-based, second and third preferences is instructive:

> *The labor certification process briefly described: Generally, an individual labor certification from the department is required for employers wishing to employ an alien under preference groups 2 and 3. In issuing such certifications, the Department of Labor applies two basic standards to exclude an alien: (1) if U.S. workers are able, willing, qualified, and available for the position; and/or (2) if the employment of an alien will adversely affect the wages or working conditions of U.S. workers similarly employed.*

> *In brief, the current process for obtaining a labor certification requires employers to actively recruit U.S. workers in good faith for a period of at least thirty days for the job openings for which aliens are sought. The employers' job requirements must be reasonable and realistic, and employers must offer prevailing wages and working conditions for the occupation. The employers may not favor aliens or tailor the job requirements to the aliens' qualifications.*

> *During the thirty-day recruitment period, employers are required to place a three-day, help-wanted advertisement in a newspaper of general circulation, or a one-day advertisement in a professional, trade or business journal, or ethnic publication. Employers are also required to place a thirty-day job order with the local office of the state employment service. If employers believe they have already conducted adequate recruitment, they may ask the Department of Labor to waive the mandatory, thirty-day recruitment. If the employer does not request a waiver of recruitment or if the waiver request is denied, the help-wanted advertisements that are placed in conjunction with the mandatory thirty-day recruitment will direct*

the job applicants to either report in person to the employment service or to submit resumés to the employment service.

The job applicants are then referred to the employer or their resumés are sent. The employer then has forty-five days to report to the employment service the job-related reasons for not hiring any United States workers referred. If the employer hires a United States worker for the job opening, the process stops at that point, unless the employer has more than one opening. If, however, the employer believes that qualified, willing and able United States workers are not available to take the job, the application, together with the documentation of the recruitment results and prevailing wage information are sent to the regional office of the Department of Labor. There, it is reviewed and a determination is made as to whether or not to issue the labor certification.

In practical application, the above explanation means that the Department of Labor will deny the labor certification if the employer requires special conditions that only a foreign person can or is willing to fulfill, unless those conditions are essential to the business. Therefore a requirement that the person holding the job speak a foreign language will disqualify the labor certification unless the employer can prove that the foreign language requirement is an essential part of the job. Mere convenience or slight competitive advantage to an employer is not sufficient. Also, the employer must offer the prevailing wage for the job that is paid in the community. It must not impose higher than normal educational or experiential requirements for the position.

Obviously, the Department of Labor wants to ensure that an employer does not bypass available United States workers so that the employer can give the job to an alien of its choice. The labor certification process can be long and difficult. It very often places considerable administrative burdens on the employer as well as personal and financial strains and risks on the employee. The employer is not permitted to hire a foreign person in preference to a U.S. worker merely because the foreign worker is better qualified than the United States worker. This means that the U.S. employer is required to hire the United States worker who satisfies the minimum recognized requirements for the particular job.

Employer's Risk   Thus, there are two impediments to the obtainment of permanent residency based upon the issuance of a *labor certification*. The first is the requirement that the job be qualified as a *skilled* job; that is, the job must have a training or learning component of at least two years. If the job can be learned in less than two years, then it will not qualify as a *skilled* job. This is important because if a job is considered *unskilled*, a visa will not be available within the reasonable future. It is important to remember that it is not the industry or character of the company that is relevant, rather it is the job itself. Thus, an *unskilled* job (customer service representative, receptionist, salesperson, etc.) for a high-tech firm or even a highly remunerative *unskilled* job (salesperson for a luxury automobile dealer like Mercedes Benz or Lexus) will not result in a classification as a *skilled* worker.

The second component of risk is that even if the job itself qualifies as a skilled job, there may be U.S. persons in the local labor markets who are qualified to perform the job. If a qualified U.S. person applies for the job, the employer must either hire the U.S. person or withdraw the job offer on behalf of the alien.

It is important to remember that the U.S. employer does not have the right to offer the job (on the basis of a labor certification) to the foreign person simply because the U.S. worker is not equally skilled. The U.S. employer can only offer the job to the foreign person if the U.S. worker candidate does not meet the minimum qualifications for the job. The Department of Labor establishes these minimum qualifications and they are all listed in a publication entitled the *Dictionary of Occupational Titles (DOT)*.

While the conditions of the local job market will determine the possibility of obtaining a labor certification, certain trends are apparent. First, as a matter of practical reality, immigrant visas are only available for persons whose jobs require a minimum of two years or more of training and experience in order to perform the job. This is caused by the backlog in the category of *other workers* for the third employment-based preference. It is so long that most job offers will not survive the long delay—neither may the U.S. job sponsor or the beneficiary.

Second, the job market will be affected by the number of jobs in the particular area. As an example, it may be very difficult to prove that there is a job shortage for hotel managers in a resort area such as Miami, Florida or San Francisco, California because these jobs and geographical areas attract many qualified U.S. candidates.

There are some anomalies, however. It is generally easier to obtain a labor certification for job skills that occupy the opposite ends of the spectrum. For example, a scientist who is experienced in advanced molecular biochemistry will probably receive a labor certification. Likewise, an attendant for a coin operated laundry at the prevailing wage for that position may also be approved for labor certification. That is because in both instances the prospective employer may not be able to find a qualified U.S. worker to fill the position, either because of the high degree of training and experience required or because of the unfavorable job conditions and low wages offered. In both cases, the result is the same in that the employer is unable to fill the job position.

In general, the U.S. economy and the law favor foreign persons who have particular job capabilities and skills that are not readily obtainable in the U.S. labor market.

An employer who wishes to hire a foreign person who possesses only general administrative and sales skills will find it very difficult to obtain the labor certification. It is always advisable to consult with a qualified immigration attorney who is familiar with the job market in the area of intended employment.

Reduction in Recruitment

In certain cases, it may be possible to avoid the labor certification process by proving to the Department of Labor that the employer has, during a period of at least six months, attempted to fill the position with normal and customary efforts and has failed to find qualified workers. Under these circumstances, it may be possible to have the Department of Labor agree that there is no need for a labor certification application since the employer has already without success made reasonable and good faith efforts to fill the position. If the employer can document these good faith efforts over a sustained period of time, it will request permission for a *Reduction in Recruitment* certification that will accept the employer's efforts as dispositive of the labor market test. This will shorten the processing time for labor certification and this seems to be the wave of the future since because of budgetary considerations, both the state and federal governments are attempting to decrease the size of the bureaucracies that adjudicate these applications.

NOTE: *This is an area of practice that strongly suggests professional assistance.*

Problem of Intent

As a result of filing the immigrant visa petition, an alien may find that the ability to travel to the U.S. can be curtailed. This could happen in at least two typical circumstances:

1. the U.S. consulate in the foreign country may not grant a temporary visa to the alien or

2. (even if the alien is granted the visa) the alien's right to enter the U.S. under the temporary visa in question may be challenged by the customs and immigration inspector at the port of entry in the course of the normal border inspection interview.

Usually, this *interview* is very short and very simple. The customs and border inspector will ask what the foreign person's purpose is of the entry to the U.S. and will run the passport through a computer scan. In the normal situation, the inspector accepts the person's statement as to the purpose of entry. If the computer scan does not show any police or immigration record, the person is allowed to enter. If the inspector decides to inquire further into the person's background or reason for entry, he or she may decide that the foreign person is entering for a purpose that is inconsistent with the visa. In this case, the inspector may refuse the person entry to the U.S. The legal determination is either that the visa is no longer valid (perhaps because of a prior violation of visa status) or because the foreign person's true intention is not in accord with the visa in the passport.

This problem is caused by the legal requirement that the alien's intent as to duration of stay as well as to the alien's deemed activities in the U.S. be consistent with the visa that the alien holds. If the alien has filed a petition for permanent residency, the intent is to remain in the United States on a permanent basis. Thus, the USCIS may decide that the alien is ineligible to receive or use a nonimmigrant (temporary) visa since these visas require that the alien have an intention to remain in the U.S. for a temporary period only. An alien who wishes to travel to the United States on a temporary visit should not file the petition for permanent residency until the temporary visit has been concluded.

If aliens are already in the U.S., the filing of permanent visa petitions may disqualify them from extending or renewing their temporary visas, or changing the duration of stay under the temporary visas. These problems do not apply to persons who are attempting to obtain *L-1* or *H-1B* visas.

Special Problems

Live-in Domestic Workers

The United States does not look kindly upon live-in domestic workers. First, since domestic workers are considered *unskilled* workers, there are no visas available for this category of worker for at least ten years. Second, even though the Department of Labor acknowledges there is a shortage of live-in domestic workers, it discourages the employment of live-in workers in favor of live-out domestic workers. It is a characteristic of U.S. society that domestic workers generally are not willing to live in the household of their employers, at least not without requiring a premium in wages.

In order to obtain an immigrant visa as a live-in domestic worker, the alien must prove by documentation twelve months of paid experience in the capacity of a domestic worker abroad. However, the most difficult part of a live-in domestic worker application is the requirement that the employer prove there is an absolute *business necessity* for employing a live-in domestic. Normally, an employer must show there are no adults at home that could take care of either the young children or the adult who may require constant attention. Employers must prove that their job occupation requires frequent travel away from the home and that there is no practical alternative to a live-in worker. The Department of Labor will go to great lengths to suggest alternatives to employers as to how they could rearrange their lives, so as not to require a live-in domestic worker.

The difficulty in obtaining the labor certification, together with the over burdened third preference for unskilled workers, results in the practical elimination of visas based upon employment as a live-in domestic worker. Currently, waiting period (priority date backlog) is approximately ten years. This long delay makes it virtually impossible to obtain a job offer and enter the United States as an immigrant on this basis. Some enterprising households have sought to get around this problem by claiming that they need a well-trained child monitor or nurse or specialty cook (kosher) for the household. Obviously, the government does not look sympathetically at these types of applications.

Investors

Business entrepreneurs could technically qualify under a second or third employment-based preference visa, except that they must be entering the United States as employees. The obvious suggestion comes to mind that perhaps the investors could form companies in the United States that would hire them.

While this is technically possible, in the practical world, it is very difficult to achieve.

NOTE: *This section does not apply to investors who qualify for the new employment creation visa.*

Investors must compete with U.S. job seekers for the positions they seek to fill themselves. The Department of Labor has a negative attitude about permitting an investor to evaluate applicants who are competing with the investor for the position. The United States Department of Labor is obviously concerned that the investor may not be objective in an analysis. The Department of Labor will require that the investor prove that the labor certification selection process is conducted by objective persons, independent from the influence of the investor. If the Department of Labor determines that the employee for whom the labor certification is sought is the principal or is one of the principal investors in a company, it will routinely deny the labor certification. As a result, the investor has the burden of establishing the objectivity of the selection process.

Under the circumstances described, this would be an almost impossible burden. There have been instances in which an investor holding a small minority of stock, generally no more than five percent, has been certified for the position sought. These circumstances are rare, however, and I would advise such applicants not to invest in the company in which they are seeking employment. It would be preferable to obtain an option to purchase stock in the future based upon job performance rather than proving to the Department of Labor that the investor, as a result of minority ownership of stock, will not be in a position to unduly influence the selection process of workers for the position that he or she also is seeking.

Child Status Protection Act

In August of 2002, the President approved a law that protects many children from *ageing-out* of permanent residency eligibility. In general, a foreign person's eligibility for *lawful permanent residency* status (LPR status) as a *derivative beneficiary* (spouse or child) is determined as of the date that permanent residency is actually conferred—not the date the application or petition had been previously filed. Thus, it was possible and often tragically did occur that a child would turn 21 years of age before the parent became a lawful permanent resident. This meant that the newly designated lawful permanent resident parent had to file a separate petition for the 21 year old son or daughter. This delayed for many years the date on which the adult son or daughter would be eligible for lawful permanent residency status.

The law in question now changes this for the better. While the language of the law is somewhat complex, in general it provides that the age of a child is generally *frozen* at the time a petition for permanent residency is filed provided that there is a permanent residency number immediately available to the principal alien. This means that the government's processing delay will not cause the child to *age-out*. This is especially important for families who already live in the United States and are filing *adjustment of status* applications as either family-based or employment-based petitions.

If there is no permanent residency number immediately available (remember the numerical quota), at the time a visa number becomes available, from the beneficiary's current age there is deducted the time during which the petition had been pending in order to determine the applicable age of the son or daughter. If using this formula, the beneficiary's age is deemed to be under 21, then the *child* is eligible to file for lawful permanent residency status provided he or she does so within one year of the date of eligibility.

As can be seen from the above discussion, in its application to specific cases, eligibility under this law may require an in-depth analysis of many factors and consultation with an experienced immigration attorney is highly recommended. In certain individual cases, not even the U.S. consular officials or USCIS officials may be clear as to eligibility. It would be highly advantageous to have a well prepared legal and factual analysis to present along with the application form. In fact, most U.S. consular or immigration officials would welcome such a presentation (a *brief*). Appendix B contains a current policy memorandum from the USCIS that discusses the application of this law. This may be used as an example presentation, identifying specific issues and sections of the law that applies.

Occupations for which Labor Certification is not Required

The law identifies a group of occupations that are presumed to be in demand in the United States and for which no labor certification is required. These occupations are designated under *Schedule A* of the Department of Labor regulations. There are two groups of persons who, upon proof of their qualifications, do not need to obtain a labor certification before applying for an immigrant visa. These groups are as follows.

Group One *Physical therapists.* Physical therapist is defined in the law as follows:

> *A person who applies the art and science of physical therapy to the treatment of patients' disability disorders and injuries to relieve pain, develop or restore function, and maintain performance, using physical means such as exercise, massage, heat, water, light, and electricity as prescribed by a physician (or surgeon). (20 CFR 656.10a4 I.)*

To prove eligibility for this group, the alien must have all the qualifications necessary to take the licensing examination in the state in which he or she intends to practice physical therapy. Thus, the alien must file, together with his or her application, a letter or statement signed by an authorized licensing official in the state of intended employment stating that the alien is qualified to take the state's licensing examination for physical therapists. (20 CFR 656.22 C.)

Professional nurses. Professional nurses are also exempt from the labor certification requirement. These are defined as follows:

> *Persons who apply the art and science of nursing, which reflects comprehension of principles derived from the physical, biological, and behavioral sciences. Professional nursing generally includes the making of judgments concerning the observation, caring, and counsel of persons requiring nursing care; and administering of medicines and treatments prescribed by the physician or dentist; the participation in activities for the promotion of health and the prevention of illness in others. A program of study for professional nurses generally includes theory and practice in clinical areas such as: obstetrics, surgery, pediatrics, psychiatry, and medicine. (20 CFR 656.50.)*

In addition, the nurse alien must pass a special test approved by the Commission on Graduates of Foreign Nursing Schools Examination, as well as hold a full and unrestricted license to practice professional nursing in the state of intended employment.

Group Two   *Persons of exceptional ability.* This group includes persons of exceptional ability in the sciences or arts, including college and university teachers who have been practicing their science or art during the year before the application. The Department of Labor takes the position that the term *exceptional ability* means international renown.

> *Such aliens should be so far above the average members of their fields that they will clearly be an asset to the United States. (Federal Register, Number 5, 1976.)*

In order to qualify for this category of skilled worker (which eliminates the requirement of a labor certification application), aliens must file a considerable amount of evidence that documents their international renown and recognition by other recognized experts in the field. The documentation may include the following:

✪   documentation of internationally recognized prizes or awards;

✪   membership in international associations that require outstanding achievement of members;

✪   published treatises and materials in professional publications;

✪   evidence of the alien's participation on panels or as a judge of the work of others in the same or similar field;

✪   scholarly research contributions of major significance;

✪   evidence of the alien's scholarship and published scientific or scholarly articles;

✪   international professional journals; and,

✪   evidence of the display of the alien's work at artistic exhibitions in more than one country.

It must be emphasized that documentation is critical. Any alien who feels qualified for admission to the U.S. under this exception must accumulate as much detailed documentation as is possible. It is doubtful that such an application could be presented properly without the assistance of an attorney who specializes in immigration law.

Occupations for which Labor Certification is not Available

Just as there is a list of jobs that are recognized as being in demand, there is also a list of jobs that are deemed to be in surplus (*Schedule B*). These, for the most part, are jobs that require only a minimal level of skill or training. These jobs include parking lot attendants, general kitchen workers, etc. Of course, in a strong economy an employer may find it very difficult to recruit workers for these jobs and in those circumstances a labor certification may still be obtained, but the employer must provide additional objective justification for the need to hire foreign workers for these jobs. This is accomplished by documenting the *business necessity* for hiring these workers.

Diversity Immigrants

In addition to immigrants entering the United States based upon marital or family relationships and employment-sponsored visas, a third category exists called *diversity immigrants*. Fifty thousand visas per year will be made available for diversity immigrants and their family members on a lottery-type basis.

These diversity immigrant visas will be made available to persons who are nationals of *low admission* countries. The prospective immigrant must have at least a high school education or equivalent or have worked at least two years in an occupation that requires two years of training or experience. The *Immigration Act of 1990 (IMMACT90)* divides the world into six regions and then establishes a formula for determining which region and which state qualifies as high admission or low admission. In the recent past, the greatest number of immigrants to the United States have come from Asia and Latin America, with a smaller number coming from Europe and Africa. The purpose of the diversity immigrant visa is to provide a separate entry basis for those persons who come from low admission regions and states.

It is beyond the scope of this book to go into the details of the mathematical formula that is utilized to determine low admission as opposed to high admission areas. While the number of these regions and states will vary from year to year, it is safe to assume that those countries that presently have high admissions into the United States will continue to be, at least for the near term, high admission countries in the future, and thus, the nationals of those countries would be excluded from participating in the diversity program. The high admission countries that would probably be excluded from this visa program are as follows:

Canada	Colombia	Dominican Republic
El Salvador	Haiti	India
Jamaica	Mexico	Philippines
People's Republic of China	Russia	South Korea
United Kingdom		

The U.S. State Department is charged with the responsibility of operating the diversity immigrant program. It designates the period during which diversity visa petitions or applications must be filed for the next fiscal year. These specific rules change year-by-year as circumstances warrant.

Each diversity visa applicant can submit only one application in a given year. There will be some form of control so that if more than one visa application is received from one applicant, it will void all of the applications. It is probable that the diversity visa program will operate similar to a lottery, with a system of random selection of all eligible entries.

Nonpreference Categories

Persons Eligible to Immigrate to U.S. without regard to Quota

Immediate Relatives of U.S. Citizens. The law provides that certain *immediate relatives* of U.S. citizens may receive permanent visas without regard to the system of numerical limitations. The categories are the parents, spouse, or child of a United States citizen. The philosophy behind this, as well as other categories of immigration systems, is to provide for the maintenance of the unity of the family. It is important to understand, however, that it is the United States citizen who has the right to make a petition to the United States Government requesting that the beneficiary receive a permanent visa. Understanding this simple concept can very often avoid unfortunate consequences, especially to the spouse of a U.S. citizen.

Spouse of a U.S. Citizen. A United States citizen may petition either the USCIS or the U.S. consul abroad for a permanent visa for the alien spouse. The foremost prerequisite under the law for this category is the existence of a valid and subsisting marriage between the parties and official recognition of the marriage in the jurisdiction in which the marriage took place. The law does not recognize polygamous marriages nor proxy marriages, unless, in the latter case, the marriage has been consummated.

The law also does not recognize sham marriages or marriages where the primary purpose is to obtain immigration benefits and where the parties never intended to live together as husband and wife. In addition, however, to the fact that sham or fraudulent marriages are not recognized for the purpose of conferring immigration benefits on the alien spouse, the use of a sham marriage to apply for visas is against the law and subjects both parties as well as any other person involved in procuring the visa under these fraudulent conditions to criminal prosecution.

"I STILL NEED TO SEE YOUR MARRIAGE LICENSE"

Conditional Residence for Marriages under Two Years. Under the terms of current law, if a marriage is of less than two years duration at the time the petition for the permanent visa is filed, the alien spouse of a U.S. citizen receives only *conditional* permanent resident status. Upon the second anniversary of the granting of the original conditional permanent resident status, the alien may remove the condition and achieve the permanent resident status. The temporary resident status automatically terminates within two years except that the alien and spouse jointly *must* submit a petition within ninety days prior to the end of the twenty-four month period requesting the removal of the conditional grant of resident status. This is accomplished by filing a documented *Form I-751*. This form either confirms that the parties are still married and living together, or, in the event the marriage has been terminated, provides an opportunity for the alien spouse to prove that the marriage at inception was entered into in good faith.

After the filing of the *Form I-751* the parties may also be interviewed again by an immigration officer. If the foreign person fails to file the required form on time, together with supporting documentation, the conditional permanent resident status will be terminated and the foreign person becomes immediately deportable. Late filing of this form will be accepted only upon proof of good cause and extenuating circumstances justifying the late filing. In addition, the conditional status or temporary resident status will be terminated by the attorney general within two years if any of the following apply.

✪ The qualifying marriage was entered into for the purpose of obtaining the alien's entry as an immigrant.

✪ The qualifying marriage has been annulled or terminated, other than through the death of the spouse.

✪ A fee or other consideration was given for the filing of the petition (other than attorneys' fees for assistance in preparing petition).

The major cause for concern by an alien spouse is the second condition that states that the attorney general is authorized to terminate the visa if the marriage has been terminated other than through death.

In the event of a termination of a marriage prior to the expiration of the two-year period, it is possible that an alien may obtain a waiver with respect to the consequences imposed by the fact that the marriage was terminated, only if the alien can demonstrate the following.

✪ Circumstances arose during the period of the conditional permanent residence that would cause extreme hardship if he or she were deported.

✪ The qualifying marriage was entered into in good faith but was terminated for good cause and that the alien was not at fault in failing to meet the requirements ordinarily prescribed for the removal of the condition period.

✪ The alien spouse or his or her child has been physically battered or subject to extreme mental cruelty by his or her spouse. (The requirements for proving that the spouse is a *battered spouse* have been liberalized somewhat so that the government will consider any and all relevant and reliable evidence to establish this ground. Typical evidence in this regard consists of reports from police authorities, physicians, mental health and marriage counselors, letters and affidavits from clergy and direct witnesses and any official court records. If an alien spouse feels that he or she cannot continue in the marriage because of physical battery, he or she should consult an immigration attorney as well as a qualified matrimonial lawyer in order to document the battery properly.)

NOTE: *In cases in which the marriage has terminated through divorce, it is imperative for the alien to preserve as many as possible of third-party documents that were issued to the parties during the marriage. This is because it is incumbent on the alien to prove that the now-dissolved marriage was originally entered into in good faith. The government does not favor the use of documents and statements created after-the-fact, even though it will accept and consider these documents as proof of a bona fide marriage. Documents such as Federal Income Tax Returns (listing both parties), leases, deeds, credit card and bank statements, and other such documents are persuasive to a USCIS examiner.*

Another point to note here is that the law does not allow an alien who is merely separated from obtaining the benefits of the *good faith marriage* exception. The alien must be finally divorced in order to reap the benefits of this exception.

Related to these provisions is a requirement that an alien who obtained lawful permanent residence status as the spouse of a U.S. citizen or of a permanent resident alien is also precluded for a period of five years from obtaining approval of a visa petition seeking a second preference status on behalf of another spouse acquired after termination (other than by death) of the marriage that formed the basis for the grant of the original permanent residence to himself or herself. This restriction may be waived if the alien can establish, by *clear and convincing evidence*, that the prior marriage was not entered into for the purpose of evading the provision of the immigration laws.

The most recent immigration law amendments have established a system that will:

✪ automatically identify persons whose marriage fits the profile of a non bona fide marriage and

✪ provide for an objective method of adjudicating the termination of those visas.

Widows and Widowers. A widow or widower of a U.S. citizen may apply for an immigrant visa as an immediate relative so long as he or she had been married to the United States citizen for a period of two years prior to the U.S. spouse's death. It is necessary that the decedent have been a U.S. citizen for at least two years prior to his or her death and that the petition be filed by no later than two years following the death of the U.S. citizen. It is also required that the widow or widower not have been legally separated from the United States citizen at the time of the citizen's death.

It is difficult to imagine how this requirement will be implemented in the case of those persons who live in states where there is no legal status known as *legally separated.* In the state of Florida, for example, a marital separation exists when the parties physically or even sexually separate. There is no particular legal process to determine when the parties have done so. This is one of the peculiarities of the U.S. immigration system in that it attempts to establish a defined legal status even though the particular state may not use the same nomenclature or even agree to implement the public policy that motivates the immigration law or regulation.

Also, the widow or widower must not have remarried at the time of the petition. (It is unclear as to the policy reason for this rule.)

NOTE: *Normally, an alien does not have a vested right to immigrant status based upon marriage to a U.S. citizen. If the marriage should terminate, whether by divorce or death, prior to the granting of the visa the alien will have no right to apply for an immigrant visa, except as noted above, regardless of how long he or she has* *lived in the United States or how otherwise deserving the alien may be of obtaining the visa.*

Thus, an alien should require that his or her U.S. citizen spouse file the petition on their behalf as soon as possible after the marriage unless the marriage will soon reach the second anniversary, in which case it is advisable to wait until then in order to avoid the conditional two year visa. All of this discussion presumes that the alien is already in the United States at the time of the marriage.

If the parties are outside of the United States at the time of the marriage, then the alien will not be permitted to enter the United States until the visa petition has been approved at the U.S. consulate abroad. This process may take as long as four months! Therefore, it is advisable to plan the marriage and/or the entry to the U.S. accordingly.

Also, if the parties were married in the United States, the alien spouse should not depart the United States until such time as the alien's status has been adjusted to that of a permanent resident alien (immigrant). Again, the mere fact that an alien is married to a U.S. citizen does not convey on the alien the right to enter or remain in the United States prior to having received an immigrant visa. This simple statement should be thoroughly understood by both the U.S. citizen and alien spouse. If either spouse has been previously married, it will be necessary to prove the valid termination of the prior marriage(s).

Child of a United States Citizen. The law permits unlimited immigrant visas to persons who qualify as the *child* of United States citizens. Child as defined under the law, means an unmarried person under the age of twenty-one. If an alien does not qualify under this category as a result of age or marital status, the alien may still qualify for an immigrant visa under the first or fourth preferences, both of which are covered in this book.

A *stepchild* is also included within the scope of *child* if the marriage between the natural parent and the stepparent occurred prior to the stepchild's eighteenth birthday.

The benefits of the law apply only to *legitimate children,* unless the child was legitimated according to the law and/or recognized custom of the child's birthplace, or unless the mother of the illegitimate child is a U.S. citizen. In the case of children who are nationals of countries that have eliminated the distinction between legitimate and illegitimate children, the law requires evidence by the

U.S. father (normally) that a normal parent-child relationship was established and maintained before the child turned 21 years of age.

An *adopted child* is also recognized under the law for immediate relative status if the adoption occurred prior to the child's sixteenth birthday and the child has resided with the adopting parents for a minimum period of two years.

An *orphan* also qualifies under the law if the child was orphaned before attaining sixteen years of age and has been either adopted by the U.S. parents, or single parent who has attained the minimum age of twenty-five years or if the U.S. parents or parent, as the case may be, have satisfied the U.S. immigration authorities of their intention to adopt the orphan in the United States and that they have qualified for the adoption under law of the state where they intend to live.

Parents of a U.S. Citizen. The third category of the *immediate relative* category benefits the parents of United States citizens. The U.S. citizen, however, must be at least twenty-one years of age in order to give the parent the right of entry under the immigrant visa. The two chief requirements under this section are that the relationship of *parent* and *child,* as defined by law, must have been established at the time the family relationship was created. Thus, if an alien adopts a United States person over the age of twenty-one, the alien will not gain immigration benefits. This is because at the time of the adoption the person adopted was not a *child* as defined under the law. The adopted person was an adult and thus the parent is not the parent of a United States *child.*

If, however, the U.S. citizen was a *child* at the time of the adoption, but is an adult at the time of the filing of the petition, the parent may still obtain the benefits of this section since the legal immigration definition of *parent* and *child* were satisfied when the civil relationship was created. Under all of the previous three sections with respect to the immediate relative status, the U.S. citizen must file a *Form I-130* (a preliminary petition) on behalf of the alien.

Other Persons not Subject to the Quota System. In addition to the immediate relatives of a U.S. citizen, there are other persons who may enter the United States for permanent residency without the requirement of conforming with the worldwide numerical quota. The first of these, of course, is the permanent resident alien who is returning to the United States from a temporary visit abroad. Thus, the alien must have already been lawfully admitted for permanent residence, and the visit abroad must have been temporary without an intention to abandon the immigrant status in the United States. Usually the immigrant visa (green card) itself is sufficient documentation to enable an alien who has been temporarily abroad to return to the United States.

An alien who is planning to remain outside the United States for a period of six months or more should obtain permission *(reentry permit)* from the United States Citizenship and Immigration Services to do so. This is obtained by filling out a *Form I-131*. This form, when approved by the USCIS, establishes that the alien is not abandoning permanent residency in the United States even though the alien may be outside the country for a period of more than one year. This permit is usually valid for a period not to exceed two years.

Other persons who have special status are (certain) foreign medical school graduates who obtained (certain) *H* or *J* visas before January 10, 1978, remained in the United States, and were licensed to practice medicine in the United States on or before January 9, 1978.

Family Members Accompanying or Following to Join. The spouse and child(ren) of the petitioning alien receive a *derivative visa* that permits them to enter the United States together with the petitioning alien. In immigrant cases, this provision of law regards the spouse or child(ren) as accompanying the principal if they receive immigrant visas within four months after the principal obtains an immigrant visa or adjustment of status within the United States or within four months after the principal departs from the home country. In fact, if the principal's family members, as defined by law, *follow to join* the principal, they would be entitled to derivative status at any time after the principal acquires an immigrant visa.

Also, beneficiaries of an immediate relative petition cannot bestow permanent residency on their other immediate family members. Thus, if a foreign person becomes a U.S. citizen and obtains permanent residency petition for his or her parents, the other children of the parents do not automatically receive permanent residency.

If the relationship of spouse or child is created after the principal has obtained a visa, then the family members would not be entitled to the derived permanent visa status. This would be the case if the principal were to marry after acquisition of an immigrant visa. Also, an accompanying relative may not precede the principal alien to the United States. In either of the above cases, the family members would be required to file a separate immigrant visa petition and would be subject to the worldwide numerical limitations quota.

**Adjustment of
Status**

Normally, the permanent visa is issued at a U.S. consulate abroad. The U.S. Congress has long recognized that for many people who are already in the United States, the necessity of a trip abroad for final processing is both inconvenient and expensive. As a result, a procedure entitled *adjustment of status* enables a person in the United States to receive the permanent visa from within the United States. The alien person must be eligible to receive a permanent visa immediately. Thus, a person who is the beneficiary of a preference petition, which is presently backlogged, is ineligible for *adjustment*. As an example, the priority date for the unskilled category under the third employment-related preference is presently six-and-a-half years in arrears. Thus, a person who is in the United States and who has an approved employment third preference petition would be ineligible to file for adjustment of status until the priority date were current.

Many of the prior conditions to this procedure have been eliminated and the government now essentially encourages a person to adjust his status within the United States rather than to travel to a U.S. consulate abroad to make the application for the permanent residency visa.

Except for certain persons who are the beneficiaries of visa petitions filed by April 30, 2001, the only persons who now have the option of filing for adjustment of status are:

✪ immediate relatives of U.S. citizens and

✪ persons on whose behalf a petition based upon employment (including an application for labor certification) has been filed, provided the total time in which they have been in unlawful status does not exceed 180 days.

Adjustment of status is essentially a procedural privilege. Ineligibility for privilege does not affect eligibility for permanent residency status. It does mean that persons will have to invest in an airplane ticket to the U.S. consulate of their country of origin or in certain cases to a friendly U.S. consulate in a third country in order to obtain their permanent residency visa.

Adjustment of Status to Permanent Residence

As stated previously, immigrant as well as nonimmigrant visas are normally issued abroad at the U.S. consulate in the country of the alien's residence. With respect to an immigrant visa the alien's entitlement to permanent residence has normally been adjudicated by the USCIS either in the United States or at one of its offices abroad. Normally, the petitioner is either a U.S. citizen individual or a lawful permanent resident as is the case for the family-based preferences or a U.S. employer. After the petition has been adjudicated and approved by the USCIS, the alien then presents him or herself to the U.S. consulate who issues permission for the alien to travel to the United States and thus claim permanent resident status at the U.S. point of entry, usually an airport. This process of applying for permanent residence conducted abroad by the U.S. consular post is referred to as *consular processing*.

If the alien, however, is already in the United States, then the process of *Adjustment of Status* permits the alien to receive the status of permanent residence in the United States without having to depart the United States and without having to apply for permanent residence at the U.S. consulate abroad. The process of applying for permanent residence from within the United States is known as adjustment of status. This privilege is extremely valuable for a number of reasons.

- ✪ The alien avoids the cost and expense of traveling abroad. This is important when considering that often there is an administrative delay of several days and, in some cases, of several weeks at the U.S. consulate in processing the various parts of the application which are necessary before the immigrant visa is issued. The cost, expense, and inconvenience to the alien with respect to consular processing can be and often is considerable.

- ✪ The alien avoids the risk of a lengthy separation from family and occupation if a problem develops in the processing and issuance of the immigrant visa at the U.S. consulate.

- ✪ In many cases an alien cannot depart the United States for any reason, including application for a permanent residency visa, without incurring either the three (3) or ten (10) year bar against reentry to the United

States. As has been explained earlier in this book an alien who has remained in the United States in unlawful status for at least 180 days the departure from the United States is prohibited from seeking reentry to the United States for either three or ten years. An alien who enters the United States illegally (this is referred to formally *entry without inspection*) starts accumulating time in unlawful status from the first day of entry in the United States.

Thus, aliens subject to either the three or five year bars against reentry cannot depart the United States for consular processing of their application for permanent residency even when they are the beneficiaries of a valid family or employment-based petition for permanent residence. That is because the section of law that contains the three- and ten-year bars against reentry operates automatically against all foreign persons who have accumulated a certain amount of *unlawful presence*.

For all of these reasons, it is often necessary for the alien to be able to apply for permanent residence from within the United States and thus avoid a departure from the U.S. that would trigger the bars against reentry. Thus, adjustment of status, which is the process of applying for permanent residence from within the United States satisfies that purpose.

In order for a foreign person to apply for the privilege of adjustment of status, he or she must satisfy the following requirements.

- ✪ The foreign person must have entered the U.S. legally and must have been inspected. This is established by presenting to the USCIS a copy of the *Form I-94* which is attached to the foreign person's passport by the USCIS inspector at the point of entry (airport).

- ✪ The foreign person must be lawfully in the U.S.

- ✪ An immigrant visa must be immediately available to the foreign person. Thus, the person must either be the beneficiary of a petition filed by a U.S. citizen who bears a defined relationship to the foreign person or the person must have a current priority date based upon a prior filing of a petition by either a U.S. citizen or permanent resident or by a U.S. employer.

❂ The alien must not be a member of a class of persons who are prohibited from applying for adjustment of status. The law prohibits the following persons, as well as others, from applying for adjustment of status:

❂ alien crewmen;

❂ a person who worked without authorization;

❂ a person who is not in legal status at the time of application;

❂ aliens who have been admitted for the purpose of transiting through the U.S. to another foreign destination (TWOV);

❂ *J* visa holder who has not satisfied the two-year foreign residency requirement;

❂ persons who marry while under removal proceedings;

❂ persons who entered the U.S. under the visa waiver pilot program (unless married to a U.S. citizen); or,

❂ persons who are subject to removal for criminal causes.

Example: A permanent resident files a petition for permanent residence for his foreign born wife. Both husband and wife are in the United States. The *waiting list* for this category of immigrant is, at the time of the writing of this book, six years. Thus, even though the husband's petition is approved within a few months of his original filing, there will not be an immigrant *number* or slot available for the wife for at least another five years after her husband's original filing.

This is because at any time there are more approved petitions pending than there are immigrant visa numbers available for that year. In some cases, there will not be a number available for many years. Thus, the foreign-born wife of our hypothetical permanent resident husband cannot apply for adjustment of status to permanent residence until her priority date becomes current (in approximately five years in this example).

Referring to our example, if the wife of our permanent-resident husband has remained in the U.S. in unlawful status for more than 180 days then she cannot depart the United States in order to obtain her immigrant visa (permanent residence). This is because if she departs the U.S., she will not be permitted to reenter for a period of at least three years, perhaps not for ten years. Thus, in our example the wife must resort to adjustment of status and must remain patiently in the U.S. until her priority date becomes current.

Since the wife has been in unlawful status for a period of time while she has resided in the U.S., she is not permitted to file for adjustment of status. However, the U.S. Congress has, from time to time, improved this situation by permitting the beneficiaries of certain immigrant petitions (who are otherwise ineligible to apply for adjustment of status) to apply for adjustment of status on the condition that they pay an administrative fine of $1,000.00 (in addition to the normal processing fees) if the petition on their behalf has been filed by a certain defined date. The latest amendment allowed foreign persons to apply for adjustment of status if the petitions on their behalf had been filed prior to April 30, 2001.

In our example, since the marriage occurred before April 30, 2001, the wife will be allowed to file an application for adjustment of status when her priority date becomes current. She will be required to pay an administrative fee of $1,000.00 in addition to the normal processing fees charged by the USCIS. Of course, if she should depart the U.S. for any reason before her status is adjusted to permanent residence she will not be permitted to reenter the U.S.

Warning: Adjustment of status is, as is the entire immigration process, a dynamic process and its requirements are subject to change. The reader is forewarned to seek professional advice before applying for adjustment of status—in fact, before even filing a petition.

Dynamic Realities in Employment-Sponsored Immigration

Not too long ago, one of the most heart-breaking developments in this field was the withdrawal by an employer of a petition for a foreign worker after the worker had been waiting for a long time for either a visa number or for application approval by the government. This meant that either the foreign worker was once again thrown into unlawful status without any means of continuing his or her application for lawful permanent residency or that he or she had to start all over again in the process, in which case all the years spent on the original petition were wasted.

The enactment of a law known as *ACT21* has greatly affected this situation. Now, as long as the foreign person's application (*Form I-485*) for adjustment of status has been pending for at least 180 days the, underlying petition by the employer remains valid even if the employer later revokes the petition so long as the foreign person provides evidence that he or she will work at the same or similar job. This means, in essence, that after the *Form I-485* has been pending for at least 180 days, the foreign person's eligibility for lawful permanent residency status belongs *(vests)* to him or her and the worker can transfer to another employer without prejudice—as long as the job is the same or is similar.

When describing the process of achieving lawful permanent residency status based upon employment (sometimes known as job-based immigration), the process can be described as a series of steps. Understanding that there are always exceptions to the rule, the following discussion will be useful in explaining how this process functions.

The labor certification process does not belong to the foreign employee, rather it belongs to the U.S. employer who acts as the *sponsor* of the foreign person. This is an important point to bear in mind. The labor certification process assumes that the U.S. immigration authorities are essentially assisting a qualified U.S. employer fill its employment needs by authorizing the hiring and immigration of a qualified worker to fill the job.

Step 1 - Labor Certification

The first step in the process is the obtainment of a *labor certification*. The purpose of the labor certification is for the employer to establish to the Department of Labor that there is a shortage of qualified U.S. workers for the job in question. While the mechanics of this process may change, the philosophy behind this requirement is very stable. It is a policy that requires documentation that qualified U.S. workers in the local labor market are not being unfairly eliminated from consideration.

As noted previously, foreign persons who qualify for Employment-based First Preference Categories or as Employment-Based Second Preference Categories, whose jobs are in the *national interest,* are exempt from the requirement obtaining a labor certification.

The employer must agree, among other things, to pay to the foreign worker the prevailing wage for the job in question. He or she must also establish that the job duties have not been *tailored* to the idiosyncrasies of the foreign worker. Also, the employer's application will be denied if the foreign worker's experience or training has been obtained solely while working for the sponsoring employer. After receipt of a *labor certification,* the process then moves on to Step 2 below.

Step 2 - Employer Petition   After receiving the labor certification from the U.S. Department of Labor, the employer can now file the petition (*Form I-140*) with the U.S. immigration authorities (USCIS) to accord lawful permanent residency status to the identified foreign worker. During this stage of the process the employer must establish that it has sufficient income to pay the wage of the worker. This is normally accomplished by the presentation of the Federal Income Tax Returns for both the year in which the application for labor certification was filed with the U.S. Department of Labor as well as the year(s) in which the petition was filed and adjudicated. If the employer has over 100 employees, then this documentation is not necessary.

The foreign worker must also establish to the satisfaction of the U.S. immigration authorities that he or she is qualified by experience, training, or education to perform the job that is the basis of the labor certification. This evidence must consist of documentation as the worker's experience, training, or education gained previously—even while the worker may have been in unlawful status in the U.S. The approval of the employer's petition will then permit the foreign person, his or her spouse, and children under the age of 21 years to file for *Adjustment of Status* to lawful permanent residency.

Step 3 - Foreign Person's Application to Adjust Status

Only after Steps 1 and 2 have been successfully completed can the foreign worker finally apply to *adjust status* in the United States to that of a lawful permanent resident alien. This application is accomplished through the filing of a *Form I-485* with other supporting documents and forms. In order to file an application to adjust status, there must be a visa number immediately available to the foreign person and he or she must be eligible to apply for adjustment of status.

The first requirement is verified by checking the *Visa Bulletin* promulgated by the U.S. Department of State, and which is available for inspection on the Internet. Most employment based petitions for lawful permanent residency status are either the Second or Third Employment-Based Preferences and if they are current for the preference category of the sponsored job and for the nationality of the foreign worker, then the *I-485* can be filed.

Second, the foreign worker must be eligible to adjust status. There are several eligibility standards, but the most common are that the foreign worker must establish that he or she was lawfully admitted to the United States and that he or she has not been in unlawful status or otherwise violated his or her nonimmigrant status for more than 180 days. Section 245 of the *Immigration and Nationality Act* (INA) lists all the eligibility standards for adjustment of status.

The filing of the *I-485* accomplishes several steps. First, if the foreign person had been in or was about to be in *unlawful status* the filing of the *I-485* stops *(tolls)* the accumulation of *unlawful status*. The foreign person is now considered to be in a status *authorized by the Attorney General* (or the Secretary of the DHS) and is now no longer considered to be *removable* (deportable) solely because of his prior unlawful status. In essence, the foreign person is considered to be *legal* until the immigration authorities decide otherwise.

The filing of the *I-485* also enables the foreign worker and dependent family members to apply for *employment authorization*. When approved, this status is evidenced by receipt of an *Employment Authorization Document* (EAD). This document will then permit the foreign person to obtain a Social Security number and, in most states, a valid automobile driver license. The EAD authorizes employment for any employer in any location or state. Of course, if the foreign worker does not start or continue to work for the sponsoring employer, the USCIS could suspect fraud and could require additional evidence to establish that the original petition was in good faith.

It is recommended to obtain an EAD for all eligible foreign persons, including children. The document authorizes the issuance of a Social Security number and many public and private institutions depend upon the social security number for record keeping.

The process of applying for adjustment of status is completed by a physical examination by an authorized physician *(authorized civil surgeon)* who will examine for communicative diseases and for proof of a series of required inoculations.

As a precondition to the grant of lawful permanent residency status, the various investigative agencies of the U.S. government will also conduct an in-depth investigation of the foreign person to ensure that he or she is not an otherwise inadmissable alien. This last process is prone to delay, especially for persons with common last names *(Thompson, Rodriguez, Muhammed)* from nationals of unfriendly countries.

It must always be remembered that adjustment of status is a *privilege* and not a right. It can always be denied by the immigration examiner as a matter of discretion.

Refugees

This subsection deals with an immigration status which differs from all of the others described in this book. In order to take advantage of the benefits of the law with respect to either *refugee* or *asylee* designations, aliens must establish certain proof that relates to political, ideological, or sociological conditions in their home country that adversely and personally affect them. This proof involves issues that affect certain specific foreign policy interests of the United States and for these reasons this category has been treated separately in this book.

This area of law invites much litigation and discussion in the United States. It is subject to changes, both in interpretation of the law and in U.S. political inclination, depending upon world events. Certain political conditions may cause the United States to assume that a member of a particular group qualifies as a refugee or asylee while denying that status to other groups similarly situated.

Definition   The law defines a refugee as follows:

> *The term refugee means (A) any person who outside any country of such person's nationality or, in the case of a person having no nationality, is outside any country in which such person last habitually resided and who is unable or unwilling to return to, and is unable or unwilling to avail himself or herself of the protection of that country because of persecution or a well-founded fear of persecution on account of race, religion, nationality, membership in particular social group, or political opinion, or (B) in such special circumstances as the President, after appropriate consultation (as defined in section 207 (e) of the Act) may specify, any person who is within the country of such person's nationality or, in the case of a person having no nationality within the country in which such person is habitually residing, and who is persecuted or who has a well-founded fear of persecution on account of race, religion, nationality, membership in a particular social group, or political opinion. The term `refugee' does not include any person who ordered, incited, assisted, or otherwise participated in the persecution of any person on account of race, religion, nationality, membership in particular social group, or political opinion.*

One of the purposes of the law was to adopt the major provisions of the *United Nations Protocol Relating to the Status of Refugees* to which the United States is a signatory. Also, the law attempts to establish a permanent and consistent method of admitting refugees and asylees to the United States.

Numerical Limitations   The law provides for a separate system of numerical limitations for refugees than that which is applicable to persons seeking permanent residence in the United States under the *preference system* discussed earlier in this book.

The refugee section of the immigration regimen of the United States establishes a mechanism by which the President of the United States (with the advice and consent of the Congress) establishes the total number of refugees that will be admitted in a given year as well as the numerical limit applicable to individual countries or sections of the world. The law provides for the exercise of executive discretion in the designation of those countries or sections of the world and thus the availability of refugee admissions may vary from year to year. The concerns of U.S. foreign policy and the political conditions in other parts of the world may influence the President's decision to implement the refugee program in any given year.

Individual Eligibility

A *refugee* as defined by the law, is a person who is physically outside the United States. If a person is physically within or at the borders of the United States, then application for asylum will be considered subject to the eligibility requirements of that status as discussed later.

The key provision in the refugee section as to eligibility is the requirement that the person be unwilling or unable to return to his or her home or other country either because of persecution or a well-founded fear of persecution on account of race, religion, nationality, membership in a particular social group, or political opinion.

The law does not discriminate between socialist or capitalist nations, except in the case of Cuba. Nor does it require that the person have actually fled from his or her home country. Obviously, persons who claim persecution by a country whose government or foreign policy is hostile to the United States have a much better chance of being judged refugees, than persons who come from countries that are friendly to the United States.

In order to prove that a person is subject to these conditions, a person must prove first that the government is oppressive and tyrannical and for that reason denies to the applicant the protection otherwise afforded to nationals of that country through the legal or political institutions of that country. Second, the person must prove individual persecution or a well-founded fear of persecution.

The first requirement (proof as to the general *oppressive nature* of the foreign regime) is easier to provide than the second requirement (proof as to the *persecution* of the alien). Usually there will be more documentation available about the regime's behavior as to human rights, and in certain instances, the United States may already recognize the oppressive nature of the foreign government. There are various documentary sources and human rights organizations that maintain information as to the human rights environment in certain countries and these can be made available to an applicant for refugee status. The refugee applicant must prove that the home country's institutions and/or policies are not available for individual protection. The Department of State of the United States does not always agree with an applicant's assertion of the home country's despotic nature. In these cases, the applicants bear a heavy burden of persuasion.

The second requirement is very often the greatest obstruction to gaining a refugee status when it is asserted by an individual who is not a member of a group that has been recognized as such by the Department of State. The applicant must present documented evidence that individually or as member of a group, the alien will be subject to persecution. For obvious reasons, the USCIS will not always accept the mere self-serving statements of the applicants regarding persecution. The law provides that the burden of proof may be established solely by the testimony of the refugee or asylee, but this is not easy to accomplish.

Unless the individual is a member of a group of persons whom the United States government accepts as a persecuted group in a foreign country, the individual must provide documentary proof as to personal exposure. As a matter of experience, this requirement presents a greater burden to an applicant for asylum, since by definition that person is already outside of the home country and probably within the national borders of the Untied States. Thus, it is difficult, if not impossible, to obtain and present the type of documentary proof that the USCIS requires.

In addition to these two requirements for eligibility, the alien applicant also must be innocent of any acts of persecution and must also be a person of good moral character.

Application Process

The applicant has the burden of providing eligibility for the designation of refugee. The application itself is completed by the filing of *Form I-590*, biographic information on a *Form G-325* and a fingerprint card for each person over the age of fourteen years. In the event of a successful refugee application, the spouse and children accompanying or coming to join the principal alien are entitled to *derivative refugee status* unless they have engaged in acts of persecution themselves.

The application process is conducted abroad either by the USCIS in those countries where it maintains offices or at certain designated U.S. consular posts abroad. In every case, the applicant is subject to customary investigation for security and police purposes and is required to present a series of personal documents for verification. In addition, the applicant is subject to medical examination to rule out certain communicable diseases.

If the application is approved, the refugee is authorized to enter the United States and is authorized to work and otherwise receive remuneration. After a period of one year from the date of entry, the alien is permitted to file an application for *Adjustment of Status* to that of a permanent resident alien. Before an alien may enter the United States, there must be proof of sponsorship for employment, a residence in the United States and that the person will not become a public charge. It is for this purpose that many volunteer and philanthropic agencies become active in the resettlement of aliens, even though the same purpose may be achieved by an individual, as is so often the case with respect to relatives or other members of a closely knit religious or ethnic group.

If an alien has been firmly settled in another country, then eligibility is denied for refugee status to the United States. The criteria for being firmly settled depends upon many factors, such as the type of legal status the person has been granted, as well as the nature of any restrictions that may have been imposed that may limit the alien's ability to adapt reasonably to the new country.

Asylum

If a foreign person is already in the United States and reasonably fears persecution abroad based upon race, religion, nationality, membership in a particular social group, or political opinion, then the individual may petition for *asylum* to the United States. The standard is essentially the same as that for achieving refugee status.

The principal difference between the asylum and refugee categories is that the former applies to those aliens who are already in the United States while the latter applies to persons outside the United States. The law provides for a procedure by which an asylee who has been admitted into the United States may have spouse and/or child(ren) join him in the United States upon proof of the familial relationship.

The grant of asylum status is discretionary. The Attorney General acting through representatives in the USCIS may withhold the granting of asylum for good cause. Thus, if an alien were to secretly enter the United States and bypass the normal refugee process that was otherwise available, the grant of asylum could be denied on that basis.

Ineligible Persons   The following categories of persons are not eligible to file for asylum in the United States.

    ✪   An alien who may be removed, pursuant to a bilateral or multilateral agreement, to a third country in which the alien would have access to a full and fair procedure for determining a claim to asylum or equivalent temporary, protection, unless the USCIS finds that it is in the public interest for the alien to receive asylum in the United States.

✪ An alien who files his or her application later than one year after entry, unless the person can demonstrate to the satisfaction of the USCIS that changed country conditions have caused the delay in filing. (This would apply to an individual who entered the United States in some non-immigrant status and then because of changes in the home country cannot now return without being subject to persecution.)

✪ An alien who has previously applied for asylum and has had such application denied.

The law does not allow an alien to appeal the decision of the USCIS to any court with respect to a decision on any of the above points.

Restrictions Even though the USCIS will prepare regulations that will define the requirements and procedures for these applications, asylum is not available to an alien if the USCIS determines that:

✪ the alien ordered, incited, assisted, or otherwise participated in the persecution of any person on account of race, religion, nationality, membership in a particular social group, or political opinion;

✪ the alien, having been convicted by a final judgment of a particularly serious crime, constitutes a danger to the community of the United States;

✪ there are serious reasons for believing that the alien has committed a serious nonpolitical crime outside the United States prior to the arrival of the alien in the United States;

✪ there are reasonable grounds for regarding the alien as a danger to the security of the United States;

✪ the alien is inadmissible as a terrorist or as a member of a terrorist organization, or is removable for having engaged in terrorist activity after admission to the U.S., unless, in the case only of an alien inadmissible the Attorney General determines that there are not reasonable grounds for regarding the alien as a danger to the security of the United States; or,

✪ the alien was firmly resettled in another country prior to arriving in the United States.

Also, an alien who has been convicted of an *aggravated felony* shall be considered to have been convicted of a particularly serious crime and thus not eligible for asylum. The law also gives the USCIS the authority to create new conditions under which an alien will be ineligible for asylum. This is unusual under U.S. law in that an administrative body is generally not given the power to create additional conditions for ineligibility under the law. Nonetheless, this is the law as it stands now.

Proving Aliens rarely have the evidence at hand to document that they would be the sub-
Persecution ject of *persecution* in the foreign land. Nonetheless, the alien has the burden of proving to the USCIS that he or she would be subject to persecution abroad. The sole testimony of the alien is seldom sufficient without some outside evidence, documentary or otherwise.

It is important to remember that asylum petitions all have one common thread and that is the necessity to establish by testimony or documentation that the alien's home government is responsible, directly or indirectly, for the alien's persecution. Thus, chronic negative social conditions such as crime, general social unrest, economic malaise, etc., which may be present in a country *do not* substantiate political asylum. In fact, aliens coming from those countries have the additional burden of distinguishing those causes from those based upon a government's program of persecution as defined above.

The government is also beginning to recognize the existence of other identifiable groups of persons who may be subject to persecution. This ever-expanding definition now include homosexuals.

There are various organizations in the United States that compile dossiers of documentary evidence about the human rights violations of countries and these may be helpful in a particular case. *Amnesty International* would be an excellent starting point for anyone who felt that he or she was eligible for a grant of political asylum. Contact the organization:

Amnesty International
705 G Street, S.E.
Washington, D.C. 20003

In addition, the Internet has ample resources to develop these secondary sources of country conditions.

NOTE: *As a result of the recent changes in the law governing asylum both as to procedure as well as substance, a prospective asylee is well served to seek competent legal assistance in the preparation of an asylum petition.*

3 TEMPORARY NONIMMIGRANT VISAS

In this section, we shall discuss the most important and common nonimmigrant visas. With the exception of the *H-1B* visa, there is no annual quota on the number of nonimmigrant visas that may be issued. The United States issues many more nonimmigrant than immigrant visas.

Typically, a person will apply for a U.S. nonimmigrant visa abroad at the U.S. Consulate within the country of residence. If the visa is issued, it is prima facie evidence of the person's eligibility to enter the United States. Foreign persons will first use the visa when they show the visa to the international carrier's airline or ship representative as a precondition to boarding the airplane or vessel.

Upon arrival at the United States border, the foreign person is inspected by a U.S. immigration inspector. If the foreign person is admitted into the United States, a small white card or piece of paper known as a *Form I-94* is issued. This is the official entry document. This form proves that the person has lawfully entered the United States and also establishes the visa category of admission as well as the designated duration of stay. The *Form I-94* should be kept in the passport and physically carried by the foreign person at all times. Few people are aware of this requirement and USCIS officers often chastise the alien for not having the passport and *Form I-94* immediately available. (While this is an archaic requirement, it is still the law.)

The length of time that the foreign person may remain in the United States is determined in the *Form I-94* and *not* by the terminology of the visa that is stamped in the passport. Thus the legend on the *B-1/B-2* Visa, which states that the bearer is entitled to unlimited entries to the United States, does not mean that the person may remain in the United States for an indefinite period of time, nor that reentry may be made into the United States as the individual wishes. It simply means that the person does not need to reapply for another visa within any particular time period. The duration of time for remaining in the United States is limited to the date indicated in the *Form I-94*.

Characteristics   There are several characteristics of nonimmigrant visas that set them apart from the immigrant visas discussed in the previous chapters.

First, the nonimmigrant visa grants the foreign person the privilege of entering the United States for only a temporary and defined period of time. This of course requires that the alien's intention as to intended duration of stay must also be temporary.

Second, each particular visa imposes certain restrictions and conditions on the activities that the alien may engage in while in the United States. In other words, there are different visas for different activities to be conducted in the United States. Thus, the tourist or visitor visa does not authorize employment, the student visa authorizes study at only a certain institution, the treaty investor visa authorizes employment only in a defined enterprise and so forth.

Very often, a nonimmigrant visa is more aptly suited to the needs of a foreign person than the immigrant visa, especially for investors, business visitors, and professionals. The nonimmigrant visa can be obtained in much less time than an immigrant visa. Since most nonimmigrant visas are much more readily obtainable than immigrant visas, some foreign persons attempt to use the nonimmigrant visa as a substitute for the immigrant visa. This is often viewed as fraud by both the U.S. consular officials and the USCIS. One of the most peculiar characteristics of bureaucratic action is an almost total lack of flexibility. Once an individual demonstrates an intention to accomplish a particular end, a governmental official will often find it outside his or her point of reference to imagine that an applicant can sincerely modify his or her goals so as to remain in conformity with the law.

Due to these factors, there has been an increase in the demand for the nonimmigrant visa. This demand for nonimmigrant visas has, in turn, resulted in an increased scrutiny of nonimmigrant petitions *(applications)* by the U.S. immigration authorities. Therefore, a thorough understanding of the limits, conditions, and purposes of the various nonimmigrant visas to the U.S. is essential for proper planning by the foreign person or entity. I cannot overemphasize the importance of advanced and thorough planning by the foreign person. It may very well mean the difference between denial or approval of the visa petition by the visa officer.

NOTE: *There are many types of nonimmigrant visas that will not be discussed in this book because they pertain to a very limited class of persons and are very specialized in their application. Examples of these visas are the NATO visa for NATO officials, the A-1 visa for diplomatic personnel, and the I visa for news media reporters and representatives.*

Tourist/Business Visitor (B-1/B-2)

The *B-1/B-2* visa is by far the most common visa issued by the United States consular authorities for entry to the United States. For most foreign persons, this is the easiest of all the nonimmigrant visas to obtain. The *B-1* visa is used for specific categories of business in the United States, while the *B-2* visa is issued to tourists or visitors for pleasure. In neither case, however, may the holder of the visa engage in activities that will result in financial compensation such as wages, tips, fees, commissions, etc.

The *business* contemplated by the *B-1* visa does not include the active management of a business or commercial enterprise in the United States. A *B-1* visa holder may properly attend business meetings, court hearings, etc., and may engage in professional or commercial undertakings so long as any compensation is earned and paid from abroad. The *B-2* visa holders, as already indicated, are limited to nonbusiness, visitor activities.

In order to qualify for the *B-1/B-2* visa, the foreign person must hold a valid passport or other travel document and must establish to the satisfaction of the U.S. visa officer the following.

✪ He or she has a permanent domicile outside of the United States which he or she has no intention of abandoning.

✪   He or she has the necessary financial capacity to conduct a business or pleasure trip in the United States and has a round trip ticket from the transportation carrier.

✪   He or she is not otherwise disqualified *(excludable)* from entering the United States for reasons such as having a criminal record, etc.

While the documentary and qualitative requirements are fairly simple to meet, persons from developing countries may find it difficult to obtain this visa. In every case, a foreign person must establish a personal motivation to depart the United States within the time period established by the immigration officer at the border.

The United States consular officers very often use *profiles* to determine whether a person might be a poor risk for receiving a *B-1* or *B-2* visas. As an example, a young, unmarried person without a job or other visible means of support would probably be denied a *B-1/B-2* visa because there would be insufficient motivation for that person to return to the country of origin. The situation would be worsened if, in addition to the above, the young person has close relatives in the United States and comes from an underdeveloped country.

In a situation in which one or more of the above factors may be present, I recommend that the visa applicant prepare for the consular officer's inquiry by organizing documentary proof that there exists a strong motivation to depart the United States at the conclusion of the visit. This might entail proof of a good job in the home country, the ownership of valuable property, as well as the existence of other strong economic, emotional, and cultural ties to the home country. Remember, the presumption is that the visa applicant is not entitled to the visa until proven otherwise to the satisfaction of the consular visa officer. In any event, it is advisable to have all the evidence properly organized before approaching the United States consulate for the visa.

The *B-1/B-2* visa is obtained at a U.S. consular post abroad and is valid for an initial entry of up to six months. This period may be extended for good cause for an additional period of six months but extensions beyond that are very difficult to obtain.

Occasionally I am asked by foreign visitors if these time limitations can be legally avoided by merely taking short trips out of the United States shortly before the expiration of stay that is listed in the *Form I-94*. My answer is to remind my client that the border inspection officer has the right to deny entry to a foreign person if the border officer is convinced that the person is living in the United States permanently or is otherwise acting *out of status*. The officer is able to assume that someone who has spent the majority of time (perhaps the last sixteen months) over a lengthy period (perhaps the last eighteen months or so) of time in the United States is probably a *de facto* immigrant, that is, an intending immigrant without a proper visa, and is therefore, removable.

Canadians, especially, should be aware of this fact. Canadian citizens do not need visas to enter the United States *if they enter as visitors*. The border crossing formalities are minimal for Canadians—so long as they are entering as visitors. Many Canadians forget that all the other immigration law restrictions still apply to them. Thus, if a Canadian citizen attempts to cross the land border towing a trailer loaded with personal effects and furniture, the U.S. immigration border will probably deny entry on the basis that the person is not entering as a visitor. A Canadian citizen who tries to board an airliner destined to the U.S. at the Toronto International Airport while carrying a one-way ticket may be denied entry on the suspicion that he or she is not a bona fide visitor. (Remember, the inspector does not have to prove that the foreign person is not a bona fide visitor. It is the foreign person who has the burden of proving his or her visitor status to the satisfaction of the immigration inspector.)

Extension of Stay

The duration of stay under the *B-1/B-2* visa may be extended. A first *extension of stay* is possible, but it is not automatic. The visitor must prove possession of a return transportation ticket and must prove financial means of supporting oneself and timely activities while in the United States. The USCIS will carefully scrutinize the reason for the extension and if the foreign person fits the profile of a risk for absconding or of otherwise violating the B-visa status, the extension will be denied. (It is recommend that an extension request be taken seriously and that a competent immigration lawyer be consulted to prepare the extension request.)

Regardless of how strong the foreign person's relationship is with the visa officer in the U.S. consulate of his or her home country, it counts for very little while the foreign person is in the United States. A second extension is almost unobtainable.

The *Immigration Reform and Control Act of 1986* established a *Visa Waiver Pilot Program* that provides that aliens from designated countries can enter the United States as visitors for a period of up to three months without a visa. The program was initially limited to visitors from the United Kingdom. Visitors from the United Kingdom are defined to be persons who have the right of permanent abode there and are unrestricted in their travel within the United Kingdom. The Visa Waiver Pilot Program now includes the following countries (and others may be added):

Andorra	Australia	Austria
Belgium	Brunei	Denmark
Finland	France	Germany
Iceland	Ireland	Italy
Japan	Liechtenstein	Luxembourg
Monaco	The Netherlands	New Zealand
Norway	Portugal	San Marino
Singapore	Slovenia	Spain
Sweden	Switzerland	United Kingdom

Visitors from these countries who enter on the basis of the Visa Waiver program are subject to certain restrictions, such as the inability to extend their stay, change their nonimmigrant status or adjust to permanent residence. The visitor may still be barred from entering the United States at the border if unable, for any reason, to substantiate the claim that entry into the United States is as a visitor. Under all circumstances, it is essential that anyone entering the United States, even under this Visa Waiver Pilot Program, be able to substantiate and support all the requirements for entrance under the *B* visa.

(I do not recommend that a prospective business investor or executive utilize this program for preparatory or research visits to the United States unless the person is certain that an extended stay or change of status to the visa category will not be necessary. This is due to the inflexibility of the program that prohibits extensions of stay or change of status.)

Treaty Trader/Investor (E-1/E-2)

This is one of the most important nonimmigrant visas to the United States. The United States has signed treaties of navigation and commerce with certain other nations that provide among other things that nationals of those countries may enter and work in the United States under certain defined conditions. If the treaty trader or treaty investor is a company, then the employee in the United

States must have the same nationality as the company. The employee must usually perform managerial or executive functions, although if the employee possesses some specialized skill not otherwise obtainable in the United States, then a purely staff or labor position could support the *E* visa.

The visa authorizes an initial duration of stay of up to two years and there is no limit to the total time period that the employee may remain in the United States with proper extensions, provided a continued employment that originally supported the visa. The *E* visa holder's spouse and minor dependents are also accorded the same visa. Another advantage of the *E* visa is that it is unnecessary to establish that the visa holder continues to maintain a home in the foreign country to which the intention is to return.

E-1 Visa
The *E-1* visa is known as the *treaty trader visa* and benefits nationals of the treaty partner who are engaged in a substantial volume of trade with the United States. While it is not possible to define precisely what the term *substantial* means, it requires a volume of trade that is sufficient to at least support the employee in the United States. The trade transactions do not have to be individually large, as long as they are numerous and the total percentage volume of trade must be at least fifty-one percent by and between the United States and the treaty country.

NOTE: *The term trade includes the exchange, purchase, or sale of goods and/or services.*

Goods are tangible commodities of merchandise having intrinsic value, excluding money, securities, and negotiable instruments. *Services* are economic activities whose outputs are other than tangible goods. Such activities include, but are not limited to, banking, insurance, transportation, communications and data processing, advertising, accounting, design and engineering, management consulting, and tourism. This new definition greatly expands the applicability of the treaty/trader provisions since the government now accepts the modern reality that much of international trade has to do with the movement of services rather than goods and commodities. This new interpretation permits the utilization of this visa for many types of businesses that are not capital intensive.

There is a disadvantage of this visa compared to the *E-2* visa. The *E-1* requires that the trade continue principally between the U.S. and the foreign treaty country during the life of the visa. It is possible for an otherwise successful entrepreneur to become disqualified from the visa if the majority of trade volume shifts from the treaty trader country to that of a third country. This is indeed an anomaly that is possible and of which the wise entrepreneur should be aware. The USCIS regulations suggest that if this occurred the alien would not become disqualified from the visa, but there is no explicit acceptance of this contingency.

One way of avoiding this problem would be for the entrepreneur to create another company in which trade to other countries would be channeled. Another method would be to utilize, if possible, the treaty trader country as a purchase and distribution center so that all invoices and payments are channeled between the United States and the treaty country. If at all possible, utilize the *E-2* visa instead of the *E-1*.

The countries that have *E-1* treaty privileges include:

Argentina	Australia	Austria
Belgium	Bolivia	Bosnia & Herzegovina
Brunei (Borneo)	China (Taiwan)	Colombia
Costa Rica	Croatia	Denmark
Estonia	Ethiopia	Finland
France	Germany	Greece
Honduras	Iran	Ireland
Israel	Italy	Japan
Korea (South)	Latvia	Liberia
Luxembourg	Macedonia	Mexico
Netherlands	Norway	Oman
Pakistan	Paraguay	Philippines
Slovenia	Spain	Suriname
Sweden	Switzerland	Thailand
Togo	Turkey	United Kingdom
Yugoslavia		

E-2 Visa   The *E-2* visa is known as the *treaty investor visa*. It is issued to an alien who is a national of a treaty country and who is entering the United States to develop and manage a business enterprise into which he or she has invested or is committed to invest a substantial amount of capital and which investment is not marginal.

The United States has signed treaties of friendship and commerce providing for *E-2* treaty investor benefits with the following countries:

Albania	Argentina	Armenia
Australia	Austria	Azerbaijan
Bahrain	Bangladesh	Belgium
Bolivia	Bosnia & Herzegovina	Bulgaria
Cameroon	Canada	China (Taiwan)
Colombia	Congo	Costa Rica
Croatia	Czech Republic	Ecuador
Egypt	Estonia	Ethiopia
Finland	France	Georgia
Germany	Grenada	Honduras
Iran	Ireland	Italy
Jamaica	Japan	Jordan
Kazakhstan	Korea (South)	Kyrgyzstan
Latavia	Liberia	Lithuania
Luxembourg	Macedonia	Mexico
Moldova	Mongolia	Morocco
Netherlands	Norway	Oman
Pakistan	Panama	Paraguay
Philippines	Poland	Romania
Senegal	Slovak Republic	Slovenia
Spain	Sri Lanka	Suriname
Sweden	Switzerland	Thailand
Togo	Trinidad & Tobage	Tunisia
Turkey	United Kingdom	Ukraine
Yugoslavia		

Eligibility. The investment must be of a *substantial* nature and must not be *marginal*. The law does not establish a particular amount of money to fulfill the requirement of substantial, nor is the term substantial defined clearly, nor is there a mathematical formula that can be used to discover this meaning. In addition, the term substantial is subject to varying interpretation in different consular posts, and indeed, perhaps between different consular officers in the same post.

The requirements of an *E-2* Treaty Investor are:

✪   treaty nationals only;

✪   substantial investment;

✪   active (entrepreneurial) risk;

✪   direct and manage or supervisory/executive employee;

✪   cannot be marginal—must create jobs or profit; and,

✪   investment must be committed.

With respect to the start up of a new enterprise that is being originally developed by the investor, whether or not a particular amount of capital is considered substantial is very often determined by a comparison of the size of other similar types of businesses. In addition to the overall size of the business, the number of employees contemplated is also very important in predicting the success of the visa application. The more employees there are, the less emphasis there will be on the question of whether or not the investment is substantial.

In start-up enterprises, there is usually less of a problem in establishing to the satisfaction of the U.S. consul that the investment is committed, as a precondition to the issuance of the visa. Since there was no pre-existing business structure in place prior to the foreign person's investment, it is not logical to expect the business to function before the visa is issued to the alien. The foreign investor must establish that he or she is past the point where liability can be escaped by failing or refusing to complete this transaction. The details of this item of evidence will vary from case to case. Newly developed business enterprises present other problems, however, these will be covered in Chapter 5 in the sections on *Franchises* and *Business Opportunities*.

The investor is at greater business risk in a newly developed enterprise than would be the case where the investor is purchasing an existing business. Most business consultants would agree that, all else being equal, it is preferable to acquire either an existing, ongoing business enterprise or a franchised business opportunity. The United States has a relatively free economy which, while providing the freedom to succeed, also provides the environment to fail.

The statistics kept by the Small Business Administration of the U.S. Department of Commerce indicate that the majority of new enterprises fail within the first two years of existence. One can only deduce that for foreign persons who do not have very much insight into the norms and customs of the commercial community into which they venture, the risk of failure is at least as high as it is for United States residents. I suspect that the percentage of failure by foreign investors with respect to start-up enterprises is higher than it is for United States residents.

Because of these realities, most foreign individuals would rather invest in an enterprise that is already in existence and is already functioning. Enter the world of immigration. The rules and regulations require that a foreign person invest a relatively high percentage of the price of the business opportunity. Indeed, much higher than sellers require of U.S. resident purchasers. My *rule of thumb* for determining what is substantial with respect to the purchase of an existing business is that the investor should purchase the largest business possible with a direct investment of at least fifty percent of the price of the business.

Substantiality. There is no mathematical formula or fixed minimum amount for determining *substantial*. The regulations of the Department of State articulate the question as follows.

> **Substantial amount of capital.** A substantial amount of capital constitutes that amount that is:
>
> *(1)(i) Substantial in the proportional sense, i.e., in relationship to the total cost of either purchasing an established enterprise or creating the type of enterprise under consideration;*
>
> *(ii) Sufficient to ensure the treaty investor's financial commitment to the successful operation of the enterprise; and*
>
> *(iii) Of a magnitude to support the likelihood that the treaty investor will successfully develop and direct the enterprise.*
>
> *(2) Whether an amount of capital is substantial in the proportionality sense is understood in terms of an inverted sliding scale; i.e., the lower the total cost of the enterprise, the higher, proportionately, the investment must be to meet these criteria.*

Substantiality is very often determined by the use of a *proportionality* or *relative* test. There are two methods.

1. In the case of the acquisition of an existing business enterprise, the capital invested by the alien must be proportional to the total value or cost of the particular business enterprise as follows:

    ✪   If the cost of acquisition is $100,000.00 or less, the required percentage of capital investment should be between 90–100%.

    ✪   If the cost of acquisition is between $100,000.00 to $500,000.00, the required percentage of capital investment should be between 60–75%.

    ✪   If the cost of acquisition is between $500,000.00 and $3,000,000.00 the required percentage of capital investment should be over 50%.

    ✪   If the amount invested is over $1,000,000.00 the investment will probably be considered substantial *per se*.

2. In the case of the creation of a new business by the foreign person, the capital invested must be an amount normally considered necessary to establish a viable business enterprise of the type contemplated.

As a general guideline, the minimum amount of cash required to meet the test of substantiality is $100,000 U.S., as long as that amount is proportional to the cost of acquisition. In certain U.S. consulates abroad, $100,000 would be considered minimal; thus, this figure must be considered only as a rule-of-thumb and must be analyzed in light of the type of business, the investment, the proportion of capital to acquisition cost, the rate of return, and all of the other factors described in this section. Nonetheless, an investment of less than this sum might seem to many U.S. consuls as insubstantial, *per se* unless one could establish that the business does not require more capital than that invested and that the sum invested represents all or almost all of the price of acquisition.

If the business enterprise, by its nature, does not require a high capital cost (such as a service business) then a relatively small amount of capital, say $50,000.00 might be considered substantial. This would be especially true where the investor possesses special and unique skills and talent such as an artist or architect. As an example, in the case of an architect, engineer, or other designer who purchases and installs state-of-the-art computers, software, and printers containing advanced computer aided design (CAD) features, the office headquarters might not require much more than standard office furniture in order to be a complete and properly functioning enterprise.

The proposed proportionality tests are not mandatory and may be modified in individual cases, but I fear that the bureaucratic tendency is to use these guidelines as *white line* tests. If a particular investment does not fall within the proportions outlined, there may be a presumption of ineligibility. This is especially unfortunate since often the foreign person may be very experienced and knowledgeable in business while the examining consular officer who has the authority to issue or deny the visa may be lacking in business experience and intellect. (In my home state of Florida, businesses are usually purchased for considerably less than the amounts required by these regulations.)

One technique that may avoid the economic problem inherent in the proportionality test is to subdivide the transaction so that the foreigner's capital is proportionately invested in the purchase of key assets or components of the business; other assets could be purchased later in a related, though separate, transaction. There are many variations of this technique that may be applicable in particular circumstances. It is imperative that proper planning be conducted prior to the execution of any documents for the acquisition of the business enterprise. The employment of a competent immigration attorney and knowledgeable business consultant is essential in this type of situation.

With an investment of a large sum of capital in the amount of $1,000,000.00 or more, *substantiality* will be presumed as a result of its sheer size, even though it may not approximate the recommended percentages. In most instances, the concept of substantiality is dependent upon the type of business that is being developed as well as the proportion of equity invested by the alien.

The investment also cannot be *marginal*. Very often, the concepts of substantial and marginal are interrelated. The concept of marginality will be explained in greater detail further on in this chapter. The following is an example of the substantiality concept.

Example: An investment in a heavy marine construction firm would obviously require millions of dollars, since each individual piece of equipment is quite costly; i.e., the cost of barges, cranes, tug boats, and additional equipment. Compare this type of investment with an investment in a wholesale distribution business for which the only capital investment required other than the wholesale inventory would be warehouse space, office furniture, perhaps the purchase of certain intangible assets, such as contract rights, etc. This business could be sufficiently capitalized with, let us say, $75,000.00.

In the warehouse business, it is very likely that the USCIS or the U.S. consul abroad will require an investment of at least ninety percent of the total amount required for the business; whereas, for the first company in our example, a lesser percentage is probably acceptable if the investment were large and if the investor were still directing the enterprise.

Investor's Own Funds. The U.S. consul abroad will usually require documentary proof that the funds invested are the investor's own funds. Any person interested in this visa should begin to gather documentation to trace the funds from the account in the home country into the United States. The U.S. consul will want documentary proof as to the origin and/or ownership of the funds and will usually not settle for anything less than this. This may be a problem for certain investors who live in countries where there is a restriction on the conversion of local funds into foreign currency or that may have various restrictions on the expatriation of capital.

It is not uncommon for persons of means in these countries to move certain amounts of their funds to a third country and to use various legal and accounting maneuvers to isolate these funds from themselves. Thus, it may be excessive for that person to reveal actual ownership of funds that the individual now seeks to move into the United States. Even though this may be a common practice in a particular country, the U.S. consul will still require documentary proof that funds brought into the United States belong to the investor.

Where an individual secretly takes large amounts of cash out of one's country and appears at the U.S. border and files the appropriate customs declarations with respect to the funds that the individual is bringing into the United States, the U.S. consul or USCIS, for purposes of complying with the *E-2* requirements, may still require that the foreign investor prove that the cash funds transported to and declared at the U.S. border are in fact his or her funds.

While the rules and regulations require that the foreign investor utilize one's own funds, loans that are guaranteed by the personal credit of the investor will suffice to meet the standard of substantiality as long as the loan is not also collateralized by the acquired assets. Loan proceeds that are collateralized by the assets that are being acquired by the foreign investor do not count as part of the foreign person's capital requirement for *E-2* visa purposes.

The investor is not limited to a capital investment of cash only into the enterprise. Equipment, fixtures, inventory, and other valuable tangible assets are also valid assets for investment. Even intangibles such as patent rights, royalty, or other contract rights can be used in the valuation of the alien's investments as long as they can be objectively appraised.

Investor to Direct and Manage. It is imperative that the alien prove that he or she is entering the United States to direct and manage the investment/enterprise. This requirement is dependent upon proof that the investor owns and/or controls the enterprise that is the subject of the visa application. While ordinarily the alien must establish ownership of at least fifty percent of the equity in the enterprise, it may be possible to demonstrate control by contracts or other agreements that essentially place the management and control of the enterprise in the hands of the alien.

Logic alone would indicate that if the alien is not in control of the investment and does not need to be present in the United States in order to manage it, the visa would be unnecessary.

Active Enterprise. The rules and regulations also require that the investment be an active enterprise as opposed to a passive investment. Investments in vacant land or in stocks, bonds, mutual funds, etc., will not qualify the investor for an *E-2* visa, regardless of the amount involved. The *E-2* visa was created to bring key individuals into the United States whose presence is required to direct and manage a business enterprise. Obviously, if the investment is one that does not require the personal involvement of the investor, the *E-2* visa would not be appropriate for that person.

Of course, this is a generality, and there may be some rare exceptions that will require close analysis if the line between a passive and an active enterprise is not clear. An example is someone who invests in the business of land or home development. While the ownership of land *per se* is insufficient as an entrepreneurial investment, someone who assumes the active entrepreneurial risk of developing land for commercial purposes could be an investor for *E-2* designation.

These points may be difficult to rationalize in certain cases. I remember specifically a situation some years ago when a prominent real estate broker brought two wealthy European investors to my office. These gentlemen were about to purchase a large tract of orange groves, already under lease to an orange grove operator. The investors would not be involved at all in the orange grove business and sought to make their profit by reselling the grove in the future. The foreign individuals were about to invest more than a million dollars, U.S. cash, for the property, since it provided a favorable rate of return and was fairly secure.

The investors, however, had one condition on their investment—that they obtain an *E* visa, so they could enter the U.S. and spend extended periods of time here at will. After analyzing the investment and their participation in the investment, I came to the conclusion that the investment would clearly not qualify for the *E-2* visa. The investors were disappointed that the large investment that they were willing to make would not entitle them to the visa but were happy to find this out prior to making the commitment to complete the transaction.

Marginality. The USCIS regulations state the following as to the question of marginality:

> *For purposes of this section, an enterprise may not be marginal. A marginal enterprise is an enterprise that does not have the present or future capacity to generate more than enough income to provide a minimal living for the treaty investor and his or her family. An enterprise that does not have the capacity to generate such income, but that has a present or future capacity to make a significant economic contribution is not a marginal enterprise. The projected future income-generating capacity should generally be realizable within five years from the date the alien commences the normal business activity of the enterprise.*

The terminology of the regulation is full of legal significance and must be carefully considered.

First of all, the meaning of a *minimal living* is not clear. This term is very often defined by the treaty visa officer abroad in the context of the usually expensive cost of living in the principal city where most U.S. consulates are located. Thus, what may be a minimal living for a person residing within commuting distance of the city of London may be a comfortable living for someone who resides in a rural community in the United States. Second, there is no definition of *significant economic contribution*. Thus, it is not clear if this terminology permits the creation of an enterprise in which just low skilled jobs are created is sufficient.

It is not entirely clear whether an enterprise that currently is or promises in the future to be highly profitable, but that creates little or no employment, is satisfactory. How about a business that doesn't provide high direct employment, but does provide much indirect employment, as would be the case of a company such as a building constructor in which most of the labor is provided by independent contractors? These are all dynamic concepts that require interpretation based upon all of the above factors, not the least of which is the particular U.S. consulate involved.

It is also obvious that most *E-2* investor applications should be augmented by a comprehensive business plan. The plan should be written in clear and simple language so that a person who has little or no training in business matters can understand it.

This is very often a difficult concept for the foreign person to grasp because it is a negative concept; that is, in order to be successful in a visa application the investor must prove that the proposed investment does not have the characteristic of *marginality*.

A component of *substantial economic contribution* is whether or not the investment will provide employment for U.S. citizens and/or residents. If the proposed business investment will provide for employment of other persons, it is less likely the investment will be found to be marginal. Thus, if the business will only support the investor and one or two other subsidiary employees, an investment may not support an *E-2* visa unless the other factors described are present in a substantial degree. If the nature of the business is such that large numbers of employees are not normally necessary, such as would be the case if the alien investor were a commercial artist, then the employment requirement can be relaxed.

This is because the nature of the business or endeavor, i.e., the creation of art, depends upon the unique and particular talent of the investor, whose efforts cannot be delegated to other employees. However, the business must still justify that it makes a *significant economic contribution*. It is clear that the focus is on the purely economic benefits of an enterprise rather than its other possible noneconomic benefits.

The more U.S. persons that will be employed by the business, the less attention or importance will be placed on the profitability of the business. The requirements are all interrelated and are somewhat interdependent.

Example: A restaurant is offered for sale by a U.S. seller at a price of $175,000. The transaction requires a total cash investment of only $75,000, since the present U.S. owner is willing to finance the balance ($100,000.00) of the purchase price. Indeed, this is a debt to equity ratio that would be customary in many areas in the United States. Furthermore, let us assume in our hypothetical transaction that the alien investor reasonably expects to derive a salary of $25,000 per annum and does not have income from any other source for support.

The USCIS and/or the Department of State (U.S. consulate abroad) will probably decide that a $75,000 investment is not in and of itself substantial under these circumstances. Secondly, they will decide that a $25,000 return, where there is no other income from any other sources indicates that the investment is one that will merely provide this person with a minimum salary. Thus, this investment will probably fail for lack of substantiality and for being marginal in nature.

If, on the other hand, the investor could show rehabilitation of a troubled business and thereby saving the jobs and—better yet—if the foreign investor could show an increase in the number of employees, the investment might be approved, especially if the investor could show that the amount invested was more than the norm or more than what would typically be required to establish or purchase a similar restaurant in the area. One cannot overemphasize the importance of documentary evidence to establish the accuracy of all assertions concerning the concept of *substantial investment* and the required lack of marginality.

Personal Residence Purchase. As stated previously, the Department of State and the USCIS are wary of alleged investments that may be nothing more than an attempt to immigrate to the United States in circumvention of the normal immigrant visa process. Consequently, these authorities look for evidence of immigrant intent in nonimmigrant visa applications. In my judgment, the purchase by an investor of a home in the United States before issuance of the nonimmigrant visa can be a tactical error.

In the case of an *E-2* visa applicant for instance, the money invested in a private dwelling (house or condominium apartment, for example) is basically wasted as it reduces the amount of capital available to satisfy the substantiality requirement of the law. This is especially true when the proportion of cash investment in the home exceeds that in the business. It does seem in these instances that the cart is before the horse.

In my geographic area in particular, the state of Florida, most prospective foreign investors with whom I speak are either planning to or have already acquired an expensive home, sometimes for cash. I generally advise my clients that, unless they are sufficiently wealthy, the purchase of the home should represent an insignificant economic undertaking and should be deferred until their investment is firmly rooted. I have spoken to foreign persons who erroneously believed they met the substantiality requirement by acquiring an expensive home for cash and then investing a small percentage of cash in the business enterprise.

In certain instances, the purchase of a personal residence at the inception of a business investment can be objectively justified—but generally I do not believe it prudent to impose that additional burden on the application. It is better to approach the situation conservatively and patiently by concentrating on the business first and then personal accommodations. The law now does not require the alien to maintain a home abroad nor does it require specific evidence of the alien's intent to return to the country of origin. Nonetheless, it is an excellent technique, especially in investment applications based upon a modest investment, to be able to demonstrate voluntarily that the alien does in fact maintain a foreign residence and that the alien's interest in acquiring or developing the U.S. enterprise is purely financial.

Advantages of the E-2 Visa. The *E-2* visa may be renewed indefinitely so long as the investment originally supporting the *E* visa continues in existence, although the visa is initially granted for up to five years at most United States consuls. The duration of the initial *E-2* visa is reciprocally dependent upon the duration of similar visas extended to U.S. investors by the other signatory country. Also, the *E-2* visa investor does not need to maintain a foreign domicile to which his or her intent is to return. Thus, the expense of maintaining two residences can be avoided. However, as a result of the attitude and working philosophy of the U.S. consulate, I still recommend to my clients, at least during the application period, they have maintained a foreign domicile as well as other close contacts with the home country in order to establish the temporary intent that is still required of an *E-2* visa applicant.

Additionally, employment by family members is not normally viewed as a violation of status even though the rules do not specifically sanction such employment. However, under the terms of the *Immigration Reform and Control Act of 1986,* it is doubtful whether a family member would be employable in the United States as employers now face criminal and civil sanctions for employing a person who is not otherwise authorized to work.

However, as a result of recent modifications to the law spouses of the principal *E-2* visa holder are now eligible to apply for employment authorization documents (EADs). Thus, there is no reason for the spouse of an *E-2* visa holder to ever worry about this problem.

Another advantage of the *E-2* visa is its *flexibility*. There is no requirement for the foreign person to have previously conducted business in a particular legal entity in the home country. Unlike the situation with the *L-1* visa, individuals (by investing the funds) can qualify for the *E-2* visa even if they have operated in the past and intend to operate in the future as a sole proprietor. Additionally, the investors do not need to prove that they are an executive or manager, etc., but merely prove that they are in a position to direct and manage the enterprise. This has been interpreted by rule and regulation in case law to mean that they must be in control of the enterprise. This distinction eliminates many of the technical problems involved in proving the status of executive or manager as indicated previously.

Procedure. It is preferable to process this visa application at the U.S. consulate abroad even though the USCIS has adopted the policy of *dual intent.* The acknowledgment of dual intent enables foreign persons to apply for the *E-2* visa in the United States even if they have had a petition for permanent residence filed on their behalf.

The *E-2* visa application may be filed in the United States if the foreign person is already in the United States in a valid nonimmigrant visa status. After the change of status is granted by the USCIS, the alien can remain in the United States and start working in the investment. If the alien departs the United States then, in order to reenter, he or she must apply for and obtain from a U.S. consulate an *E-2* visa. Often the United States consulate will require an entirely new *E-2* visa application and will reserve the right to adjudicate it anew. As a result of the obvious inconvenience and risk inherent in this situation, an entrepreneur should plan to minimize the problem of visa issuance—especially since in this situation the enterprise has already commenced.

There is another variation of the intent problem already discussed in previous chapters that may affect holders of nonimmigrant visas. Since it is often easier to obtain one particular visa as opposed to another (for example, the *B-2* visitor visa) an alien might be tempted to enter the United States on one visa and then once in the United States, file an application for a change to a different visa. There is nothing wrong with this procedure if the change of intent is genuine. However, if the USCIS believes that the alien entered the United States with a preconceived intent to apply for a change of visa after arrival, then the requested visa may be denied just for that reason.

Furthermore, even if the USCIS approves the change of status, this is no guarantee that the U.S. consulate abroad will issue the visa in the event the foreign person is required to travel outside the United States. The U.S. consulate may deny issuance of the *E-2* visa even if the foreign person has commenced business operations in the United States under the authority of the USCIS. The rationale is that the Department of State is required by law to exercise its own independent judgment with respect to visa issuance.

Be advised that the Department of State jealously guards its prerogatives. One sure way to earn the animosity of the treaty visa officer is to indicate by word or deed that one is merely seeking to have the visa stamped into the passport.

Each U.S. consulate has developed a method for processing *E* visa applications, even though most of them use the same form (*OF-156* with *E Supplement*). Every consul will require proof of all the elements outlined in this chapter, so an individual applying for an *E* visa should have all of the requirements thoroughly documented. Even though not required, it is strongly recommended that an individual applying for this visa, as well as certain other temporary visas, utilize the services of an experienced immigration professional for assistance in organizing the evidence required and to answer any of the questions of the U.S. consul. There is a saying that there is no second chance to make a favorable first impression, and it would be imprudent to submit an *E* visa application that did not evidence care and consideration. In many cases, a consul will appreciate having a professional handling the application because many problems can be avoided.

In addition, as a result of the passage of the *North American Free Trade Act,* both Canadian and Mexican citizens are now eligible to obtain the *E* visas.

Employees of E Visa Traders or Investors

If the *E* visa applicant is not the Trader or Investor principal, then the applicant's job must be of either executive and supervisory in nature or must have *special qualifications.*

The regulations state the following requirements for an *E-2* employee.

> *Executive and supervisory character.* The applicant's position must be principally and primarily, as opposed to incidentally or collaterally, executive or supervisory in nature. Executive and supervisory duties are those which provide the employee ultimate control and responsibility for the enterprise's overall operation or a major component thereof. In determining whether the applicant has established possession of the requisite control and responsibility, a Service officer shall consider, where applicable:
>
> (i) That an executive position is one which provides the employee with great authority to determine the policy of, and the direction for, the enterprise;
>
> (ii) That a position primarily of supervisory character provides the employee supervisory responsibility for a significant proportion of an enterprise's operations and does not generally involve the direct supervision of low-level employees; and,
>
> (iii) Whether the applicant possesses executive and supervisory skills and experience; a salary and position title commensurate with executive or supervisory employment; recognition or indicia of the position as one of authority and responsibility in the overall organizational structure; responsibility for making discretionary decisions, setting policies, directing and managing business operations, supervising other profes-

sional and supervisory personnel; and that, if the position requires some routine work usually performed by a staff employee, such functions may only be of an incidental nature.

Special qualifications. Special qualifications are those skills and/or aptitudes tat an employee in a lesser capacity brings to a position or role that are essential to the successful or efficient operation of the treaty enterprise. In determining whether the skills possessed by the alien are essential to the operation of the employing treaty enterprise, a service officer must consider, where applicable:

(i) The degree of proven expertise of the alien in the area of operations involved; whether others possess the applicant's specific skill or aptitude; the length of the applicant's experience and/or training with the treaty enterprise; the period of training or other experience necessary to perform effectively the projected duties; the relationship of the skill or knowledge to the enterprise's specific processes or applications, and the salary the special qualifications can command; that knowledge of a foreign language and culture does not, by itself, meet the special qualifications requirement and

(ii) Whether the skills and qualifications are readily available in the United States. In all cases, in determining whether the applicant possesses special qualifications which are essential to the treaty enterprise, a Service officer must take into account all the particular facts presented. A skill that is essential at one point in time may become commonplace at a later date. Skills that are needed to start up an enterprise may no longer be essential after initial operations are complete and running smoothly. Some skills are essential only in the short-term for the training of locally hired employees. Under certain circumstances, an applicant may be able to establish his or her essentiality to the treaty enterprise for a longer period of time, such as, in connection with activities in the areas of product improvement, quality control, or the provision of a service not yet generally available in the United States. Where the treaty enterprise's need for the applicant's special qualifications, and therefore, the applicant's essentiality, is time-limited, Service officers may request that the applicant provide evidence of the period for which skills will be needed and a reasonable projected date for completion of start-up or replacement of the essential skilled workers.

Planning Tip. From a discussion of the above requirements of documentation and proof, it should be apparent that it is much easier to establish whether or not a given business investment satisfies the *substantiality* requirement if the business is acquired rather than developed from the very beginning. The price established between two independent parties is accepted by the government as the *going* or *market value* for that particular business enterprise.

If the business must be developed from the very beginning, then the government can, and frequently does, require independent proof that the investment is substantial for that particular type of business. This can require a written opinion from an independent expert, as well as an audited financial statement from a certified public accountant. It must be remembered that the immigration authorities do not generally have personnel who are competent or otherwise trained in business matters. The prospective investor must therefore generally prove and document to a nonbusiness person what to the investor may be obvious.

Bilateral Investment Treaties

In addition to the treaties of navigation and commerce, which are the basis of the *E-2* visa, there recently has come into vogue the use of *Bilateral Investment Treaties* (BIT) between the United States and other nations that are specifically designed to provide for various investment advantages to both sides. These BITS also provide for the issuance of *E-2* visas to nationals of the foreign country. Here is a list of the countries with which the U.S. has BITS in effect at the time of the printing of this book. It is important to verify the status of these BITS before undertaking any contracts for the acquisition of business assets with a view towards qualifying for an *E-2* visa.

Albania	Argentina	Armenia
Bangladesh	Bulgaria	Cameroon
Congo (Kinshasa)	Congo(Brazzaville)	Czech Republic
Ecuador	Egypt	Estonia
Georgia	Grenada	Jamaica
Kazakhstan	Kyrgyzstan	Latvia
Moldova	Mongolia	Morocco
Panama	Poland	Romania

Senegal	Slovak Republic	Sri Lanka
Trinidad	Tobago	Turkey
Tunisia	Ukraine	Zaire

Canada and Mexico: Special Advantages

Canada has traditionally been treated in a special and generally preferred manner by the immigration regimen of the United States. Canadians (together with certain classes of Mexican citizens) do not need visas to enter the United States. Of course, this does not mean that the immigration law does not apply to Canadians; rather that Canadians entering the United States merely have to demonstrate to the officer at the border that they were otherwise qualified to enter in whatever visa category applied.

The *North American Free Trade Act* (NAFTA) was passed by the U.S. Congress in 1994. NAFTA addresses primarily topics such as trade, commerce, and tariffs but in order to facilitate the overall trade purposes of the Act, also made some major sweeping changes in the immigration procedures. The immigration provisions do not replace the existing substantive immigration law, but rather modify the existing law. The immigration provisions of NAFTA present very favorable changes for both Canadian and Mexican business persons/investors.

As an example, the legislation and administration Rules and Regulations makes the Treaty/Trader Investor visa *(E-1, E-2)* classification available to Canadian and Mexican citizens. All of the provisions and requirements as described in this book, that apply to *E* treaty applicants, now apply to Canadian and Mexican citizens. Canadian citizens applying for an *E* visa in the western hemisphere do not need to possess a passport and may have their visa issued on a separate document (*Form OF-232*). Unlike Canadians, Mexican citizens applying for an *E* visa must have a passport.

The provisions of NAFTA apply only to citizens of Canada and Mexico. Canadian Landed Immigrants are not benefited. In order to qualify under the appropriate division of NAFTA, an individual must fit within the prerequisite definition of a *business person*—someone who is engaged in the trade of goods or services or investment activities. *Temporary entry* is defined as entry without the intent to establish permanent residence. With respect to the latter requirement, all of the previous discussion on intention applies.

There are four groups of nonimmigrants covered by NAFTA. They are as follows.

Business Visitors Business visitors may come temporarily to the United States for research and design, growth, manufacture and production, marketing, sales, distribution, after-sales service, and general service. An alien who qualifies under this provision is not entitled to receive salary or remuneration from a United States source. However, a business visitor may receive incidental expenses from a United States source.

In accordance with the statutory scheme, a person who is granted a visa under NAFTA is designated as having *TN* visa status, while the family dependents are designated as having *TD* visa status. TD designated persons are not authorized to work.

The initial entry is for one year and the regulations state that an extension may be granted in one-year increments. At the date of the publication of this book, the limit on the total number of extensions permitted under this category was an unsettled issue it seems that there is no precise limitation as to how many extensions may be granted after the original one-year admission. The reader should note, however, that the *TN* visa (unlike the *H-1B* or the *L-1*) does not provide for dual intent. The foreign person must always establish either at the border during the initial application or with the appropriate service center of the USCIS for the extension that the foreign person has not abandoned his foreign domicile and intends to return as soon as the job is over.

Logically, then it would seem that at some, as yet undetermined time, the USCIS may take the position, either by individual adjudication or by policy directive, that there is a limit as to the number of extensions permitted. Accordingly, *TN* holders must make their plans accordingly and not assume that past extensions will always result in future extensions. The *TN* visa should be viewed as not only a temporary visa but also as a temporary status for the foreign person.

Of course, accompanying family members (spouse or children) may be admitted under the same terms and conditions of the principal. There is an annual numerical limitation of 5500 *TN* visas for Mexican citizens. Accompanying dependents of Mexican TN professionals are also counted against this annual limitation.

Canadian and Mexican Traders and Investors

NAFTA extends the benefits of the *E* Treaty Trader provisions to citizens Canada and Mexico. A Canadian or Mexican citizen seeking admission under this section must apply for a visa from a U.S. consular officer abroad in order to enter in *E* status.

Regulations as to the issuance of these visas have been issued by both the Department of State and legacy INS (now the USCIS) so that the adjudicatory mechanism and philosophy of these agencies has now been established.

NOTE: *These definitions now include the provision of services as "trade." Previously, the term trade was limited to the traffic in tangible goods while now it is has been accepted by the government that services such as banking, insurance, etc. can now be the subject of trade and thus substantiate the issuance of treaty trader status.*

Intracompany Transferee

The only substantial change in the application of the *L-1* visa provisions to Canadian citizens is that the citizen may have the option of presenting all supporting documents, etc. at the designated border points, thus circumventing the need for previously approved petitions by the USCIS. I believe this will be difficult to implement as the volume of documentation required for these visas can sometimes be quite onerous and unless one arrives at the border point early (three hours is recommended), it is doubtful that the border official will be able to properly analyze the documents. Unless the USCIS border inspector has sufficient time to review the alien's documents, the foreign person will be admitted under parole and an appointment will be scheduled at the USCIS office nearest the Canadian citizen's intended place of work in order to have the supporting documents thoroughly reviewed.

Mexican citizens will still have to apply for the *L-1* visa at the Northern Regional Service Center of the USCIS.

Canadian and Mexican Citizens Seeking Classification in Activities at a Professional Level

Under the provisions of the NAFTA, Canadian and Mexican citizens can enter the United States temporarily to *engage in business activities at a professional level.* In order to qualify under this category, individuals must provide proof of Canadian or Mexican citizenship and documentation showing that they are engaged in one of the professions listed in Schedule Two to Annex 1502.1. Schedule Two follows this subsection.

An important advantage of this provision is that the Canadian citizen will be able to enter the United States without first having a petition filed by an employer requesting the alien's admission. NAFTA provides that individuals who lack a baccalaureate or licenciatura degree must demonstrate at least four years of experience, or the equivalent of the time normally spent acquiring a baccalaureate degree in the United States.

A Canadian or Mexican citizen who otherwise qualifies, will be provided with a *Form I-94* under the classification symbol *TN* with an initial entry period not to exceed one year. Extensions of stay may be granted in increments of one year.

Although NAFTA does not require that a petition be filed on behalf of a Canadian business professional, the implementing regulation specifies that the level of documentation be on a par with that required for nonimmigrant classifications for which petitions are required. Mexican citizens will have to file a formal visa petition (*Form I-129*) at the Northern Regional Service Center. Canadian citizens do not need to file a visa petition and may present their credentials and documentation of job offers directly to the USCIS inspector at the border. For either Mexicans or Canadians the following documentation must be presented:

✪ the professional activity to be engaged in;

✪ the purpose of entry;

✪ the anticipated length of stay;

✪ the educational qualifications or appropriate credentials that demonstrate that the Canadian or Mexican citizen has professional level status;

✪ proof that the Canadian or Mexican citizen complies with all applicable state laws and/or licensing requirements for the occupation to be engaged in; and,

✪ the arrangements for remuneration for services to be rendered.

Extensions of stay may be granted in increments of one year. The application for an extension of stay is to be accompanied by a letter from the employer confirming the continuing need for the alien's temporary services and specifying the additional time needed.

In addition to specific documentation, NAFTA provides for the admission of Canadian and Mexican citizens who are coming to engage in certain professional activities. A list of those specific professions that have been identified by the Act and enabling legislation is reproduced below.

(For purposes of brevity, the term baccalaureate degree includes the *licenciatura* degree issued in Mexico.)

- ✪ Accountant—baccalaureate degree;

- ✪ Architect—baccalaureate degree or provincial license;

- ✪ Computer Systems Analyst—baccalaureate degree;

- ✪ Disaster Relief Claims Adjuster—baccalaureate degree or three years experience in the field of claims adjustment;

- ✪ Economist—baccalaureate degree;

- ✪ Engineer—baccalaureate degree or provincial license;

- ✪ Forester—baccalaureate degree or provincial license;

- ✪ Graphic Designer—baccalaureate degree, or post-secondary diploma and three year's experience;

- ✪ Hotel Manager—baccalaureate degree and three year's experience;

- ✪ Land Surveyor—baccalaureate degree or provincial/federal license;

- ✪ Lawyer—member of bar in province, L.L.B.; J.D.; L.L.L., or B.C.L;

- ✪ Librarian—M.L.S. or B.L.S;

- ✪ Management Consultant—baccalaureate degree or five years experience in consulting or related field;

- ✪ Mathematician—baccalaureate degree;

✪ Medical/Allied Professionals:

✪ Clinical Lab Technologist—baccalaureate degree;

✪ Dentist—D.D.S., D.M.D., or provincial license;

✪ Dietitian—baccalaureate degree or provincial license;

✪ Medical Technologist—baccalaureate degree;

✪ Nutritionist—baccalaureate degree;

✪ Occupational Therapist—baccalaureate degree or provincial license;

✪ Pharmacist—baccalaureate degree or provincial license;

✪ Physician—(teaching and/or research only) M.D., or provincial license;

✪ Physio/Physical Therapist—baccalaureate degree or provincial license;

✪ Psychologist—provincial license;

✪ Recreational Therapist—baccalaureate degree;

✪ Registered Nurse—provincial license; or,

✪ Veterinarian—D.V.M.; D.M.V., or provincial license;

✪ Range Manager (Range Conservationist)—baccalaureate degree;

✪ Research Assistant (Working in a Post-Secondary Educational Institution)—baccalaureate degree;

✪ Scientific technician/technologist—must work in direct support of professionals in the following disciplines: Chemistry, geology, geophysics, meteorology, physics, astronomy, agricultural sciences, biology, or forestry; must possess theoretical knowledge of the discipline; must solve practical problems in the discipline; must apply principles of the discipline to basic or applied research;

✪ Scientist:

> ✪ Agriculturist (Agronomist)—baccalaureate degree;

> ✪ Animal Breeder—baccalaureate degree;

> ✪ Animal Scientist—baccalaureate degree;

> ✪ Apiculturist—baccalaureate degree;

> ✪ Astronomer—baccalaureate degree;

> ✪ Biochemist—baccalaureate degree;

> ✪ Biologist—baccalaureate degree;

> ✪ Chemist—baccalaureate degree;

> ✪ Dairy Scientist—baccalaureate degree;

> ✪ Entomologist—baccalaureate degree;

> ✪ Epidemiologist—baccalaureate degree;

> ✪ Geneticist—baccalaureate degree;

> ✪ Geologist—baccalaureate degree;

> ✪ Geophysicist—baccalaureate degree;

> ✪ Horticulturist—baccalaureate degree;

> ✪ Meteorologist—baccalaureate degree;

> ✪ Pharmacologist—baccalaureate degree;

> ✪ Physicist—baccalaureate degree;

✪ Plant Breeder—baccalaureate degree;

✪ Poultry Scientist—baccalaureate degree;

✪ Soil Scientist—baccalaureate degree; or,

✪ Silviculturist (forestry specialist)—baccalaureate degree;

✪ Teacher for any of the following institutions:

✪ College—baccalaureate degree;

✪ Seminary—baccalaureate degree; or,

✪ University—baccalaureate degree;

✪ Technical Publications Writer—baccalaureate degree, or post-secondary diploma and three year's experience;

✪ Urban Planner—baccalaureate degree; or,

✪ Vocational Counselor—baccalaureate degree.

The Canadian and Mexican citizen must present to the USCIS inspector at the port of entry a verification of citizenship, a letter and any other required documents that demonstrate that the individual possesses the requisite educational background and experience for the profession claimed. Canadian citizens must also establish that they are qualified to engage in the employment indicated. A dependent spouse and children may also be admitted under the same visa category so long as these are also NAFTA nationals. If the dependents are not NAFTA citizens, they may be admitted as *B-2* visitors.

Canadian citizens in this classification may be re-admitted to the United States for the remainder of the period authorized on the original *Form I-94* that they received at the border at the time of the initial entry, without presentation of the original letter or documentation. A Canadian admitted under this section may apply for an extension of stay on *Form I-539*, which is standard for requests of extensions of stay. The application for extension shall be accompanied by a letter(s) from the United States employer(s) confirming the continued need for the NAFTA citizen's services and stating the length of additional time needed.

A Mexican citizen seeking the *TN* visa must file a formal petition on *Form I-129* and will be adjudicated as if the petition were a normal *H-1B* visa petition. The petition must be filed at the Northern Service Center of the USCIS. The *Notice of Approval* must then be presented to the appropriate U.S. consulate in Mexico which will issue the visa.

A request to change U.S. employers is also made on the *Form I-539*. This must then be accompanied by a letter from the new employer describing the services to be performed, the time needed to render such services and the terms of remuneration for services. Employment with a different or with an additional employer is not authorized prior to approval by the USCIS of the request for extension of stay.

In addition, NAFTA provides for a procedure that allows for certain Canadian business persons to enter the United States temporarily. This would enable these persons to enter the United States for the purpose of extending performance of after-sales, service and training throughout the life of a warranty or service agreement.

A Canadian is permitted to present a *Form I-129* petition together with supporting documentation at a U.S. port of entry rather than having to file the petition in advance at a regional USCIS office. Since these visa petitions generally require much documentation, it is recommended that individuals appear at the border at least three hours in advance of their scheduled departure.

Intracompany Transferee (L-1 Visa)

The *L-1* visa is one of the most flexible and sought-after temporary visas that provide for employment. Section 101(a)(15)(L) of the *Immigration and Nationality Act* establishes the requirements for the *L-1* visa, one of the most useful nonimmigrant visas available to employees of foreign companies. The purpose of the *L-1* visa is to facilitate the transfer of *key employees* to the United States from companies that are affiliated with or related to United States corporations. This visa is very useful because it is not limited to specific countries with which the United States may have entered a treaty. Nationals of all countries are eligible, provided the specific qualifications for the visa are satisfied.

Duration of Stay

The *L-1* visa has a duration of seven years for *managers* and *executives* and five years for persons of *specialized knowledge*. The duration of stay is issued for an initial period of three years and may be extended for additional periods of two years. In the case of a new office, the visa is issued for one year and may be extended for two periods of three years.

Duration of Employment

The employee who is to be transferred must have been continuously employed by the overseas (extra-United States) company for a period of at least one year out of the last three years prior to entry into the United States. Short business or pleasure trips to the United States during the one year period will not disqualify the employee from the visa; however, extended trips or visits to the United States may be considered by the USCIS as an interruption of the one-year foreign employment requirement.

Intracompany Relationship

The prior employer/foreign company must be related to the U.S. company, either as a subsidiary, affiliate or division. This unity of identity is satisfied by any of the above legal relationships, and must in most cases, be documented to the USCIS. The documentation of the U.S.-foreign corporation relationship may not need to be documented in the case of large, well-known multinational corporations such as Ford Motor Company, Monsanto, Dupont, etc.

Requirements

In order to establish that the foreign-domestic entities are one and the same for immigration purposes, it is necessary that the corporations be controlled by the same person(s) (affiliate) or that one corporation controls the other (subsidiary). In order to document the above, one must show that the U.S. corporation owns at least fifty-one percent of the shares of the foreign corporation, (or vice-versa), or in the alternative that the same stockholders own fifty-one percent of each of the corporations.

Another alternative, is to show that the foreign corporation is a branch or division of the U.S. corporation or vice-versa. The requirement of common control can be satisfied in certain instances even where the controlling entity does not own fifty-one percent of the stock. Thus, where persons own less than fifty-one percent of the foreign corporation, they must demonstrate effective control of that corporation through legal documents, contracts, or some other documented arrangement.

The regulations pertaining to the definition of an *affiliate* now provides for some degree of flexibility as to the percentage of ownership required for each owner. The law states affiliate means:

✪ one of two subsidiaries both of which are owned and controlled by the same parent or individual or

✪ one of two legal entities owned and controlled by the same group of individuals, each individual owning and controlling approximately the same share or proportion of each entity.

The operative concept here is the adverb *approximately*. Most experienced practitioners equate this concept with effective control, be established that the power or control relationships are the same as between the two companies, then they will be considered as affiliates. As a result of the above ambiguities, consultation with an experienced immigration attorney is very much advised as to managing these issues.

Example: A Taiwanese family owns seventy-five percent interest in a Taiwanese manufacturing concern. The same family acquires a U.S. company, but instead of owning it in the same fashion as they own the Taiwanese parent, the family forms two foreign holding corporations (organized in the country of Barbados) which in turn own all the stock in the U.S. affiliate company. Even though the family indirectly owns the U.S. affiliate company in the same proportion as they own the Taiwanese company, the USCIS may make a technical objection on the basis that the forms of ownership of the companies differ.

This scholarly attitude on the part of the USCIS may change on this subject, but as of the writing of this book, it represents the current posture of the USCIS. The reason why a foreign person may decide to hold U.S. business and real property interests using a multi-tiered corporate structure may be due to sound tax and other reporting requirement concerns, but there is no automatic understanding or acceptance by the USCIS of these otherwise very valid motivations.

In addition, the petitioning company must continue to be a *qualifying organization*. Thus, the foreign company must continue to function as a viable business entity throughout the employment period of the *L-1* visa holder. If the foreign entity ceases to exist or ceases to function as a viable business entity, then the L-visa status of the employee is jeopardized. This is an extremely important point for a small company to bear in mind.

Other Qualifying Companies. The immigration regulations permit entities other than a corporation to serve as a qualifying company. Partnerships and even sole proprietorships can serve as qualifying companies for *L-1* visa purposes. In a noncorporate setting it is important to establish that the employing company is a separate entity from the employee being transferred. This fact is easier to establish with a corporation since a corporation is recognized as a separate legal entity from its owners. In the case of a larger, well-established company which operates in a legal form other than a corporation (or its equivalent), the *L-1* visa may still be available but there will be a heavier burden of proof to establish the separate business and economic identity of the company.

In the case of a company that is contemplating the creation of a U.S. subsidiary or affiliate office, it is recommended that either the company incorporate or that it create a separate corporation that will then act as the qualifying company for the *L-1* visa. It must be remembered that mere creation of a corporation is insufficient. It will be necessary to transfer active and viable business activities to the corporation in order to allow it to serve as a qualifying company. Advanced and careful planning is the key to success in these endeavors.

Employee's Qualifications. The law defines *manager, executive,* and *person of specialized knowledge* as follows:

Manager:

- ✪ primarily manages the organization, or a department, subdivision, function, or component of the organization. The addition of the concept *function* gives the definition more usefulness for smaller companies or companies in which a key function is primarily managed and run by the same person;

- ✪ primarily supervises and controls the work of other supervisory, professional, or managerial employees, or manages an essential function within the organization, or a department or subdivision of the organization. In order to qualify as a manager under these regulations, a *first-line supervisor* must supervise professional persons. Thus, a manager would not qualify as such if he or she is the first-line supervisor of actual production personnel;

- ✪ has the authority to hire and fire or recommend those as well as other personnel actions if another employee or other employees are supervised; if no other employees are supervised, functions at a senior level within the organizational hierarchy or with respect to the function managed; and,

✪ exercises discretion over the day-to-day operations of the activity or function for which the employee has authority.

Executive:

✪ directs the management of the organization or a major component or function;

NOTE: *This is similar to the third point under manager as defined above.*

✪ establishes the goals and policies of the organization, component, or function;

✪ exercises wide latitude in discretionary decision-making; and,

✪ receives only general supervision or direction from higher level executives, the board of directors or stockholders of the organization.

Person of specialized knowledge:

✪ must have special or unique knowledge of the petitioning organization's product, service, research, equipment, techniques, management, or other interests and its application in international markets, or an advanced level of knowledge or expertise in the organization's processes and procedures;

✪ *special knowledge* is knowledge that is different from or exceeds the ordinary or usual knowledge of an employee in a particular field; and,

✪ a specialized knowledge professional is a person who has specialized knowledge and is a member of the professions.

There is no requirement that the position to be filled by the employee be identical to that previously held abroad, or that it have all of the same responsibilities, but the position in the United States must be at least of the equivalent classification as the employee's position abroad.

Newly-Formed Companies

The original purpose of the law was to provide for the transfer to the United States of managers and key persons from and by multinational corporations. However, the letter of the law as written also permits small companies to benefit from the *L* visa—even companies that are composed of no more than two or three individuals.

The USCIS regulations have the following additional requirements for newly formed companies. A *newly-formed company* is a company that has been in business for less than one year. A newly formed U.S. company that is a subsidiary or an affiliate of a foreign company must establish that it has obtained a place for conducting business, that the beneficiary had been employed abroad as a manager or executive and will continue in that capacity in the United States.

If the *L-1* visa employee is a major stockholder of the company, proof must be submitted that the employee will be transferred abroad at the completion of temporary duties in the U.S.

All of the above points must be minutely documented to the USCIS. Indeed, one should provide, among other things: copies of the lease for the premises, copies of any business contracts, a cash projection for the business, and copies of accounting and bank records to indicate that both the foreign company and the United States parent are viable entities. Proof of economic viability usually requires documentation that establishes that the United States entity has the financial ability to cover the transferee's salary for at least the first year of operation. It is also recommended that documentation regarding the qualifying company's economic strength be included as well. The petition, together with the supporting documentation, must then be filed with the appropriate district office of the USCIS for processing.

It cannot be overemphasized the importance of presenting a well-organized and probative set of corroborating documents together with the *Form I-129*. The success or failure of the petition will be based for the most part on the strength of the documentary evidence submitted in support of the petition. After approval of the petition, the employee may bring the letter of approval to the nearest U.S. consular post in order to apply for the issuance of the visa.

The purpose of this regulation is to prevent relatively small companies from sponsoring visas for their sole or family owner/manager when the real intention is to immigrate permanently to the United States. The regulation however, ignores economics and business realities and often results in an overly mechanistic view of a business organization.

The regulations further state that in defining *executive or managerial* for *L* visa purposes, the USCIS will review the size of the company and the total number of employees employed by the company. The regulations seem to be creating an additional requirement of size and/or structure that is not contained in the original law and is subject to attack in the court systems. This new development requires close study and analysis by any foreign company seeking to expand operation into the United States.

Company must be doing Business. The law also requires that the petitioning company be in the business of providing regular, systematic, and continuous goods and/or services. The regulations specifically exclude the mere presence of an agent or office of the qualifying organization in the U.S. and abroad as being acceptable. The law clearly favors entrepreneurial activities rather than passive investments. Indeed, if the person is not needed to actively manage or supervise a key function of the organization, that person probably does not need to be physically present in the United States—or at least that is the attitude of the government on this issue.

Alien's intent. An important consideration for this visa (as is the case with all of the others discussed in this book) is the question of *intent*. This applies both as to the employer and the employee. In both cases, it is required that the intention be one of a temporary nature. In the context of the *L-1* visa , the problem of intent has been largely eliminated.

It is now permissible for an employee to have a *dual intent* with respect to intention as to the duration of stay. That is, the employer and employee may have the present intention of remaining in the United States on a temporary basis in compliance with the requirements of the *L-1* visa, while at the same time, having an intention to file a petition for a permanent visa at some point in the future. The USCIS must be satisfied that both the employer and the employee agree that the employee will return abroad if the permanent visa is not approved during the valid period of the stay authorized by the *L-1* visa. Putting the intention into words, it can be thought of as saying:

> *It is my intention to remain in the United States on a temporary*
> *basis during the period of time that my L-1 Visa is valid. I may*
> *decide to remain in the United States as a permanent resident by*

filing an application for a permanent visa but I agree that I will depart the United States in the event that the L-1 Visa expires before I obtain my permanent visa.

Usually, the mere statement of intention by the employer is sufficient to establish the petitioner's intention to comply with the law, unless the transferee is also a principal owner of the company and/or the U.S. corporate enterprise is a new venture. In these cases, additional documentation is required to establish the circumstances under which the transferred employee will depart the United States. This visa does not require that the foreign employee maintain a home abroad but if he or she does, it is obviously helpful on the issue of temporariness.

The reason for this high degree of attention to the question of intent by the USCIS is that the *L* visa, at least with respect to executives and managers, lends itself to a relatively easy conversion to a permanent visa.

Normally, an alien must have received a job offer from a U.S. employer that has been certified by the Department of Labor as not displacing qualified local workers or negatively affecting the U.S. labor market. This process can take a long time. A manager or executive who holds an *L-1* visa can qualify for a first preference employment-based permanent visa as a multinational manager or executive without the necessity of a labor certification. This is a highly coveted advantage.

As a result of the long time delays in obtaining a permanent visa, an employee may need to extend his or her *L* visa before the permanent visa is approved. A new policy determination by the USCIS states that the filing of a request for labor certification or of a petition for a permanent visa will not *per se* disqualify a person from obtaining an extension to the *L* visa. In other words, the USCIS representative will look at other evidence to determine whether or not—at the time a person applies for an extension of an *L* visa—that person has a true intention to return home in the event that the permanent visa is denied.

Even though the distinction between dual intent and a preconceived permanent intent may be somewhat unclear, the distinction must be thoroughly understood by the employee and the employer in order to avoid difficulties with USCIS. This is especially the case where the person is the employee of a small business or a business in which a substantial interest is held.

Change of Status

If the alien is already in the United States and otherwise qualifies for the *L-1* visa, he or she may elect to file for a *change of status*, while he or she is in the United States so as to avoid the necessity of a trip abroad to a U.S. consulate. Persons holding a *B-1* status who file for an application for a change of status to *L-1* should be aware of a hidden issue. That is, the time in which a person has been in the U.S. in *B-1* status may cause an interruption in the required one year period of employment abroad. Thus, before filing for a change of status an *L-1* petitioner must ensure that the one year period of employment abroad has been satisfied prior to the employee's (beneficiary) last entry to the U.S. The USCIS and its predecessor has always interpreted the one year prior foreign employment as a bright line test. One must establish a full prior year of foreign employment and the USCIS examiner will compute the days to ensure that the foreign worker has worked at least 365 days abroad.

As a result of the legal complexity concerning the requirements of the L visa, the employer and/or employee should seek the advice and counsel of a qualified immigration attorney before any definite steps are taken.

Employment Authorization for Certain Spouses

The law now provides for the issuance of employment authorization to the spouse of a holder of either an *E-1/E-2* or *L-1* visa status. This fairly new provision corrects a prior anomaly in the law that assumed that the spouses of aliens would not have a career of their own. As far as the *E-1/E-2* visa is concerned, this law allows for some flexibility in maximizing the income earning potential of a family. It may be possible, for instance, for a married couple to decide strategically which one of them should apply for the *E* visa. This allows the other spouse, who may have a greater job marketing availability or income earning availability, to avail him or herself of other job and career opportunities in the U.S.

Furthermore, the accompanying spouse could then actively pursue a labor certification and permanent residency while the *E* visa holder continues to develop the U.S. investment or the *L* visa holder continues to work for the sponsoring multinational enterprise.

In order for the other spouse to take advantage of this provision, it is only necessary as a matter of documentation to prove the existence of the marital relationship. This is accomplished by providing a copy of the marriage certificate together with the application form (*Form I-765*).

Temporary Workers

H-1B Visa   This is one of the most important nonimmigrant visas available to qualified foreign persons wanting to come to the United States in order to work. An *H-1B* classification applies to an alien who is coming temporarily to the United States:

> *(1) To perform services in a specialty occupation (except registered nurses, agricultural workers, and aliens of extraordinary ability or achievement in the sciences, education, or business) described in section 214 (i)(1) of the Act,... and for whom the Secretary of Labor has determined and certified to the Attorney General that the prospective employer has filed a labor condition application under section 212 (n)(1) of the Act;*
>
> *(2) To perform services of an exceptional nature requiring exceptional merit and ability relating to a cooperative research and development project or a co-production project provided for under a Government-to-Government agreement administered by the Secretary of Defense;*
>
> *(3) To perform services as a fashion model of distinguished merit and ability and for whom the Secretary of Labor has determined and certified to the Attorney General that the prospective employer has filed a labor condition application under section 212(n)(1) of the Act. 8 C.F.R. Sec. 214.2(h)(ii)(B).*

This visa is highly sought because, unlike many other types of visas, the position that is being filled by the alien can be permanent; it is only the need for the alien that must be temporary. Furthermore, the foreign national is not required to have any prior employment experience with the same employer nor does the employer have to be international in character.

Specialty Occupation. A specialty occupation is defined as—

> *an occupation which requires theoretical and practical application of a body of highly specialized knowledge in such fields of human endeavor including, but not limited to, architecture, engineering, mathematics, physical sciences, medicine and health, education, business specialties, accounting, law, theology, and the arts, and*

which requires the attainment of a bachelor's degree or higher in a specific specialty, or its equivalent, as a minimum for entry into the occupation in the United States.

This definition describes a classic profession that requires the application of a theoretical body of knowledge to particular circumstances.

In the field of fashion modeling, prominence is defined as a high level of achievement evident by a degree of skill and recognition substantially above that ordinarily encountered to the extent that a person described as prominent is renowned, leading, or well known in the field of fashion modeling.

Employer's Requirements. Before filing an *H-1B* petition, the prospective employer (petitioner) must file a labor condition application with the Department of Labor. The *labor condition application* is a representation that the petitioner has agreed to pay the *H-1B* beneficiary the prevailing wage for the job.

The labor condition application is not a document to be taken lightly. It presupposes that the employer has made a determination as to the prevailing wage for the job and then will pay the foreign employee accordingly. If it is determined by the government that an employer has violated the terms of the labor condition application, the employer can be fined. One of the conditions of the *H-1B* visa is that the employer is obligated to pay the cost of transporting the foreign employee abroad in the case of termination. (The law does not provide for a sanction in the event of a violation of this provision. It is difficult to imagine how this provision could be enforced or who could enforce it.)

Employee's (beneficiary) Requirements for a Specialty Occupation. In order to qualify as a specialty occupation, the beneficiary-employee must meet one of the following criteria:

- ✪ hold a United States baccalaureate or higher degree as required by the specialty occupation from an accredited college or university;

- ✪ hold a foreign degree determined to be equivalent to a United States baccalaureate or higher degree required by the specialty occupation from an accredited college or university;

✪ hold an unrestricted state license, registration, or certification that authorizes full practice of the specialty occupation and be immediately engaged in that specialty in a state of intended employment.

✪ If a temporary license is available and the foreign person is allowed to perform the duties of the occupation without a permanent license and an analysis of the facts demonstrate that the alien under supervision is authorized to fully perform the duties of the occupation, *H* classification may be granted. (This might be the case for certain health-related occupations such as physical therapists, for which occupations a state might provide a temporary license pending completion of all requirements for permanent licensure.)

✪ In certain occupations that generally require licensure, a state may allow an individual to fully practice the occupation under the supervision of licensed supervisory personnel in that occupation. In such cases, if the facts demonstrate that the alien under supervision can fully perform the duties of the occupation, *H* classification will be granted. (For example, this might be the case with architects who might be able to fully perform their functions as long as they work under the authorization of an employer-architect's state license.)

✪ have education, specialized training, and/or progressively responsible experience that is equivalent to completion of a United States baccalaureate or higher degree in the specialty occupation and have recognition of expertise in the specialty through progressively responsible positions directly related to the specialty;

✪ proof of the filing of a labor condition application must accompany a petition for fashion modeling for *H-1B* classification;

✪ an evaluation from an official who has authority to grant college-level credit for training and/or experience in the specialty at an accredited college or university that has a program for granting such credit based on an individual's training and/or work experience;

✪ the results of recognized college-level equivalency examinations or special credit programs such as the College Level Examination Program (CLEP) or Program on nonCollegiate Sponsored Instruction (PONSI);

✪ an evaluation of education by a reliable credentials evaluation service that specializes in evaluating foreign educational credentials;

✪ evidence of certification or registration from a nationally recognized professional association or society for the occupational specialty that is known to grant certification or registration to persons in the specialty who have achieved a certain level of competence; or,

✪ a determination by the USCIS that the equivalent of the degree required by the specialty occupation has been acquired through a combination of education, specialized training, and/or work experience in areas related to the specialty and that the alien has achieved recognition of expertise in the specialty occupation as a result of such training and experience. (For purposes of determining equivalency to a baccalaureate degree in the specialty, three years of specialized training and/or work experience are required by the USCIS for each year of college-level training the alien lacks.)

In addition, the USCIS requires that the alien produce at least one type of documentation such as:

✪ recognition of expertise in the specialty occupation by at least two recognized authorities in the same specialty occupation;

✪ membership in a recognized foreign or United States association or society for the specialty occupation;

✪ published material by or about the alien in professional publications, trade journals, books, or major newspapers;

✪ licensure or registration to practice a specialty occupation in a foreign country; or,

✪ achievements which a recognized authority has determined to be significant contributions to the field of the specialty occupation.

Duration of Stay. The *H-1B* visa is issued for three years and may be extended once. Foreign persons who are issued an *H-1B* visa in order to work on a Department of Defense project are issued a visa valid for five years.

Annual Quota. Currently there is a maximum of 65,000 visas to be issued annually for this visa status. This annual limitation is subject to change depending upon the perceived needs of U.S. employers. Consequently, one should verify the number of *H-1B* visa that can be issued in any given year prior to filing.

Employers must always establish that they have the financial resources to pay the alien's salary and are otherwise a viable economic entity. If aliens are an owner or part owner of the business, they must convince the USCIS that their intention to remain in the United States is only of a temporary nature, regardless of their ownership interest in the company. If the company does not have other employees or does not have the other indicia of a going enterprise then the *H* visa petition may be denied.

Once the visa is obtained, it may be extended for an additional three-year period. This provides for a maximum six-year duration of stay. In filing a request for the extension, the employer will have to justify the need to maintain the employee on a temporary basis for an additional three years, and the employee will have to prove an ongoing temporary intent that he/she will, in fact, leave the United States as soon as the duration of stay of the visa expires. The filing by the *H-1B* foreign national for a labor certification as the first step in a petition for a permanent visa, will not in and of itself disqualify the alien from obtaining the *H-1.*

Physicians. The law originally provided a *loophole* permitting foreign physicians to enter the United States to practice medicine (direct patient care). The loophole has been partially closed and foreign physicians may perform direct patient care if they:

- ✪ have a license or other interim authorization otherwise required by the state of intended employment to practice medicine and

- ✪ have a full and unrestricted license to practice medicine in a foreign country or have graduated from a medical school in the United States or a foreign country.

If the physician is being admitted primarily to teach or conduct research for a public or nonprofit private educational or research institution, only the second condition requires compliance. As far as the petitioning employer is concerned, it must establish that the alien is coming to the United States primarily to teach or conduct research as described above or, if coming to provide patient care, has passed the Federation Licensing Examination (FLEX) or equivalent and is competent in English or is a graduate of an accredited medical school. In order to demonstrate competency in English the alien must pass the English proficiency test given by the Educational Commission for Foreign Medical Graduates (ECGMG).

Further details about the experience of implementing these new rules will determine the feasibility of utilizing this visa category for aliens who intend to practice medicine in the United States, albeit on a temporary basis. It is possible to enter the United States with this visa and then adjust status to that of permanent residency if conditions and circumstances warrant.

Aliens of Extraordinary Ability

O-1 Visa. This visa category benefits aliens of extraordinary ability in the sciences, arts, education, business, or athletics. For persons other than in the motion picture and television industry, extraordinary ability is shown by *sustained national or international acclaim.* It appears that at least with respect to business, sciences, and education, the standard for eligibility could be quite high—perhaps the equivalent of a Noble Prize winner.

In the case of foreign persons who are engaged in the motion picture and television industry, extraordinary ability is shown through a *demonstrated record of extraordinary achievement.* The documentation required will include letters and print-media articles of acclaim, copies of awards, as well as portfolios indicating the nature and extent of the performer's activities.

Consultation with local industry groups. The law also requires that the USCIS consult with union and management groups in the motion picture and television industry on an advisory basis prior to issuance or denial of the visa. The rule provides that petitioners for both *O* and *P* aliens must obtain an advisory opinion before submitting the petition. If the petition lacks the advisory opinion, then the USCIS will ask a peer group or labor union for an advisory opinion only if the USCIS agrees that the petition merits expeditious handling. If the USCIS does not feel that the case merits expeditious handling, it will deny the petition.

Needless to say, the USCIS is generally not sympathetic to the custom in the entertainment industry of last-minute scheduling and promotion, and a petition should also provide proof as to the expeditious nature of the contracting arrangement. The attitude of many of the USCIS personnel is that the failure of the petitioner to plan properly does not mandate that the USCIS adopt a *crisis* approach to the adjudication of the petition. There is some logic to this position.

The USCIS rules provide that a labor union or peer group must act on an USCIS request for an advisory opinion within fifteen days after receiving a copy of the petition.

In the event there is no union or other peer group with which to consult, the USCIS may issue the visa regardless. The law is an improvement over the prior one practiced under the old *H-1* regulations, which did not provide for consultation with management or labor groups. The advisory opinions by unions or management groups which recommend denial must be in writing and the USCIS must attach such opinions to its final decision.

Duration. There is a three-year limitation on the initial duration of this visa. The duration of the visa shall be sufficient for the completion of the event(s) or activity but for no longer than three years. However, extensions of stay are granted only in order to complete the event(s) or activity.

Standards for Extraordinary Ability. The administrative Code of Federal Regulations establishes the standards for determining extraordinary ability as follows:

- ✪ receipt of a major internationally recognized award such as the Nobel Prize and

- ✪ at least three of the following forms of documentation:

    - ✪ documentation of the alien's receipt of nationally or internationally recognized prizes or awards for excellence in the field of endeavor;

    - ✪ documentation of the alien's membership and association in the field for which classification is sought that requires outstanding achievement of their members as judged by recognized national or international experts in their disciplines or fields;

    - ✪ published material in professional or major trade publications or major media about the alien relating to the alien's work in the field for which classification is sought, that shall include the title, date, and author of such published material and any necessary translation;

✪ evidence of the alien's participation on a panel or individually, as a judge of the work of others, in the same or in an allied field of specialization as that for which classification is sought;

✪ evidence of the alien's original scientific scholarly or business-related contributions of major significance in the field;

✪ evidence of the alien's authorship of scholarly articles in the field in professional journals or other major media;

✪ evidence that the alien has been employed in a critical or essential capacity for organizations and establishments that have a distinctive reputation; or,

✪ evidence that the alien has commanded and/or commands a high salary or other remuneration for services evidenced by contracts or other reliable evidence.

The rules establishing the standards for determining extraordinary achievement or extraordinary ability in the arts are reproduced from the Federal Register (Vol. 57, No. 69, April 9, 1992) as follows:

(A) Evidence that the alien has been nominated for or has been the recipient of significant national or international awards or prizes in the particular field such as an Academy Award, an Emmy, a Grammy, or a Directors Guild Award; or (B) At least three of the following forms of documentation:

(1) Evidence that the alien has performed and will perform services as a lead or starring participant in productions or events which have a distinguished reputation as evidenced by critical reviews, advertisements, publicity releases, publications, contracts, or endorsements;

(2) Evidence that the alien has achieved national or international recognition for achievements evidenced by critical reviews

or other published materials by or about the individual in major newspapers, trade journals, magazines, or other publications;

(3) Evidence that the alien has performed in a lead, starring, or critical role for organizations and establishments that have a distinguished reputation evidenced by articles in newspapers or trade journals;

(4) Evidence that the alien has a record of major commercial or critically acclaimed successes as evidenced by such indicators as title, rating, standing in the field, box office receipts, credit for original research or product development, motion picture or television ratings, and other occupational achievements reported in trade journals, major newspapers, or other publications;

(5) Evidence that the alien has received significant recognition for achievements from organizations, critics, government agencies, or other recognized experts in the field in which the alien is engaged. Such testimonials must be in a form which clearly indicates the author's authority, expertise, and knowledge of the alien's achievements; or

(6) Evidence that the alien has commanded or now commands a high salary or other substantial remuneration for services in relation to others in the field, as evidenced by contracts or other reliable evidence; or

(C) If the above standards do not readily apply to the beneficiary's [alien] occupation, the petitioner may submit comparable evidence in order to establish the beneficiary's eligibility.

O-1 aliens can petition for themselves and thus, do not need to be hired by a U.S. employer.

O-2 Visa. This visa is used for those foreign persons who accompany and/or assist the *O-1* alien in the athletic or artistic performance. The person must be an integral part of the performance of the *O-1* visa person and must have critical skills and experience with the *O-1* alien that are not of a general nature and cannot be readily replicated by other individuals.

O-2 visa applicants who assist persons in the movie and television industry must have a pre-existing and long-standing working relationship with the *O-1* alien and in the event of filming, must be needed for purposes of maintaining continuity of filming both inside and outside of the United States.

Unlike *O-1* aliens, *O-2* visa applicants must show that they have a foreign residence, which they have no intention of abandoning; consultation is also required for this group but only from labor organizations experienced in the skill involved. The current regulations provide for a fairly efficient time schedule for the obtainment of a peer review consultation. Normally, the USCIS will forward the petition to the recognized peer group or labor organization within five days of its receipt of the petition. The peer group will then be given twenty-four hours within which to advise of its position concerning all the issues appropriate to the consultation. If the peer group does not respond within the time period given, the USCIS can adjudicate the petition without receiving the peer group report. These peer group consultations are always advisory only and the USCIS is not bound by the peer group determinations.

Dependent family members of *O-1* and *O-2* aliens are issued *O-3* visas, but they are not authorized to work.

P-1 Visa. This visa is for two types of internationally recognized individuals:

1. athletes who compete individually or as part of a team at an *internationally recognized level of performance* and

2. entertainers who perform as part of a group that has received international recognition as *outstanding* for a *sustained and substantial period of time*.

The rules and regulations establishing the standards for these terms are reproduced as follows from the Federal Register (Vol. 57, No. 69, April 9, 1992):

(A) *A P-1 athlete must have an internationally recognized reputation as an international athlete or he or she must be a member of a foreign team that is internationally recognized. The athlete or team must be coming to the United States to participate in an athletic competition which has a distinguished reputation and which requires participation of an athlete or athletic team that has an international reputation.*

Standards for an internationally recognized athlete or athletic team. A petition for an athletic team must be accompanied by evidence that the team as a unit has achieved international recognition in the sport. Each member of the team is accorded P-1 classification based on the international reputation of the team. A petition for an athlete who will compete individually or as a member of a United States team must be accompanied by evidence that the athlete has achieved international recognition in the sport based on his or her reputation. A petition for a P-1 athlete or athletic team shall include:

(1) a tendered contract with a major United States sports league or team, or a tendered contract in an individual sport commensurate with international recognition in that sport, and

(2) Documentation of at least two of the following:

(i) Evidence of having participated to a significant extent in a prior season with a major United States sports league;

(ii) Evidence of having participated in international competition with a national team;

(iii) Evidence of having participated to a significant extent in a prior season for a United States college or university in intercollegiate competition;

(iv) A written statement from an official of a major United States sports league or an official of the governing body of the sport which details how the alien or team is internationally recognized;

(v) A written statement from a member of the sports media or a recognized expert in the sport which details how the alien or team is internationally recognized;

(vi) Evidence that the individual or team is ranked if the sport has international rankings; or

(vii) Evidence that the alien or team has received a significant honor or award in the sport.

(B) A P-1 classification shall be accorded to an international group to perform as a unit based on the international reputation of the group. Individual entertainers shall not be accorded P-1 classification to perform separate and apart from a group. [I]t must be established that the group has been internationally recognized as outstanding in the discipline for a sustained and substantial period of time. Seventy-five percent of the members of the group must have had a sustained and substantial relationship with the group for at least one year and must provide functions integral to the group's performance.

Standards for members of internationally recognized entertainment groups. A petition for P-1 classification for the members of an entertainment group shall be accompanied by:

(1) Evidence that the group, under the name shown on the petition, has been established and performing regularly for a period of at least one year;

(2) A statement from the petitioner listing each member of the group and the exact dates for which each member has been employed on a regular basis by the group; and,

(3) Evidence that the group has been internationally recognized in the discipline. This may be demonstrated by the submission of evidence of the group's nomination or receipt of significant international awards or prizes for outstanding achievement in its field or by three of the following different types of documentation:

(i) Evidence that the group has performed and will perform as a starring or leading entertainment group in productions or events which have a distinguished reputation as evidenced by critical reviews, advertisements, publicity releases, publications, contracts, or endorsement;

(ii) Evidence that the group has achieved international recognition and acclaim for outstanding achievement in its field as evidenced by reviews in major newspapers, trade journals, magazines, or other published materials;

(iii) Evidence that the group has performed and will perform services as a leading or starring group for organizations and establishments that have a distinguished reputation evidenced by articles in newspapers, trade journals, publications, or testimonials;

(iv) Evidence that the group has a record of major commercial or critically acclaimed successes, as evidenced by such indicators as ratings, standing in the field, box office receipts, record, cassette, or video sales, and other achievements in the field as reported in trade journals, major newspapers, or other publications;

(v) Evidence that the group has achieved significant recognition for achievements from organizations, critics, government agencies, or other recognized experts in the field. Such testimonials must be in a form that clearly indicates the author's authority, expertise, and knowledge of the alien's achievements; or,

(vi) Evidence that the group has commanded or now commands a high salary or other substantial remuneration for services comparable to others similarly situated in the field as evidenced by contracts or other reliable evidence.

(C) Special provisions for certain entertainment groups—(1) Alien circus personnel. The one-year group membership requirement is not applicable to alien circus personnel who perform as part of a circus or circus group, or who constitute an integral and essential part of the performance of such circus or circus group, provided that the alien or aliens are coming to join a circus that has been recognized nationally as outstanding for a sustained and substantial period of time as part of such a circus.

(2) Certain nationally known entertainment groups. The director may waive the international recognition requirement in the case of

an entertainment group which has been recognized nationally as being outstanding in its discipline for a sustained and substantial period of time in consideration of special circumstances. An example of a special circumstances would be when an entertainment group may find it difficult to demonstrate recognition in more than one country due to such factors as limited access to news media or consequences of geography.

The one year membership requirement may be waived if the new member is replacing another member because of illness or other urgent circumstances or in the event the new member adds to the group by performing a critical role.

NOTE: *Entertainers who perform individually cannot be issued this visa.*

The Attorney General of the United States acting through the District Director of the applicable USCIS District office may waive the *international* requirement or consider other types of evidence to sustain the substantial recognition factor for the entertainment group. This provision will benefit entertainment groups that may be quite talented and recognized in their country or region but who do not yet have an international acclaim or recognition.

P-2 Visa. The *P-2* visa is issued to artists and entertainers participating in a reciprocal exchange program between foreign-based organizations and U.S.-based organizations that are engaged in the temporary exchange of artists and entertainers. This applies to both individuals and groups. Future administrative regulation will define the details for the eligibility and documentary requirements for these visas.

P-3 Visa. This visa is applicable to artists and entertainers who perform *under a program that is culturally unique.*

Duration of stay for the P Visa. The duration of stay under both *P-2* and *P-3* visas is the time needed for the specific performance or event. *P-1* athletes, however, may be allowed a duration of stay of up to ten years. This is a very sound provision since many professional athletes are required or encouraged to sign multi-year contracts with the team organizations for which they are playing.

Other eligibility requirements. P visa applicants must have a residence in a foreign country which they have no intention of abandoning (this requirement does not apply to *O* visa applicants) and foreign persons must be entering to work in their respective fields of endeavor.

Educational/Training Visas

These sections will discuss each of three types of educational-training visas that are available to qualified foreign persons. They all share the common purpose of serving to upgrade the educational and/or vocational skills of foreign persons but differ markedly about the approaches that are taken to fulfill these goals.

H-2A and H-2B Visas
The *H-2A* visa applies to persons coming to the United States to perform agricultural work of a temporary or seasonal nature. This is a specialized visa process and the USCIS has published a handbook that provides details to prospective farm employers on the requirements of this visa.

The *H-2B* visa applies to persons whose job skills or occupation do not rise to the level of an *H-1B* applicant and who are coming to the United States to perform temporary work for a United States employer. The need for the employee must be temporary even though the job itself may not be of a temporary nature. Thus, if the employer needs a worker for a one-time occurrence or to meet seasonal or intermittent needs, then the employer may hire the foreign person after obtaining a labor certification from the Department of Labor to the effect that there are no U.S. persons available to perform the job requested and the employment of the alien will not adversely affect wages and working conditions of workers in the United States. In fact, because of the expense and inconvenience involved in obtaining the labor certification, I personally do not feel that this visa category is very useful, at least not in my experience. The visa is only issued for a one year period, so that only very unique positions and circumstances would justify the expense and trouble involved in obtaining this visa.

This visa is used by U.S. companies to employ both skilled and unskilled aliens on a temporary basis. There are two parts of the *temporariness* concept that must be noted. First, the position that the alien is filling must be of a temporary nature, and secondly, the company's need for the designated position must also be temporary. This visa is issued for a duration of one year at a time and may be extended, with some difficulty, up to a maximum period of three years. Another feature of the *H-2* visa that differentiates it from the *H-1B* visa is that a Department of Labor *certification* must usually be issued as a precondition to the issuance of the visa. This is a marked difference from the *H-1* visa that does not require a Department of Labor certification.

Eligibility Requirements. Most of the eligibility requirements for this visa pertain to the employer rather than the employee even though, of course, the alien employee must be qualified for the position. As previously stated, a United States employer is required to file a request for a labor certification from the Department of Labor as a prerequisite to the filing of an *H-2B* petition. It is incumbent upon the employer to prove to the Department of Labor that there are no U.S. workers available in the location of the job offering who are willing and able to perform the required work at current and prevailing wage rates. In addition, the employer will need to prove that the employment of the alien workers will not adversely affect the U.S. labor market.

The procedure above is identical to the procedure required for a Department of Labor certification for an immigrant visa, except that the Department of Labor is only interested in *Part A* of the Labor Certification request, which deals with the employer's needs and job offering. *Part B* of the *ETA-750* lists the alien's qualifications, and does not have to be completed. If the Department of Labor denies the certification, it is still possible to obtain the *H-1B* visa if the employer can convince the USCIS of the unavailability of local labor to perform the job. This is not an easy task and, frankly, is probably not worth the effort.

Temporariness. Assuming that the Department of Labor issues a labor certification, the employer must still prove to the satisfaction of the USCIS that the need for the position is temporary and that the position itself is temporary. An example of these conditions is where a United States employer starts a new manufacturing operation and requires the assistance of a foreign expert who can train the employer's existing U.S. workers and give consulting advice to the management on the organization and administration of the new operation. In this example, the position is temporary in that it has a defined beginning and end; and the need is temporary since the employer's need will terminate with the completion of the job.

It is important to note that the mere designation of a termination date is insufficient proof of *temporariness* to the USCIS. Rather, it is required that the employer give operational evidence as to the projected termination of the position as well as the employer's need for that position in order to support the visa.

Alien's Qualifications. In order for alien to be the beneficiaries of an *H-2* petition, they must establish their qualifications to perform the job requested. The job may be skilled or unskilled and can range from a high degree of technological expertise to that of a seasonal, unskilled laborer. In any event, aliens must prove that they are qualified by work experience or training or both to perform the job.

In addition, aliens must prove that their intention in entering the United States is temporary and that they maintain a home in a foreign country to which they intend to return as soon as their job tour is over.

Special Problems. It is nearly impossible to adjust the *H-2* visa to that of a permanent resident alien. The USCIS has consistently maintained in a series of judicial and administrative rulings that the initial certification by an employer that the position as well as the employer's need were temporary preclude a later contention that the same position and need has now changed to that of permanent nature. In essence, the USCIS treats the initial petition as a warranty by the employer that the temporary character of the position will not change in the future to that of a permanent position to justify the employment of the alien.

It is possible for an employer to file a permanent visa petition or a petition to change the status on behalf of an employee's temporary visa so long as it is for a different employment position with different responsibilities than those that formed the basis for the issuance of the original *H-2* visa.

Application Requirements. The application for an *H-2* visa consists of essentially two steps. The first is the completion of the Department of Labor certification by the employer and the second is the processing of the actual petition via *Form I-129* by the employer with the USCIS. It is not necessary that the employer obtain the Department of Labor certification as a prerequisite to the issuance of the *H-2* visa. That is, if the labor certification request is denied, the employee may offer rebuttal evidence to the USCIS, together with the letter of denial by the Department of Labor and attempt to persuade the USCIS to issue the visa, notwithstanding the Department of Labor denial. However, the USCIS normally gives much weight and credence to the finding of the Department of Labor in these matters.

Issuance of the H-2 Visa. In the event the visa is granted, then the USCIS will issue its approval notice on a *Form I-171C* that is sent to the employer. The employer will then forward this original form, together with its petition to the appropriate U.S. consulate abroad. The U.S. consulate will then make a file for the beneficiary (or beneficiaries) and issue the individual visas. The petition filed by the employer can be for multiple workers for the same position.

Duration of Time and Extension Process. The *H-2* visa is granted for a one-year period and may be extended for additional periods of one year to a maximum of three years. The extension request is accomplished by filing an additional *Form I-129*, which is now used as an extension application and requires both an additional Department of Labor certification and additional filing fee.

Obviously, the necessity of having to go through a second Department of Labor certification militates against extending the *H-2* visas beyond the original one-year period. It is very difficult to file successfully a change of nonimmigrant status from a different nonimmigrant classification to an *H-2* classification. The likelihood that an alien who is in the United States in another nonimmigrant status and coincidentally discovers a temporary job for which he or she is immediately qualified is rare. The reverse, however, is not as unlikely, in that it may be possible to change an *H-2* visa to that of a different nonimmigrant classification so long as the beneficiary is eligible for that visa, and the visa is for a totally different position from that which supported the *H-2* petition.

H-3 Visa

This visa is offered to qualified foreign trainees who enter the United States with the purpose of participating in an established occupational training program. The visa anticipates that the alien will not be entering the United States for the purpose of engaging in productive employment, even though some degree of productive employment may be permissible so long as it is incidental to the training and is otherwise inconsequential in nature.

Eligibility. Most of the eligibility requirements pertain to the U.S. company or entity under whose auspices the alien will be entering the United States. In order to support an *H-3* visa, the United States company must file a preliminary petition with the USCIS to participate in an established training and/or educational program. If the company does not have its own approved and fully structured in-house training program, then it will have to seek the assistance of one or more blanket agencies that have already been authorized by the United States Information Agency to sponsor the entry of qualified foreign persons as *J-1* trainees. Training of the foreign persons cannot anticipate an eventual job offer by the U.S. employer. The law assumes that the *H-3* visa holder will undergo training that will be useful in the alien's home country. The documentary proof must show that the employer is not seeking to train the foreign person for eventual U.S. employment, but rather for employment abroad.

In addition to the above, the U.S. employer must prove that the type of training it offers the alien is unavailable in the alien's home country. This very often can be established by showing that the U.S. company's activities in the United States (or even on a worldwide basis) are unique.

Aliens must prove that their intention is to enter the United States only for a temporary period of time, and that they will return to a home or foreign domicile that they have no intention of abandoning.

Duration of the Visa. This *H-3* visa is valid for the documented length of the approved training program, which usually means an outside limit of two years. It is technically possible to extend the visa beyond a two-year period of time, but such a request will generally be met with skepticism by the USCIS. Where a number of foreign trainees will be undergoing the same training, it is possible to include all of them in a single petition filed by the U.S. company or training agency. The U.S. employer must establish that the majority of time spent by the alien in the United States will be a bona fide training-instructional program, as opposed to on-the-job productive employment. If from a description of the position and its attentive duties, it seems as if the employer is gaining direct benefits from the alien's activities in the United States, then the *H* visa may be denied.

F-1 Visa

The *F-1* visa is available to persons who seek to enter the United States for the purpose of engaging in a full time academic program. The visa extends to persons enrolled at the elementary school level through the postgraduate and doctoral level of university education. In theory, the requirements for obtaining a visa are simple and straightforward. However, it is often difficult for persons from certain countries where there is a high incidence of visa fraud to obtain this visa.

Duration of Stay. The *F* visa is granted for a period of stay known as *duration of status* (DS). That is, the visa is valid for the entire period of the proposed academic program. If an individual enrolls in a four-year college program leading to an engineering degree, the visa will be valid for the entire four-year university program, so long as the individual otherwise maintains an educational status and does not violate the terms of the visa. Upon the completion of the academic program—the basis for the visa—the foreign students must then apply for an extension of that visa if they decide to pursue an additional course of study. If a student changes institutions before the completion of the academic program, an extension application is not required even though the USCIS must be notified of the change.

Conditions of Eligibility. The foreign student must be coming to the United States to engage in a full-time course of study, all of which is defined by regulations. Generally, full time status requires a minimum of twelve semester hours (or credit hours) on the university level or an equivalent—assuming that the university considers this to be a full-time course of study and charges a full time tuition rate. For secondary or elementary grade school programs, the student must be enrolled in a course of study that the institution normally considers as minimum in order to obtain the diploma. Enrollment in associate degree institutions is also acceptable to support an *F* visa as long as the student is involved in a full-time course of study; usually, requiring a minimum of twelve hours.

Since the institution will be certifying on a *Form 1-20A* that the student is in fact enrolled in a full-time course of study, that institutional certification is almost always accepted by the Department of State as proof that the full-time course of study requirement will be met.

Visa Processing. In order to obtain the *F* visa, the student must apply for and receive admission to an approved educational institution in the United States. In addition to any other required documentation, the student will also receive a completed *Form I-20A-B* that will be filled out by the school and will require little information from the student other than a signature in two places. Most of the information that is on the *Form I-20A-B* is provided by the school so the student should review the form to make sure that it is accurate. The existing *Form I-20A-B* is an eight-page document that is submitted to the visa office at the time the student applies for his or her visa. In addition, the student will prepare and execute a *Form OF-156* that is a general nonimmigrant visa application form. It is important that all questions are properly answered.

There is an exception to the above procedure. Occasionally prospective students will not yet have chosen a particular institution at which they will study and may enter the United States on a *B-2* visa and then make a change of nonimmigrant visa when they have made their selection. In this case, students will appear before the visa officer and prove their student intention and financial ability and may then receive a *B-2* visa that will be stamped *prospective student/school not chosen.* This will be very helpful when the students later make an application to change their status after they have chosen their school.

This notation is very important because without it, students may find it very difficult to change their status to that of an F visa from a tourist visa. That is because the USCIS very often considers these change requests as evidence that the prospective student entered the United States on a fraudulent basis (pre-conceived intent), bypassing the normal F visa application process. A notation will thus avoid that problem since it will establish that there has been no fraudulent intent.

Persons seeking to enter the United States under *F* visa status must present a valid passport with the F visa stamped therein, together with the *Form I-20A-B.* Students will then be examined at the border with respect to the school that they will be attending and the duration of the program. If the immigration officer is satisfied that the person is entitled to the *F* visa, then the student will be given the I-94 arrival/departure record with the notation *DS* stamped therein, *(duration of status),* as well as a portion of the *Form I-20* (i.d. copy). The alien must keep both documents. Certain types of on-campus employment are permissible if it is the type of employment that is normally done by students and does not displace U.S. labor. Thus, the position of library or laboratory assistant employment is permissible.

Eligible Institutions. In order to qualify for the *F* visa, the student must be enrolled in an institution that has been approved for that purpose by the attorney general. All public elementary, secondary, and post-secondary institutions are approved by the attorney general and most private institutions with established reputations and recognizable names are also approved. When applying for enrollment in an educational institution, unless it is public, the alien should inquire that the private institution is in fact approved by the attorney general. The student must be enrolled in an educational program that provides academic training as opposed to purely vocational-type training. A vocational or business school whose curriculum is basically nonacademic would not support an *F* visa.

Financial Requirements of the Student. Prospective students must prove to the U.S. consul abroad that they have sufficient funds to pay for the educational training as well as their maintenance for the duration of the program. This requirement very often causes great difficulty to applicants for this visa. The funds must be currently available and not be based upon some speculation of funding by the student. In this regard, the Department of State (the Visa Office) will want proof that the student—himself, herself, or through family—has sufficient funds to pay for the expenses. Where a student has family or close friends that agree to provide room and board, an affidavit to this effect and supported by proof of their financial stability would be very helpful.

The *Designated School Official (DSO)* may authorize a foreign student to work part-time on-campus if the work is integral to the student's course of study and is based upon the economic need of the student. The work is limited to part time (20 hours) during the school session and full time during vacation periods if and while the student is still matriculated in the school.

In addition, the DSO may authorize a student to work off-campus based upon a severe and unanticipated economic need of the student. This typically occurs when the student's home country suddenly experiences economic or political crises but may also be documented with personal family emergencies. The student's derivative family members in *F-2* status are not authorized to work.

English Language Proficiency. The student must be proficient in the English language or must be enrolled in a course of study that will enable proficiency in English. These matters are all covered in *Form I-20A-B*, which is filled out by the educational institution and serves as a prerequisite for the issuance of the visa.

"I SEE YOU'RE APPLYING FOR A STUDENT VISA!"

Proof of Temporary Intent. Perhaps the largest stumbling block for persons applying for the F visa is the requirement that the persons have a purely temporary intent and that they have a domicile to which they shall return at the completion of the educational program. This requirement can cause great difficulty for those persons who are of modest financial means, young, and are traveling to the United States alone or at least without immediate family. Under these circumstances the Department of State is concerned that the individuals may be entering the United States only for the purpose of employment and will disappear into the U.S. economy as soon as they leave the airport.

It is highly recommended that when a student is interviewed by the visa officer of the U.S. consulate, in addition to the required documents, such as the *Form I-20A-B* and the other nonimmigrant visa petition documents, the student also bring proof of ties to a home country to document this temporary intent. In this regard, family photographs and/or information as to membership in various civic and social organizations would be important. Perhaps proof that the student will be returning to a job at the completion of schooling or any other evidence of ties to the home country would be very helpful.

Practical Training. A student may also apply for a period of practical training which cannot exceed a total of twelve months, including time spent in such practical training during the normal course of the student's academic training: summer vacations, mid-semester breaks, etc. The requirements are essentially that the practical training is related to the course of study of the alien's educational training in the United States and that the student be unable to receive practical training in his or her home country.

In both instances, this is a matter of documentary proof and the USCIS will have to rule on the application. In general, the fact that a school official will certify that the practical training sought by the student will benefit academic training is normally sufficient. In this regard, a *Form I-538* is filled out, together with documentary information as to the unavailability of that type of training in the student's home country.

J-1 Visa

The *J-1* visa assumes that the foreign employee will be actively engaged in on-the-job training under employment circumstances equivalent to that of a U.S. employee in the same position. In other words, it is expected that the employer will be gaining some productive benefits from the foreign employee's activities even though the main purpose of the employee's presence in the United States is to gain on-the-job, practical training.

Duration of Stay. The duration of stay under the *J-1* visa is limited to the time required to complete the particular program for which the foreign person was admitted.

Eligibility. Again, most of the eligibility requirements focus on the U.S. employer determining whether or not the sponsor has been designated by the United States Information Agency as an exchange-visitor program sponsor. Thus, a company having its own established program may seek to bring foreign employees to the United States in accordance with its already-approved program. In the event it does not have such a program, it may seek to bring the foreign employee under one of various umbrella programs that have already been designated by the United States government.

These umbrella programs are sponsored by other organizations who, at the request of the U.S. employer, will place a foreign exchange visitor with the sponsor in a United States company. Under some circumstances, the United States company may decide to establish their own exchange-visitor program by filing an application directly with the United States Information Agency. Obviously, this is a time-consuming and expensive step and it would only be feasible under the rarest of circumstances. A small to medium-sized company that did not have experience with foreign exchange visitors in the past might find it difficult to obtain such approval from the United States Information Agency.

NOTE: *This visa is very often used for the purposes of bringing* au pairs *to the United States.*

This visa is useful for advanced courses of training such as for medical school graduates who must have at least passed Parts I and II of the National Board of Medical Examiners Examination or the Foreign Medical Graduate Examination in Medical Sciences (FMGEMS).

The visa is obtained at the U.S. consulate abroad. The alien must obtain and complete a *Form IAP-66* and a *Form OF 156, Application for Nonimmigrant Visa,* must show evidence of means of support while in the United States, proof of an intention to depart the United States upon completion of the program, and provide the appropriate fee. The alien must also prove proficiency in the English language.

The *J* visa holder's dependent family members will also receive *J-2* visas which will enable them to accompany the *J-1* visa holder to the U.S. There is no prohibition against the *J-2* visa holder engaging in employment so long as the employment is not for the purpose of providing financial support for the *J-1* visa holder.

Requirements. The foreign business trainee must be employed on a full work week basis and must receive compensation equal to at least the prevailing minimum wage and under the prevailing working conditions for the particular industry involved. The purpose of the training must be to improve the visitor's skills for use in the visitor's home country. Consequently, the alien must maintain a foreign residence that he or she has no intention of abandoning. Any indication by foreign exchange visitors that they may be harboring an intention to remain in the United States on a permanent basis may cause the visa to be denied to them.

Two-year Foreign Residency Period. One of the most unusual characteristics of this visa category is that the foreign exchange visitor will be barred from filing a permanent visa petition or for applying for a change of status to a foreign *H* or *L* visa for a period of two calendar years from the date of U.S. training completion. This rule is applicable to those exchange visitors whose programs have been financed in whole or in part by:

✪   the United States government;

✪   their own governments; or,

✪   by persons who are nationals of countries that the United States Information Agency has determined require the skills and services of people with the alien's special training.

Since the nature and purpose of the *J* visa is to encourage sponsorship entry of third world persons to the United States, neither the United States nor the home country would want the foreign exchange visitor to remain in the United States at the completion of the training program. This would be self-defeating with respect to the program and probably makes poor politics between the United States and the alien's home country. Nonetheless, there are procedures to waive the two-year foreign residency requirement, but they are not liberally granted.

While the nature of the waiver application process is beyond the scope of this book, it is possible to highlight the general four conditions which provide for the waiver.

1. A waiver may be requested by a United States governmental agency on behalf of the exchange alien. (This is usually couched in terms of being beneficial to the United States security interest or to that of the public good.)

2. A waiver may be obtained when the foreign residence requirement would result in exceptional hardship to the U.S. citizen or permanent resident spouse or child. (What constitutes *exceptional hardship* is very often difficult to establish in advance, and generally requires intervention of legal counsel. Thus, when a United States citizen marries a foreign exchange visitor while that person is in the United States, it would be very difficult to justify extreme hardship since the U.S. citizen voluntarily embraced the situation. In any event, legal assistance is generally required to properly present an extreme hardship.)

3. Another ground for obtaining a waiver of the two-year foreign residency requirement is on the basis of a *no-objection letter* issued by the alien's government to the United States Information Agency stating that the foreign government has *no objection* to the alien remaining in the United States. (The United States government is not bound by this no-objection letter and if the United States government will be paying all or a substantial portion of the foreign exchange visitor's costs, then such a letter would have little influence. In any event, these no-objection letters are *unavailable* to foreign medical graduates.)

4. If the alien can prove that he or she would be subject to persecution in the home country on the basis of race, religion, political opinion, nationality, or membership in a particular social group, then the two-year waiting period may be waived. (Proof as to the exception should be conducted along the same line as a request for political asylum.)

Application Process. The most practical method of bringing an exchange alien into the United States is under an established umbrella program. The sponsoring agency who has already been designated by the United States Information Agency will issue a certificate of eligibility for the exchange visitor status (*Form IAP-66*) directly to the foreign national and will help arrange the transfer of the alien to the United States for practical training. The *J* visa holder must present a passport with a valid J visa stamped in it together with a *Form IAP-66* upon arrival at the border.

Q Visa

The *Q* visa category permits entry of a person into the United States for purposes of participating in a program designed to provide practical training or employment and the sharing of the history, culture, and traditions of the alien's home country. This exchange program will be administered by the USCIS instead of the United States Information Agency. The visa is valid for a period of fifteen months and may be applied for either at the U.S. consulate in the alien's home country or in the United States by way of an application for a *Change of Status*.

NOTE: *Until October 2005, the law allows certain Irish citizens to enter the U.S. as Q visa holders for the purpose of job training and career enhancement. These persons must be selected by appropriate agencies in Ireland and then must enter the U.S. to participate in an approved program. This population of Q visa holders is markedly different than all other potential Q visa holders.*

The law establishes a series of requirements that the U.S. employer must establish in order to be eligible to sponsor or hire foreign persons in this visa status. While the *Q* visa holder will be employed and remunerated, there must also be cultural component to the program. The cultural component must be designed, on the whole, to exhibit or explain the attitude, customs, history, heritage, philosophy, or traditions of the international cultural exchange visitor's country of nationality. A cultural component may include structured instructional activities such as seminars, courses, lecture series, or language camps.

In addition the performances and program must be available to the general U.S. public. As is often the case in these matters, the viability of an application for *Q* visa status will in large part depend upon the U.S. employer's fulfillment of numerous requirements.

K Visa

This visa is issued by the U.S. consulate abroad to the fiancé of a United States citizen. It is a temporary visa that requires that the foreign person contract marriage within ninety days of entry into the United States. The visa presumes that upon the celebration of the marriage, the foreign person will then apply for a permanent visa to the United States and will adjust his or her status in the United States.

The essential requirements are that the parties must establish that they have physically met within the last two years and are intent on getting married. In the case of those persons whose religious principals prohibit their meeting before the wedding, the Department of State has relaxed the requirement of a physical meeting but requires proof of the parties' membership in the religion that in fact prohibits the physical meeting prior to the marriage.

The proofs required in order to substantiate the physical meeting have no limitation. In cases that I have handled, I have offered photographs taken of the parties together in myriads of circumstances including: birthday celebrations, other weddings involving other parties and even a ribald photograph or two taken while the parties were celebrating in a nightclub. The United States consular officers are not squeamish in this regard and will accept documentation that establishes the statutory and regulatory requirements. (Remember, a picture is worth a thousand words.)

The United States citizen is the petitioner and must establish that he or she is a United States citizen. Both parties must establish that they are otherwise free to contract marriage. Thus, if he or she has been married before, proof of the termination of the previous marriage must be submitted.

If the foreign person marries a person other than the original petitioner, he or she will be precluded from adjusting status to permanent residency in the United States. Rather, upon approval of a *Form I-130* from the United States citizen or permanent resident spouse, the beneficiary will have to travel abroad to have the visa issued by the United States consulate abroad.

In any event, the beneficiary is still subject to the two-year *conditional* visa provision as explained in the section concerning permanent residency based upon marriage to a United States citizen on page 28 of this book.

"ER-EXCUSE ME BUT I HAVE JUST A FEW MORE QUESTIONS ON YOUR "K" VISA FORM..."

R Visa   This nonimmigrant visa category closely follows the immigrant visa category for special immigrant religious workers. The immigrant religious worker category expired on October 1, 2000, but the *R* visa category will continue to apply indefinitely.

The principal difference between the immigrant religious worker visa and the *R* nonimmigrant visa is that the *R* visa category has a five-year limitation. There is no requirement in the INA that applicants for *R* status establish that they have a residence in a foreign country which they have no intention of abandoning.

The criteria for classification of an *R* religious worker are the following.

✪   The alien is a member of a religious denomination having a bona fide nonprofit, religious organization in the United States.

✪   The religious denomination and its affiliate, if applicable, are exempt from taxation, or the religious denomination qualifies for tax-exempt status.

✪   The alien has been a member of the organization for two years immediately preceding admission.

✪ The alien is entering the United States:

✪ solely to carry on the vocation of a minister of that denomination or

✪ at the request of the organization, to work in a religious vocation or occupation for that denomination or for an organization affiliated with the denomination, whether in a professional capacity or not or

✪ is the spouse or child of an *R-1* nonimmigrant who is accompanying or following to join him or her; and,

✪ the alien has resided and been physically present outside the United States for the immediate prior year, except for brief visits for business or pleasure, if he or she has previously spent five years in this classification.

Characteristics of a Religious Denomination. A religious denomination will generally have the following elements or comparable indications of its bona fides:

✪ some form of ecclesiastical government;

✪ a recognized creed and form of worship;

✪ a formal code of doctrine and discipline;

✪ religious services and ceremonies;

✪ established places of religious worship; and,

✪ religious congregations.

Requirements for a Nonprofit Organization. A bona fide nonprofit organization, as described in the Internal Revenue Code of 1986, must meet the following criteria.

✪ No part of the net earnings of the organization may benefit any private shareholder or individual.

✪ No substantial part of the organization's activities may involve propagandizing or otherwise attempting to influence legislation.

✪ The organization may not participate or intervene in any political campaign, including publishing or distributing statements on behalf of (or in opposition to) any candidate for public office.

Membership. Aliens must establish that they have been a member of the qualifying organization for at least two years immediately preceding application for a visa or for admission. Unlike an applicant for a special immigrant visa as a religious worker, an applicant for *R* nonimmigrant classification needs only to have been a member of the organization for the required two-year period and needs not to have been engaging in qualifying ministerial, vocational, or occupational activities in addition to membership.

Ministers of Religion. Only individuals authorized by a recognized religious denomination to conduct religious worship and to perform other duties usually performed by authorized members of the clergy of that religion may be classified as ministers of religion. The term does not include lay preachers or other persons not authorized to perform such duties. In all cases, there must be reasonable connection between the activities performed and the religious calling of a minister. Evidence that a person qualifies as a minister of religion is normally available in the form of official ecclesiastical recognition such as certificates or ordination, licenses, formal letters of conferral, etc.

Ordination of Ministers. Ordination of ministers chiefly involves the investment of the individual with ministerial or sacerdotal functions, or the conferral of holy orders upon the individual. If the religious denomination does not have formal ordination procedures, other evidence must be presented to show that the individual has authorization to conduct religious worship and perform other services usually performed by members of the clergy.

A deacon of any recognized religious denomination may be considered to be a minister of religion. Practitioners and nurses of the Christian Science Church and commissioned officers of the Salvation Army are considered to be ministers of religion.

Buddhist Monks. The ceremony conferring monkhood status in the Buddhist religion is generally recognized as the equivalent of ordination. Whether or not a Buddhist monk qualifies as a minister of religion depends upon the activities he is seeking to pursue in the United States. However, in order to qualify for R status, a Buddhist monk must both establish his own qualifications as a minister of religion and must demonstrate that he is seeking to enter the United States for the sole purpose of conducting religious worship and providing other traditional religious services.

Evidence Forming the Basis for R Classification. An alien seeking classification as a religious worker makes application directly to a consular officer, or if visa exempt, to an immigration officer at a U.S. port of entry. No petition, labor certification, or prior approval is required. The alien shall present evidence that establishes to the satisfaction of the consular or immigration officer that he or she will be providing services to a bona fide nonprofit, religious organization or its affiliate, and that he or she meets the criteria to perform such services. The alien shall present evidence that the religious denomination, or its affiliate, qualifies as a nonprofit religious organization in the form of:

- ✪ a certificate of tax-exempt status issued by the Internal Revenue Service or

- ✪ in the case of a religious denomination that has never sought tax-exempt status, documentation demonstrating that the organization would qualify for tax exemption, if such status were sought. In all cases involving claimed eligibility for tax exemption, the consular officer must forward all pertinent documentation along with an evaluation of the evidence presented to the State Department for an advisory opinion.

Certification from Employing Religious Organization. An authorized official of the specific organizational unit of the religious denomination or affiliate that will be employing or engaging the alien in the United States must prepare a letter certifying the following:

- ✪ if the alien's religious membership was maintained (in whole or in part) outside the United States, the foreign and United States religious organizations belong to the same religious denomination;

- ✪ immediately prior to the application for the nonimmigrant visa or application for admission to the United States, the alien has been a member of the religious organization for the required two-year period;

- ✪ that (as appropriate):

- ✪ if the alien is a minister, he or she is authorized to conduct religious worship for that denomination and to perform other duties usually performed by authorized members of the clergy of that denomination. The duties to be performed should be described in detail;

- ✪ if the alien is a religious professional, he or she has at least a United States baccalaureate degree or its foreign equivalent; such a degree is required for entry into the religious profession; or,

- ✪ if the alien is to work in a nonprofessional religious vocation or occupation, he or she is qualified in that vocation or occupation. Evidence of such qualifications may include, but need not be limited to, evidence establishing that the alien is a monk, nun, or religious brother or sister, or that the type of work to be done relates to a traditional religious function.

- ✪ the arrangements made for payment for services to be rendered by the alien, if any, including the amount and source of any salary, a description of any other types of compensation to be received (including housing, food, clothing, and any other benefits to which a monetary value may be affixed) and a statement whether such payment shall be in exchange for services rendered;

- ✪ the name and location of the specific organizational unit of the religious denomination or affiliate for which the alien will be providing services within the United States; and,

- ✪ if the alien is to work for a bona fide organization that is affiliated with a religious denomination, a description of the nature of the relationship between the affiliate and the religious denomination.

A consular officer may request any appropriate additional evidence that is necessary to verify the qualifications of the religious denomination, the alien, or the affiliated organization.

Aliens in *R-2* status (spouses and dependents of the *R* alien) are not authorized to accept employment. The consular officer shall take this into account in evaluating whether family members have furnished adequate evidence of their self-support while in the United States. *R-2* nonimmigrants are permitted to study during their stay in the United States.

NOTE: *R visa recipients should have all qualifying documentation available when applying for admission in the event that it is requested by a USCIS officer at the port of entry.*

Length of Stay. The initial period of admission for an *R* nonimmigrant may not exceed three years. To extend a religious worker's stay, the organizational unit of the religious denomination or affiliate must file *Form I-129*, petition for the nonimmigrant worker at the USCIS Service Center having jurisdiction over the place of employment, and provide a letter from an authorized official of the organizational unit confirming the worker's continuing eligibility for *R* classification. An extension may be authorized for a period of up to two years. The religious worker's total period of stay may not exceed five years.

4 | MAINTAINING VISA STATUS

Now that you have obtained your visa to the United States, at great expense and after much preparation and hard work, it is important that you understand how to maintain your visa so that you do not inadvertently lose it. There are traps for the careless that can jeopardize either a nonimmigrant or an immigrant (permanent residency) visa. This chapter will give some examples.

Problems for Nonimmigrants

Overstay of I-94

The first and most important danger in maintaining visa status is for a nonimmigrant to inadvertently *overstay* the duration of stay permitted by the *Form I-94*. This form is the small white card that is inserted in the alien's passport upon inspection and admission to the United States by the USCIS inspecting officer.

Just for a moment let us review the situation. Foreign persons obtain visa status in one of two ways:

1. by obtaining their visas from a U.S. consulate abroad, in which case the visa is affixed in their passports or

2.   by receiving the desired visa status through a *Change of Status* approved by the USCIS while they are already in the United States.

With respect to the visa stamped into the passport, the time period of visa validity measures the time within which an alien may seek to enter the United States in that particular visa category. In other words, the visa in the passport establishes the time period in which a person may seek to cross the border into the United States. The duration of time the foreign person is allowed to remain in the U.S.A., after entry is not determined by the validity period of the visa. This time period is known as *Duration of Stay* and is determined by the date designated on the *Form I-94 (Arrival-Departure Record)*.

For example, when a person enters the U.S. with a *B-1/B-2* visa, which normally has a duration of ten years, the immigration officer at the border will normally allow the arriving alien to remain in the U.S. for a period of six months. The date of required departure will be designated on the *Form I-94*. If a person enters with a different type of visa, say an *H-1* or an *L-1*, the lawful period of stay may be one or two years.

If the foreign person remains in the United States beyond the date stated in the *Form I-94* by even one day, without first having filed an application for an *Extension of Stay*, the underlying visa is automatically and immediately terminated—the visa becomes void. This means that if the person attempts to use that visa again to reenter the United States, he or she is subject to (removal) exclusion from the United States on the basis of not holding a valid visa. Understand further that if a person is formally *removed*, that is to say, is turned away at the border, he or she will not be able to reenter the United States for a period of five years. The only exception to this penalty occurs if the immigration inspector allows the foreign person to withdraw his or her application for entry.

If a foreign person is removed from the United States at the border, the person will need to return to the country of nationality and reapply for another visa as a condition of reentry. The risk, of course, is that the U.S. consulate may not issue the visa again if the foreign person has already violated the terms of the original visa. Obviously if the overstay is only for a slight period of time (one or two days) and is only a technicality, there is a better chance that the U.S. consulate will reissue the visa. However, if there has been a substantial overstay, then there is a good chance that the U.S. consulate will not reissue the visa. There is no appeal from a denial by the U.S. consulate.

Dependents   All of these issues apply to the principal visa holder's dependents as well. Following is an example of a problem that often occurs with dependents and visa maintenance.

Example: Assume that a foreign person, Mr. Schiller, holds an *L-1A* visa as the executive of a large subsidiary of a foreign owned company. He is married to Olga and has two children, ages eight and eleven. Olga does not work outside the home and takes care of all household duties and especially the education and upbringing of the children. The Schillers are a typical busy young family and Olga is very active in the school parents/teachers association and also directs the children's various outside activities. This includes driving both children around to soccer and hockey practice and games as well as gymnastics and music education.

Olga does not work outside the home and takes care of all house-

In the jargon of visa law, Mr. Schiller is known as the *principal* visa holder, while Olga and the children are known as *derivative* visa holders. Mr. Schiller is required by the conditions of his job to travel often in and out of the United States. Olga and the children do not accompany Mr. Schiller on any of these trips. Inadvertently, the *duration of stay* as noted on the *Form I-94* expires as to Olga and the children and they remain beyond the period of authorized stay for seven and a half months. This is only discovered at a holiday party when one of Olga's friends casually remarks to her that she has heard that the wife and children of executives must also file for an extension of stay. This family now faces a life changing crisis that cannot be easily remedied. This is because Olga cannot now *extend her stay* of visa status and must return to her country of origin in order to reapply for a visa. More important, she is subject to the three-year bar against reentry.

How did this happen?

Upon entry to the United States the principal visa holder, as well as the derivative visa holders, received *Forms I-94* that allowed each of them to remain in the U.S. for an entire year. Every time a visa holder departs and then reenters the United States, he or she will receive permission to remain in the U.S. for another year or perhaps two years and this will be noted on a new *Form I-94*. This is how Mr. Schiller continued to receive new *Forms I-94* each of which extended his duration of stay for a period of one year from entry. He has always remained in status. However, if the derivative visa holders have not departed and reentered the United States, they will need to file a form known as an *Application to Extend/Change Nonimmigrant Status* (*Form I-539*) in order to remain longer than the year which they originally received. Olga and the children never departed the United States after their initial entry. They never paid attention to their own visa affairs, expecting that if Mr. Schiller were in status, these would be, too.

Neither Mr. Schiller nor his employer considered the duration of status of Olga and the children as separate from Mr. Schiller's status. Since Olga and the children, the derivative visa holders, did not file an application to extend their status (*Form I-539*) with the USCIS they overstayed their *duration of stay* and thus their visas became void. What is more important, since Olga overstayed the *Form I-94* by 180 days or more, when she travels to her home country to apply for a new visa, she will then automatically trigger the three-year ban to the United States. There are no waivers or exceptions to these bureaucratic consequences. The Schillers must either return to their country of origin in order to remain together as a family unit or Mr. Schiller must remain alone in the United States while Olga lives out her three-year ban from the United States.

This is not fiction nor is it farfetched. It is a real problem based upon real events.

A nonimmigrant can also lose his or her nonimmigrant visa status by engaging in activities that are inconsistent with the visa that the person holds or for causing the USCIS border inspector to believe that to be the case.

Issues Regarding E-2 Visas

In addition to the requirement of not violating the terms of the duration of stay a treaty investor also has a substantive problem with which to contend for purposes of visa maintenance. Remember that one of the requirements for obtaining an *E-2* investor visa is to ensure that the investment is not *marginal*. The regulations state in the negative that a marginal enterprise is *one that does not have the present or future capacity to generate more than a minimal living for the treaty investor and his or her family.*

On a positive note the regulations also state as follows:

> *Marginal Enterprise. A marginal enterprise is an enterprise that does not have the present or future capacity to generate more than enough income to provide a minimal living for the treaty investor and his or her family. An enterprise that does not have the capacity to generate such income, but that has a present or future capacity to make a significant economic contribution, is not a marginal enterprise. The projected future capacity should generally be obtainable within five years from the date the alien commences normal business activity of the enterprise.*

If the company has been relatively successful, the investor/owner has a choice as to whether to fund the company's expansion with its own profit or to borrow from an outside source. Most conservative economists would encourage most businesses to fund their own growth and not borrow from outside sources. This, however, is not always a good idea in the *E-2* visa context because a government examiner who may know very little about business may deny the reissuance of the visa if the company's financial books do not reflect a net profit. Indeed, in certain hostile consulates the treaty officers seem to be looking for excuses to deny treaty visas, not withstanding that the investor has in good faith already relocated his or her person, family, assets and life's energy to the U.S. Thus under most circumstances it would be advisable to borrow from a third party, perhaps using the profit as collateral by the creation of some sort of sinking fund or other special account, to fund the growth and expansion.

A complex financial statement that attempts to demonstrate that the enterprise utilized its financial surplus to fund its acquisition of personnel, equipment, or inventory creates a problem for the investor. Most government examiners are not financial analysts. They are looking for conceptually clear and simple evidentiary guideposts. A financial statement or income tax return that clearly demonstrates a healthy net income is good. A similar report that documents the hiring of many employees is also good.

It is recommended that a treaty investor/entrepreneur hire a competent financial professional that can advise him or her on the best method of demonstrating income and profitability and funding the continuing growth of the enterprise.

Additionally, the comprehensive business plan that served as the basis for original visa issuance should be carefully prepared so that it does not become the basis for the denial of the *E-2* visa reissuance. The business plan should be realistic and also express the conditions that support the financial projections. So, if some of these conditions change and the company is not as profitable as anticipated, the investor will at least have a basis for explaining any income differential from the original projections and modifying the business plan accordingly. Indeed, the original comprehensive business plan should be a *living* document and the company's performance should be charted against it throughout the life of the investment.

Issues Regarding L-1A Visa

For new companies, the *L-1A* visa is issued somewhat liberally for the first year. Thereafter in order to extend the term of the *L-1A* visa as well as the duration of stay beyond the first year, the business must demonstrate that it is making legitimate progress in its development and is engaged in the actual provision of goods and services. Therefore, a new company should commence operations as soon as possible after visa issuance. Additionally the company must demonstrate that its executive or manager is not merely acting in the capacity of the actual provider of the company's service. The government examiner will search for defined levels of employment and function. It thrives on organization and flow charts. The argument that the young company may be better off with fewer levels of employees and departments will probably be lost to deaf ears.

It is recommended that as much as is reasonably possible, new businesses should put into place the most dramatic increases in capital and personnel growth before the end of its first year. The company should concentrate on meeting a three, four, or five year plan rather than try to justify its costs on its single and first year basis and that it organizes itself accordingly. The government examiner who is adjudicating the petition has, in all probability, not had to contend with meeting a payroll or satisfying a contract at all costs and does not sympathize with the plight of the manager who must do anything and everything to get the job done. Also, as with the *E-2* visa, the comprehensive business plan should be considered as a living, dynamic document against which the company's performance should be documented.

The Power of Expedited Removal

The law gives the immigration inspector at the border the power to turn a person away from the United States, without a hearing and without review of any kind, if the inspector determines that the person is either entering the United States with fraudulent documents or entering for a purpose other than that which is authorized by the visa. This power was clearly meant to apply to aliens who attempt to enter the U.S. with no documents or with fraudulent documents. But the law as written also applies to a person who has a valid visa but who is determined by the USCIS inspecting officer to be entering the U.S. for a purpose other than that permitted under the particular visa.

The Three- and Ten-Year Bars against Reentry

The law states that if a foreign person is illegally present in the United States for 180 days but less than one year, upon that person's departure from the United States he or she will be prohibited from reentering the U.S. for a period of three years from the date of the departure. *Illegal presence* is a period of time that accrues after the expiration of the duration of stay as noted on the *Form I-94*, or after the government has declared in some formal manner that the foreign person has either violated the terms of the non-immigrant visa or that the person's visa status has been terminated.

In the example with the Schillers, the consequences to the principal visa holder's wife, who does not extend her *I-94* at the expiration of the year and then remains illegally present in the United States for 180 days, includes:

✪   her *L-2* visa is void from the day after the expiration of the *Form I-94*;

✪   she cannot extend her visa status from within the U.S.;

✪   she will be required to apply for a new *L-2* visa in her country of last residence; and so,

✪   upon her departure from the United States, she will be barred from reentering the United States for a period of either three or ten years.

NOTE: *There are no waivers to these consequences available to nonimmigrants.*

Furthermore, if a person overstays the expiration date noted on *Form I-94* by more than one year, he or she is then prohibited from reentering the United States for a period of ten years.

There are some very limited waivers available for persons who can prove that the application of either of these bars to reentry would cause an *extreme hardship* to a U.S. citizen or permanent resident, spouse, child, or parent. Needless to say, even if a foreign person were eligible to apply for these limited waivers, it is very difficult to obtain these waivers, and for nonimmigrant persons they are unavailable.

Thus, a person who is entering the United States with a *B-1/B-2* visa may be turned away at the border if the inspector feels that this person is entering the United States in order to reside permanently (perhaps to join with a U.S. citizen or permanent resident of the opposite sex in a long term relationship) or to engage in unauthorized employment. These activities are inconsistent with that of a *B-1* or *B-2* visa. So, if an immigration inspection officer makes a determination at the border that the foreign person is not entitled to enter the U.S. on the basis of the visa that the foreign person holds, then the officer has the right and the authority to turn the alien away (*removal*) without offering the opportunity to make a phone call or provide any other evidence to support the foreign person's case.

Furthermore, removal by the officer prohibits that person from reentering the United States for a period of five years. There is no appeal to this decision by the inspecting officer. Indeed, there is not even a method under the law for the government itself to undo the action of an inspecting officer that may clearly have been wrong. Obviously this is a very dangerous provision. It poses a special problem for foreign persons who own real estate in the United States, who may have close relatives in the United States, and who may not have a standard type job outside the United States.

Example: Harold Smith is a single, young-looking man in his mid-forties from England who earned a lot of money as a commodities trader. He has always been a freelance or independent consultant to established commodities and stock brokerage houses in Europe. He does not actually maintain an office but is always *on-call* to his clients. He has purchased an expensive and nice condominium apartment on the beach on the west coast of Florida and uses it at least two times a year. His trips to the United States are usually for periods of one month or so at a time. This year, however, he has already been in the U.S. for a total of three months.

He decides to come once again to his U.S. beach apartment to experience and enjoy the traditional Thanksgiving holiday in order to relax a bit and to work on a proposal which he intends to make to a large international commodities brokerage house. He brings all of his research documents with him as well as the telephone numbers of his most important clients so that he can *stay in touch*. He receives a bargain price for round trip airfare on an airline which flies through Memphis, Tennessee.

Upon inspection at the USCIS immigration counter, the inspector questions why this relatively young person is traveling for a third time to the U.S. The inspector also finds out that Harold owns real estate in the U.S., while only renting a flat in his home country. The inspector also finds various documents in Harold's luggage which relate to his work including a list of work items that he must complete in the U.S. These include a number of clients to telephone and some research to be done on the financial status of a U.S. mining company. Harold did not bring any documentation as to the nature of his job, other than that he is an independent consultant. Finally, the USCIS inspector finds a Florida driver license as well as a Florida issued credit card, all in Harold's name. Harold explains that the driver license is a matter of convenience for writing checks and for otherwise providing personal identification in Florida and the credit card was issued as a courtesy by his Florida bank for starting a checking account.

The USCIS inspector speaks rudely to Harold, addressing him disparagingly by his first name and suggests that Harold is really coming to the U.S. to work illegally. Harold becomes irate and says things to the USCIS inspector that he later regrets. Harold is placed back on the next airplane and is removed from the U.S. He cannot come back for at least five years, not even to arrange the sale of his apartment and its contents.

How could Harold have avoided his disastrous encounter with the USCIS border inspector? What might anyone who is similarly situated do or not do in order to avoid bureaucratic difficulties at the border? The following is a list of suggestions and recommendations applicable to most nonimmigrants though it is clearly not complete and may not be applicable to all persons in all circumstances.

First—do not travel to the U.S. with a U.S. state issued driver license or U.S. issued credit cards or bank check books. Leave these here in the U.S. Their presence on your person will only cause questions and suspicions. Also, the law of the state of your final destination may be different from the law of the state in which you are attempting to clear U.S. immigration. The USCIS examiner may be unfamiliar with the law of any state other than his or her own. It may be difficult, for instance, to convince the inspecting officer that the state of your destination requires all residents who reside therein for sixty consecutive days to obtain a state issued driver license. The same advice applies to U.S. issued credit cards and check books.

Carry travelers' checks as well as travel and resort brochures. In the case of business travelers who hold employment authorized visas, do carry documents which identify your employment in the United States.

Second—foreign persons should purchase a round trip ticket from a point outside the United States. The money saved by buying and using *back to back* round trip airline tickets is not worth the frustration and difficulty at the border with a suspicious USCIS inspector.

Third—if a foreign person owns a U.S. home or apartment, that person should carry in his luggage proof of ownership or lease of a residence outside the U.S. as well as evidence of his or her foreign income or financial means. If one has purchased a holiday home in the U.S., preserve all the marketing materials, brochures, etc., which were used to market the property as these will often confirm that the property is suitable as a holiday home. This is important if a foreign person seeks admission at a port of entry other than the state of final destination. In the example above, the USCIS inspector will not necessarily know (or care) that the west coast of Florida is a popular destination for Europeans and that there is a large vacation or holiday home industry there.

Fourth—avoid entering the U.S. at new or developing U.S. international destinations. Always try to enter in the state of final destination.

Fifth—foreign persons should not carry work related documents with them upon entry to the U.S. Often these documents create confusion and suspicion in the minds of USCIS inspectors and may require explanations which a foreign person may be unable to make in the limited and intimidating environment of an immigration border inspection. These suggestions also apply to letters from and to persons of the opposite sex with whom a foreign person may be involved, since the USCIS inspector may determine that the purpose of entry is to reside permanently in the U.S. with the love interest.

Sixth—a foreign person should carefully examine the *Form I-94* before leaving the inspection counter to make sure the date of required departure is clear. Also the foreign person should carefully document the date of expiration of the *Form I-94* and arrange to either file an extension or depart the U.S. on a timely basis.

Seventh—during the inspection interview, always be honest and forthright and remain courteous and respectful of the USCIS examiners regardless of their attitude or demeanor. Most USCIS inspectors are courteous persons who are merely enforcing the law and regulations that others in the government have enacted. Outbursts of angry words or return sarcasm directed at the occasionally rude border inspector by a foreign person will not be helpful. The immigration inspector has tremendous authority and will probably not be in a mood to be counseled as to good manners by a foreign person. (When patience is about to fail, the foreign person should retain the attitude that he or she is dealing with a ruthless and strong bully who is guarding the entrance to a place which the foreign person wishes to visit.) Of course, the foreign person should not engage in gainful employment or in any business activity which is unauthorized by the visa in the passport.

Finally—illegal conduct that results in a conviction in a U.S. court can be a permanent bar from entering the United States. Do not believe what is depicted in the movies or is otherwise bandied about in pubs and train stations. The United States' immigration laws *are* enforced.

It is important to understand the difference in cultures between the bureaucracy that is administering these visa regulations and that of a typical foreign person entering the United States. A nonimmigrant visa for a person entering the United States on a temporary basis is usually not an end in itself. Rather, it is a means to an end. A person is either coming to be a student, to run a business, to get married, or any number of things, and the visa is the way to accomplish them. Normally after a person has entered the United States, the visa status is relegated to a secondary importance. However, for the U.S. visa immigration authorities, the visa is of the utmost importance—it is their life. Consequently, what may be an inadvertent oversight to a foreign person is a grievous violation to the bureaucrat, who is charged with the responsibility of administering the laws.

Understand also that the United States legal regimen charges a person with the knowledge of the law, no matter how complex. Thus, even if a person seeks in good faith to extend his or her visa and then inadvertently mails it to the wrong immigration office he or she may lose the visa. This is because by the time the application is filed at the correct office the original authorized time period may have expired and the foreign person may be out of status. It is ineffective to claim that the late filing was caused by an honest mistake by the alien or that the application had been mistakenly sent to a wrong USCIS office, even by the mistake of an USCIS employee. This author has seen letters rejecting requests to extend visa status when a foreign person inadvertently mailed the extension request on a timely basis but to the wrong immigration office and by the time the application was filed at the correct office, the filing was late.

Problems for Immigrants

When a foreign person who is already a permanent resident remains outside of the United States for more than six months but less than one year, upon reentry that person is subject to the same type of inspection as would be given to any other foreign person. The fact that he or she has a permanent residency visa does not avoid the necessity of having to prove all over again to the satisfaction of the USCIS inspector at the border that he or she is entitled to reenter as a permanent resident. The burden of proof is on the foreign person to prove that he or she is still a permanent resident and not on the USCIS to prove that the person has abandoned the permanent residence. The foreign person must prove that he or she has not abandoned by intention or action his or her permanent residence. (Only in *visadom* is it standard to require a person to prove a negative.)

One of the easiest ways of abandoning permanent residence of the United States, other than by remaining outside of the U.S. for at least one year without first having obtained a *reentry permit*, is by failing to pay taxes within the United States or by failing to maintain a United States domicile.

If the permanent resident remains outside the United States for a period of one year without having first received or obtained a reentry permit, the government will assume that person has abandoned residency unless the person can prove by documents and otherwise that he or she has not abandoned residency.

One can also lose permanent residence by a series of actions that when taken in their totality, indicate to the government an abandonment of permanent residency. A person who maintains a residence as well as a job outside the United States and only lives a short period of time each year in the United States, say two months, can be considered to have abandoned his or her residency. This is because the inspector believes that the foreign person is domiciled outside the United States and is just visiting the United States for the purpose of maintaining the visa. In these cases if the person must travel abroad. It is strongly recommended that if he or she is going to be outside the United States for a period of six months or more, obtain in advance of departure, a document called a *reentry permit.* This document is valid for a period of two years and will allow a person to reenter with much less stress.

Here are some suggestions.

First—if the trip outside the U.S. is for longer than six months, apply for a reentry permit before departing the United States.

Second—if business or personal commitments require extensive time and travel outside the United States always arrange to file a U.S. federal income tax return and carry it with you upon reentry. Always try to return the United States within six months of departure. Try to maintain a U.S. home or residence and carry the documentation on your person upon your return to the United States.

5 TAXES, PROFESSIONAL SERVICES, AND PRE-ENTRY PLANNING

It is important that an investor or other business visitor to the United States (for brevity, we will designate all such persons *investors* in this chapter) understand some pertinent business customs and practices in the United States. This section will provide some ideas and examples that may be helpful to a business person who is contemplating an initial business visit to the United States for the purpose of completing a transaction that will have certain visa consequences.

If I had to characterize a society with a single concept, I would characterize the United States as the *information society*. We are a nation driven by the need to record statistics and data on almost any notable economic activity. While it is sometimes difficult for the lay person to discover needed information, it is almost always possible to find someone who can provide a service for the discovery, compilation, and analysis of that information. This wealth of access to information is one of the primary advantages of investing in the United States. Information is almost always available to analyze, and investments or transactions can be accomplished in a proper and professional manner. Nonetheless, many foreign persons in the United States do not take advantage of these facilities and very often encounter unnecessary problems in the development and execution of their plans.

If a person wishes to develop an enterprise or a business in a particular location in the United States, one merely has to ask for the critical information and it is usually obtainable. If it is not obtainable, then that in and of itself is a relevant finding. Here are some examples.

In the United States, almost every state has an economic development agency or industrial promotion board or some other similar bureaucracy whose function it is to stimulate investment and economic growth in that state. These agencies will gladly provide a wealth of information and statistics, free of charge. It is wise to spend some time corresponding and obtaining information from these sources about the demographic and economic trends within the state, the state's employment policies, and existing labor market. These agencies may also provide information about the individuals and professionals who may be of assistance in a particular field of endeavor.

In addition to state governmental programs, there are also local and regional chambers of commerce and related organizations, all of whom may be very helpful to a prospective entrepreneur. The best way to approach the chambers of commerce is to already have a particular plan or scheme in mind and then discuss this with the key person of that body. The local chamber of commerce can be very helpful in pointing out local trends and in making recommendations as to banks and other professional services and providers who can be of assistance. The local chamber of commerce also will have much statistical and economic data that can be helpful in further analyzing one's plans. It is often good to compare any data or other demographic information obtained from the state with the local chamber of commerce and to explore any discrepancies between the two of them.

One should also not overlook other sources of information that may be obtained from local or regional trade or industrial associations that are easily identifiable through industrial and/or trade journals. These organizations will also have statistical and economic data which will be much more specific to an industry and that will enable one to do a comparison between conditions as portrayed on a general basis by the local chambers of commerce and the information otherwise obtained from the trade or industrial association.

Legal System

The system of law in the United States is probably very different from legal systems with which most foreign persons are familiar. Our system of law evolved from the Common Law of England with its emphasis on the *rule of precedent* and the lack of a rigid (and predictable) code of law. Parties in a business environment are basically free to establish for themselves the benefits and responsibilities of their transaction or their business relationship. Subsequently, the law as it applies to any specific situation may be difficult to discover; thus, the proliferation of lawyers, both general practitioners and specialists.

While it is clearly beyond the scope of this book to engage in a general discussion of all the attributes of the legal system as they would affect the affairs of a foreign person, one point needs to be made very clearly. Most states in the United States have laws, judicial precedents, and customs that give preference to the words of a contract as opposed to the oral understanding of the parties. This is especially true with respect to the acquisition of real estate, business ventures, and other types of commercial investments. Thus, the written instrument is given considerable weight in any dispute by two legally capable parties. Foreign persons must be careful that they clearly know and understand the consequences of any documents that they sign because they will be bound to that document.

Lawyers

Much has been written and discussed about the proliferation of lawyers in the United States. While it is true that the United States does have a larger number of attorneys than other countries, it is important to remember that the attorney handles many of the functions which, in other countries, are dealt with by notaries and other judicial and quasi-judicial officers. In addition, U.S. law is based on the Common Law of England which is a jurisprudence molded by judicial precedent rather than by a detailed code. Additionally, one should bear in mind that the United States, whether as a result or a cause of the preceding, is a very complex society and has a profusion of business and legal rules that cannot be mastered by a single individual. It must also be remembered that the laws of each state may vary and may also differ from the laws of the federal government. It is also possible that both federal and state laws may deal with the same subject matter.

It is money well spent to consult with any competent attorney who is experienced or sensitive in dealing with foreign buyers before any purchase transaction is consummated. Such consultation can be very illuminating and can ensure that the transaction is structured in the most favorable terms for the foreign person. The *American Immigration Lawyers Association (AILA)* is an organization of lawyers who strive to achieve some degree of expertise in the field of U.S. immigration law. A foreign person who is interested in obtaining a visa to the United States should consider utilizing the services of a member of this organization. There are members of this organization in many foreign countries. Also, each state has a bar association that can identify lawyers who hold themselves out as experts in a particular field, including immigration law. Referral advice can also be obtained from other professional associations, such as accountants and other types of business and professional consultants.

The foreign investor should, at some point in negotiations, and certainly before any documents are signed, seek professional assistance. The list of possible consultants includes qualified accountants and an expert who is knowledgeable in the particular field or business of interest to the investor.

One of the most helpful benefits gained by this practice is learning the terms applicable to that particular business. There are many business and legal terms that are in use in various jurisdictions of the United States that have no counterpart in a foreign culture. Many terms and customs vary from state to state or town to town in the United States. In the real estate field, for example, the use of the terms *escrow agent, title insurance,* and *trustee,* are all terms that must be clearly understood by a prospective investor or entrepreneur.

In the United States, the parties are presumed to have read and understood a document that bears their signatures. It is too late after a signature has been applied to a document to state that one had a misconception as to what the document meant or what the meaning was of a particular paragraph. The United States is not a multilingual society and very little sympathy is extended for those who cannot understand the language.

Real Estate Brokers and Agents

One of the benefits of seeking to invest in the United States is that there is virtually no field or endeavor for which one cannot find a person or entity willing to provide a consulting service. This is the case with respect to the acquisition of land, buildings, shopping centers, and business opportunities. Real estate brokers are trained and licensed in each state and are presumably expert in the selling and purchasing of real estate of all types. This includes residential and commercial properties ranging anywhere from the most humble of acquisitions to major urban income-producing properties costing hundreds of millions of dollars. The same can also be said with respect to acquisition of a United States business enterprise. Real estate brokers can render valuable services in that they can identify suitable acquisitions within the structural and financial parameters that the foreign investor establishes.

While it is advisable to use the services of a real estate professional, it is important to understand that in many states a real estate broker, unless special arrangements are made at the beginning of the transaction, represents and works for the seller of property. This is the case even though the real estate broker may never have met the owner of the property that is being sold. In the United States, property listing services are often utilized by real estate professionals.

In this system, a broker who obtains authorization to sell a property (*listing*) for a person will record that property in a central listing index called a multiple listing file or multiple property list file, or some other such designation. This list will then be circulated to other real estate professionals who can read a description of the property being sold together with the price and terms, etc. When these other real estate brokers find a prospective buyer who may be interested in purchasing property with those characteristics, they will present the compatible properties from their multiple listing sources to the prospect.

The industry custom, however, is that the seller will pay a commission to whoever sells this property and the *selling* broker is usually a sub-agent of the *listing* broker. The commission is usually divided by the listing broker, that is the broker who listed the property, and the selling broker, the broker that procures the buyer. Thus, even though the selling broker may have a personal relationship with the buyer, the broker represents the seller, who, as indicated previously, may be a stranger. The broker's legal and ethical duty is to protect the interest of the seller and obtain for that seller the highest price under the most favorable terms possible.

Obviously, this typical system is not the ideal way for the foreign buyer to approach the purchase of a real estate acquisition in the United States. Since foreign persons do not normally understand the dynamics or the customs of the local market they are usually at a great disadvantage compared to local persons and may not be in a position to derive the best bargain possible.

For these reasons, it is strongly recommended that a foreign person acquiring real property and/or business enterprises in the United States utilize a real estate agent who is committed to representing the buyer only, i.e., a *buyer's broker*. In this manner, the foreign buyer will derive the most benefit from the experience and skill of the real estate professional. Normally, the foreign person will agree to pay the buyer's broker an agreed upon fee or commission but this in no way involves a price disadvantage as the broker should be able to reduce the price to the seller by the amount of the commission the buyer is paying. Again, knowing how this system works enables one to gain an advantage.

If real estate brokers state that even though they are being paid by and contracted to the seller, they will protect the interest of the buyer/investor, the buyer should be forewarned of a potential *conflict of interest* and should proceed with caution. However, if the seller acknowledges and accepts this arrangement, it is usually permissible although not recommended. The laws of most states do not permit a professional to represent both sides of a transaction. This situation is now in a state of change and many states are considering a modification of the customary rules of agency so as to allow a real estate professional to represent both parties to a real estate transaction, or in some cases, to represent neither side to a real estate transaction. This is a matter of local law and custom that must be determined on a state-by-state basis and it is the responsibility of the alien to do so. As stated, the United States is a dynamic society and constantly revises many of its legal norms and customs.

The concept of *real property* includes raw vacant land, apartment buildings, shopping centers, warehouses, and even hotels and motels. Closely related to real estate brokerage (and licensed in the same manner in many states) are business brokers. These are people who specialize in the acquisition and sale of commercial business enterprises which may or may not have any real estate as part of their assets.

FIABCI   Additionally, there is an international association of real estate brokers who specialize in international real estate transactions. This organization is known by the initials *FIABCI* that stand for *International Real Estate Federation*. The organization is composed of real estate professionals from many countries who specialize in representing foreign purchasers (and sellers) and who are experienced in dealing with the needs of foreign persons. There probably are FIABCI members in your home country who can serve as a good referral source to a local U.S. FIABCI member for the foreign buyer. This organization is headquartered in Paris, France and has members throughout the world.

National Association of Realtors   In the United States there is a national professional real estate association known as the *National Association of Realtors* (NAR). This organization has state and local boards throughout the country and has an international subgroup named the *International Section of the NAR*. The members of this section manifest a special interest in the needs and desires of prospective foreign real estate investors.

Hotel and Motel Brokers of America   If one is interested in acquiring or developing a hotel or motel in the United States, one can also contact an organization known as the *Hotel and Motel Brokers of America*. It is headquartered in Kansas City, Missouri and its members are specialists in the acquisition and sale of hotel and motel properties in the United States. The acquisition of a hotel or a large motel, especially one that has other enterprises within it such as a restaurant and/or sports facilities, etc., is generally a good investment for a foreign buyer. This business combines the security of United States real estate with the growth potential of an entrepreneurial enterprise and can qualify an individual to obtain an *E* visa.

There are many other well qualified real estate professionals in other organizations who may also be of service to a foreign buyer, but it is important to remember the key consideration—to ensure that the real estate professional is working as a buyer's agent.

Acquiring and Developing a U.S. Business Enterprise

An existing U.S. business enterprise is the best option. I agree with the school of consultants who generally favor the acquisition of an existing U.S. business enterprise, including a franchised business, as a means of establishing the basis of an *L, E,* or *H-1B* visa. For purposes of this discussion I will refer to all of these as *business visas.*

The Small Business Administration publishes statistics on the dynamics of developing business enterprises in the United States. Perhaps in no other country in the world does the entrepreneurial zeal thrive more than in the U.S. Yet, the other side of the fabled stories of successful enterprises that are developed from the bottom up is the reality of the high percentage of business failures—especially among newly formed enterprises. While the statistics may vary slightly, the consensus is that approximately seventy-five percent of all new businesses fail within the first two years.

It is for this reason that it is generally advantageous to purchase an existing U.S. business enterprise—one that has preferably been an existence for at least five years. One of the greatest advantages of this process is that the purchaser buys an existing administrative and marketing apparatus. The existing business has at least survived the critical beginning period and has established the basis for its future growth. This is true even in the case of some troubled businesses. In fact, the troubled business also usually presents the opportunity to identify the source of the business' difficulties. Thus, the new owner can concentrate on correcting the problem areas and avoiding the mistakes of the past.

The foreign purchaser must be aware of a few key points in the business acquisition process.

First—the foreign prospective buyer should do a thorough *due diligence analysis.* The term, *due diligence* is defined as a critical analysis of the key characteristics of a business that will predict its future success or failure. The due diligence inquiry includes the study of the enterprise's financial books and records, a review of the company's past and present marketing techniques, inspection of the key items of equipment and fixtures and consideration of the competitiveness of the company's product or services.

The prospective foreign buyer should negotiate for a due diligence period of at least twenty-one days as well as for a visa contingency clause. The latter would enable the foreign person to nullify the purchase agreement in the event their visa petition is denied.

Second—the prospective buyer should take advantage of the due diligence period and conduct a thorough analysis of all the key components of the enterprise. Very often, this will involve the hiring of one or more technical or financial experts. I cannot overemphasize the importance of hiring and utilizing the best consultants that can be afforded. Foreign buyers must remember that even though they may be familiar with the nature of the business enterprise they are investigating, they are unfamiliar with the local business, administration, and legal environment of the enterprise. Assume nothing—heed everything.

Third,—the prospective buyer should remember that in business dealings in the U.S., personal relationships may be important but the formal written agreement is paramount.

Fourth—during the negotiation period the prospective buyer should remember that even though the status as a foreign purchaser may generate inconvenience to the seller, foreign status also presents an advantage to the seller. The advantage results from the fact that the buyer must invest a greater percentage of capital in the purchase transaction than the typical U.S. buyer. This fact alone should give the prospective buyer a stronger negotiating position.

Fifth—a good business broker can be invaluable in the selection of a business acquisition and in the negotiation process. The business broker (or Merger and Acquisition Specialist) is a person who specializes in the sale and purchase of existing business enterprises. The foreign entrepreneur must remember that traditionally a business broker is paid by and owes allegiance to the seller. In that capacity the broker will always attempt to place the business in the best possible light. Additionally, the broker will try to assess whether or not the buyer is financially qualified to complete the acquisition and whether or not the buyer is qualified to manage the business.

Therefore, while buyers should be candid with their broker, they should not offer information that could prejudice their bargaining position. Very often reputable business brokers will also work as an agent for the buyer or, in some cases, will agree to honor the confidences of both seller and buyer. The nature of the relationship should be established at the commencement of the transaction process, not at the end. Depending upon the particular state, the occupation of a business broker or merger and acquisition specialist is often regulated by law.

Finally—the prospective foreign buyer should not attempt to acquire and manage a U.S. business enterprise without a substantial capital reserve. At the very least, the buyer should reserve sufficient capital to cover personal living expenses for at least one year as well as a sufficient cash reserve to cover the enterprise's operating costs for approximately six months. Planning conservatively for capital needs is essential not just for success but also for peace of mind. The foreign entrepreneur will be immersed in the many details of adjusting to life in this fast-paced society and it would be inappropriate to burden oneself with unnecessary stress caused by the normal ebb and flow of the business cycle.

Franchised Businesses

For a variety of reasons, the foreign entrepreneur may prefer to establish a new business enterprise. Perhaps there are no suitable existing business enterprises that suit or interest the buyer. Or perhaps the buyer just desires to pursue a particular type of business enterprise. Perhaps one's dream requires the creation of something new, something in which the buyer can claim credit for developing. If this is the case, then there is another exciting option that, if not unique to the U.S., is nonetheless a product of the American business dynamism—a franchised business opportunity.

There are more than 500,000 franchised businesses in the United States and franchising is one of this country's fastest growing methods of doing business. A franchised business is a method of operation in which the originator or developer of a successful product or service authorizes another business operator to utilize the originator's trademark, business methods, products or services. The originator is called the *franchisor* and the *franchisee* is the one who purchases the right to use the trademark and system of business. A franchisee usually receives assistance with the site selection for the business, personnel training, business organization, marketing, and product supply. The franchisee usually pays an initial fee as well as on-going royalties. These fees enable the franchiser to provide training, research, development, and support for the entire business. In essence, the franchisee acquires the franchiser's experience, expertise, and operational system.

Franchising has a much greater percentage of success than businesses started without the benefits of a franchise system. One of the reasons for this success is the requirement by U.S. federal law that a franchiser provide the prospective franchisee with extensive documentation as to the considered business. This documentation is contained in the *Uniform Franchise Offering Circular* (UFOC). This document provides detailed information on the initial investment required, the amount of working capital, current and past litigation and monetary claims, identity and experience of the principal executives, advertising reserves, degree of managerial experience required, and much more. The UFOC provides the prospective franchisee with the tools to conduct an effective due diligence inquiry. Additionally, the prospective franchisee should contact other franchisees in the system and obtain as much information and comment as possible from these business owners.

Nonetheless, it is good sense to hire an experienced franchise consultant or attorney to assist in the analysis of the UFOC. Unlike traditional enterprises, the franchise alternative offers a lower risk of failure to the entrepreneur.

Franchising is especially relevant for foreign executives and managers because most franchisers do not want an overly individualistic person as a franchisee. Experience has demonstrated to franchisers that the ability to follow a proven business plan coupled with executive and managerial ability provides the best combination for franchise success. These characteristics are also generally beneficial for foreign buyers since it is prudent for foreign persons to allow themselves to be taught the local U.S. business customs and business practices. So there seem to be a combination of advantages which favor the franchised business for foreign entrepreneurs.

Some franchises, however, are so controlled that there is very little room for executive or managerial discretion. In that case, the franchised business might not sustain an *L-1* or *E-2* visa. That type of tightly controlled franchise is easy to identify and can be avoided. In any event, utilizing a visa contingency clause in the franchise agreement will provide the foreign entrepreneur with the ability to apply for the franchise without risking the loss of a deposit in the event the visa is denied. In fact, most franchised businesses still require a high level of executive and managerial ability (as well as time and energy) in order to succeed and there is an administrative precedent for the suitability of a franchised business for visa purposes.

Perhaps foreign persons can franchise their successful business methods from their home countries into the United States and thus provide others with the opportunity to share in their success.

Anyone interested in the option of franchising may contact:

International Franchise Association
1350 New York Avenue, N.W.
Suite 900
Washington, D.C. (U.S.A.)

Additionally, there is a permanent franchise exhibition at The Merchandise Mart, Chicago, Illinois 60654.

Tax Planning and other Economic Considerations

This section will briefly discuss the various U.S. federal income tax and estate tax consequences as they may affect a foreign person seeking entry into the United States. It is not meant to be a profound or complete analysis of all of the subjects and issues that are pertinent to such an individual, but is merely designed to acquaint a person with important topics. Any foreign person who contemplates an investment into the United States should consult a qualified international tax attorney or accountant for advice regarding the income and or estate tax consequences of the investment. Very often it will be necessary for the U.S. tax professional to consult with the client's tax and business advisors in order to ensure complete coverage of all the pertinent issues.

Taxation of Residency

The United States federal government collects taxes from its residents on the basis of a federal income tax as well as by gift and estate taxes. The agency in charge of taxes is the Internal Revenue Service. Additionally, every state as well as its various local subdivisions and municipalities may also collect taxes. The United States is one of the few countries in the world whose central government taxes its citizens and residents on their *worldwide income*. This very often is a substantial factor to be considered in the overall strategic financial planning by an inbound foreign person. For income tax purposes, there is a profound difference between a citizen, a resident and a nonresident. These designations may, in fact, have nothing to do with the immigration definition of these same terms.

A United States resident, for tax purposes, is any person who is either a U.S. citizen or a person deemed to be a resident of the United States in accordance with the Rules and Regulations of the Internal Revenue Code. A person deemed to be a resident of the United States, for tax purposes, is anyone who is the holder of a permanent visa to the United States (green card). This is sometimes called the *green card test*. This is an absolute test. If a person is a permanent U.S. resident alien, the person is automatically and absolutely a resident for income tax purposes under current U.S. law.

In addition to the so-called *green card test,* there is also the *substantial presence test.* This test imposes U.S. tax residency on foreign persons who spend a designated time in the United States. These so-called substantial presence tests are as follows.

✪ Any person who is present in the United States for thirty-one or more days in the present year is treated as a United States resident if the person has also spent 183 more days in the current year or 183 days over a three year period using the following formula.

> ✪ In the current year, one day of actual presence equals one day for the legal formula (1=1).

> ✪ In the previous year, one day of actual presence equals one-third of a day (1=$^1/_3$).

> ✪ For the next previous year, one day of actual presence equals one-sixth of a day (1=$^1/_6$).

Example: If a person were to reside in the United States for ninety days in 2004, ninety days in 2003, and ninety days in 2002, that person would not be considered a U.S. resident for tax purposes since the total of the above formula does not equal 183 days.

> ✪ 2004: 90 actual days = 90 equivalent days

> ✪ 2003: 90 actual days = 30 equivalent days

> ✪ 2002: 90 actual days = 15 equivalent days

> Total = 135 days of equivalent presence in the United States under the substantial presence test and thus, not a U.S. resident for income tax purposes.

In applying the above formula, any actual travel days in the United States must also be counted in the equation. For instance, if one enters the United States at 11:30 p.m. on a given day, that entire day is counted as one actual day of presence in the United States. Similarly, if one departs the United States at 12:30 a.m., that entire day also is counted in the equation.

There are some specific exemptions that apply to this formula. For instance, a person who remains in the United States for an extended period because of a medical emergency or who is posted in the United States as a diplomat. There are other exemptions applying to teachers, job trainees, and students. In addition to the above formula, if persons meet the substantial presence test under the mathematical computation but can prove that they maintain a home abroad and have closer connections with another jurisdiction, (i.e., they pay taxes in the other jurisdiction), then they may preserve their status as a non U.S. resident for income tax purposes. This possible exception, however, applies only to an individual who has been present in the United States for less than 183 days in the current year.

Taxation for Nonresidency

As to nonresidents, the United States taxes four categories of income.

1. *Income that is effectively connected with a U.S. trade or business.* This type of income is taxed on a net taxable income basis, using the normal progressive tax rates otherwise applicable to U.S. taxpayers. Business losses and expenses are allowed to be deducted from gross income in the calculation of net income which is subject to taxation.

2. *Income that is known as fixed or determinable annual or periodic income that is not connected with a U.S. trade or business.* This category does not include interest income generated by deposits in qualified U.S. financial institutions such as banks or insurance companies. This latter form of investment interest is not taxable at all.

3. *Capital gains income of a foreign person who is physically present in the U.S. for more than 183 days in the calendar year.* Obviously, a person physically present in the United States for more than 183 days in the calendar year will almost always be deemed to be a U.S. taxpayer in any event.

4. *Gain on the sale or other disposition of U.S. real property interests* (USRPI).

Fixed or determinable annual or periodical income is taxed at a flat rate of thirty percent on the gross amount unless that amount has been reduced by treaty. In addition to the burden of taxation, the tax amount must be withheld at the source of payment by the *withholding agent*. This person is usually the last person who has control of the income before it is transferred or conveyed to the foreign person. This type of income is normally considered passive income, such as dividends, interest, or royalties, etc.

Thus, it may be in one's financial interest to be considered engaged in a U.S. trade or business if one is receiving rents from real estate investments. Also, there may be a tax treaty in effect between the United States and the foreign person's home country that may reduce the rate for fixed or determinable annual income or periodical income.

Additionally, capital gains—that is, the amount of gain realized when a capital asset is sold, associated with United States property and other than real property—is not taxable so long as the person receiving that income has not been physically present in the United States for 183 or more days. Capital gains on the sale of real property, however, is taxable regardless of the length of time a person has been in the United States.

If the income is from a source outside the United States, then it would not be taxable unless that income is effectively connected with a U.S. trade or business. There are a number of complex rules that determine the source of income, and the application and effect of these rules usually requires professional assistance.

Withholding Requirements

A primary concern for a foreign person who owns real estate or other income producing assets in the U.S. is the requirement of withholding a certain percent of the income to cover tax liability. In order for the withholding rules to apply, the following requirements must exist.

- ✪ *There must be a withholding agent.* The Internal Revenue Service rules are very broad in defining which persons are required to withhold funds otherwise payable to a foreign person. This definition includes real estate brokers, attorneys, other trustees, lessees, or mortgagees of real or personal property.

- ✪ *Only U.S. sources of income are subject to withholding.*

- ✪ *The items that are subject to withholding are fixed, determinable, and annual or periodic income such as interest, dividends, rent, salaries, and other fixed or determinable annual or periodical gains and profit income.* Income from the sale of property, real or personal, is not considered fixed, determinable, annual, or periodic. So capital gains are not subject to withholding unless they involve real estate.

✪ *The income must not be effectively connected with a U.S. trade or business.*

✪ *The recipient of the income or money must be either a nonresident or alien, foreign partnership, or foreign corporation.*

✪ *If there is a treaty or other special rule or exception, then the withholding requirement may be avoided.*

✪ *As to partnerships, it should be noted that a domestic partnership is required to withhold and remit to the IRS all fixed determinable annual and periodic income (which is not effectively connected with a U.S. trade or business), which is included in the distributive share of a foreign partner, even if the income is not actually distributed.* If the partnership distributive income is effectively connected, then withholding is not required. However, IRS rules and regulations now require a U.S. partnership to withhold and make quarterly estimated tax payments on a foreign partner's share of partnership income that is effectively connected with U.S. trader business regardless of whether distributions of income are made to the partners.

✪ *Trusts income from a U.S. source that is fixed or determinable, annual or periodic, and which is distributed through a trust's foreign beneficiary, is subject to withholding.*

✪ *It is extremely important that a foreign person understand that the tax characterization of a business entity by the IRS may determine whether distribution is a dividend and thus taxable by thirty percent as opposed to any other type of distribution.* For example, if a foreign entity is called or designated as a trust or partnership but is defined by the IRS as a corporation, then a distribution may be determined to be a dividend. The United States has signed a network of treaties dealing with income tax and withholding requirements with other countries. The primary purpose of the U.S. income tax treaties is the prevention of double taxation. However, some treaties may provide some insular and legitimate tax avoidance opportunities. The advantages offered by U.S. tax treaties have been utilized by corporations formed or otherwise resident within the treaty jurisdiction, controlled by well-advised foreign taxpayers whose personal residences are countries not having a treaty with the U.S., or whose treaty may not be suitable for a particular transaction or investment.

General Planning Requirements

There are many planning considerations that should be addressed by a foreign person seeking to make investment in the U.S. prior to that direct investment. Some of them can be characterized as follows.

- ✪ Initially, the foreign person must establish priorities with respect to the transfer of assets to the United States. There is always the objective to minimize U.S. and other taxation earnings in this position (gains) at the various levels of operation and in avoidance of U.S. state tax. In addition, there may be some other very valid immigration objectives that may conflict with some of the above tax concerns and the foreign person will need to determine which objective shall be paramount.

- ✪ Where will the investor maintain residence?

- ✪ Are there plans in the immediate future or in the near future to relocate?

- ✪ Compare the U.S. tax regimen with the individual and corporate income tax rates and state tax rates in the country of residence or in the country where assets generating income are located.

- ✪ The availability of tax treaties that may change the withholding rules or other U.S. tax requirements otherwise applicable to a non-resident or resident alien.

- ✪ Is the investor making a unique trans-national acquisition in the United States or is the investor making a long term plan to transfer assets to the U.S.?

- ✪ Is the investor already engaged in a business outside of his or her home country? Where? What are the tax ramifications?

- ✪ If there are other existing U.S. investments, are they producing income or loss?

- ✪ Is there need for anonymity on the part of the foreign investor?

- ✪ How will the investment be financed and by whom?

- ✪ What are the home country laws concerning the repatriation of foreign income earnings for individual residents?

✪ What is the anticipated time that the investment will be held? Short term or long term?

✪ What are other relevant business considerations?

The tax rates for income that is effectively connected with a U.S. trade or business is the same as for residents and is based on a progressive schedule. In addition, the tax is imposed on the net gain of the enterprise. In certain cases a foreign person may elect to be taxed as if engaged in a U.S. trade or business. It may be beneficial to be taxed as a U.S. trade or business so as to avoid the imposition of a tax on the gross income derived from investments in the United States. (The rules for this type of election are beyond the scope of this book but the election option is mentioned here only to make the reader aware of the availability of this procedure.)

Nonresident Engaged in Trade or Business

If a nonresident alien is engaged in a trade or business in the United States, then all the income effectively connected with that trade or business is taxable at the same rates and according to the same rules as for a United States citizen or resident. There is no clear-cut definition as to what constitutes a United States trade or business. The determination usually involves a review of the activities of the person and the frequency and nature of those activities. Any business activity that involves significant contacts in the United States or that operates from, or in connection with, a fixed or permanent office may well cause the taxpayer to be treated as engaged in a trade or business in the United States.

Various countries have treaties with the United States that provide that the host country will only tax the profits of an enterprise if the alien maintains a *permanent establishment* in that country. There are various definitions as to what denotes a permanent establishment but it normally includes the maintenance of a business, an office, or factory that is in place or is expected to remain in place for a period of twelve months or more. Normally, the use of an independent contractor or agent for the representation of a foreign enterprise in the United States will not result in a finding of a permanent establishment unless that independent contractor has wide and general authority to act on behalf of the principal and normally does so.

An amendment to the United States Federal Tax Code known as the *Foreign Investment Real Property Tax Act* (FIRPTA) essentially places nonresident aliens on an equal footing with United States residents with respect to the tax on the net gains from the sale of United States real property interests. The gain is taxed as if the gain were effectively connected with a United States trade or business. A person is taxable only on the net gain realized in the business and can offset the gross amount realized with expenses, depreciation, etc.

The definition of what is a real property interest is quite broad and covers most interests in real property; i.e., land and buildings, except an interest that is purely that of a lender or creditor. Ownership by foreign persons of a hotel or motel, for example, is considered ownership of a United States real property interest.

In addition, if a United States corporation owns the United States real property interest, and that interest amounts to at least fifty percent of the sum of all property owned by that corporation, then it will be considered a United States real property holding corporation and the corporate sale of stock will also result in taxation. Payment of the tax is secured by way of a mandatory withholding of ten percent of the amount realized on disposition of that United States real property interest. The tax may not equal the ten percent, but the withholding agent is required to secure that amount and submit it to the Internal Revenue Service. This is to ensure there will be a fund of money to pay the tax when it is annually determined. The following are exceptions to this withholding requirement:

✪   the property is purchased by a person for use as a residence and the value is $300,000.00 or less;

✪   the property being sold was not considered an interest in U.S. real property; however, according to the law, a U.S. real property interest includes not only real property owned directly by an individual, but also real property owned by a U.S. corporation which, is itself, principally owned by a foreign person. If the property is held by a foreign corporation, and only the shares of stock are sold, then FIRPTA does not apply since the purchaser is only buying shares of stock in a foreign corporation; or,

✪   the transferred property's corporate stock is transferred under an established U.S. securities market, or the transferor has executed and furnished a *nonforeign affidavit* certifying that the transferor is not a foreign person.

Any nonresident alien who was engaged in a trade or business in the United States during the taxable year or had his or her income subject to tax by the

United States is required to file an IRS Form 1040NR. There are certain exceptions to this that can be discussed with a tax expert.

Thus, if United States real property taxation considerations are important to a foreign investor, the above information needs to be addressed in the preimmigration planning stages.

Estate and
Gift Taxes
The tax computation for a gross estate in the case of a nonresident alien involves calculations very similar to that for a U.S. person. The following special rules should be kept in mind by any foreign person when making an investment in the United States for acquisition of income-producing assets.

✪ The *situs* (that is, the legal residence) of real property is determined by its physical location. Thus, real property situated in the United States is considered as having a U.S. situs. Mortgages and liens on real property as a result of loans are not considered as real property for this purpose. These are considered intangible assets, but if the debt obligation is of a U.S. person, then it is U.S. situs property.

✪ As to corporate stock, stock of a U.S. corporation is U.S. situs, whereas stock of a foreign corporation is considered foreign situs regardless of the place of management or location of the stock certificates. As to foreign partnerships, the rule is somewhat unclear. The situs of the partnership is where the partnership business is carried on or managed, not necessarily where the assets are located. What is unclear is whether or not a foreign partnership, which is engaged in a U.S. business, subjects its entire partnership interest as U.S. situs rather than just its U.S.-based situs assets.

✪ The situs of currency is its physical location and it is treated just as other tangible personal property.

✪ Debt obligation of a U.S. person is considered a U.S. situs property except where the obligation of a U.S. corporation for more than eighty percent of the gross income of the organization comes from an active foreign source for a three-year prior period.

✪ The physical location of the assets of sole proprietorship determines its situs.

✪ Property held through a reputable or grantor trust, of which the decedent is the grantor, can be U.S. situs property.

✪ Intangible personal property is considered as U.S. situs if it was issued by or enforceable against a resident of the U.S., a domestic corporation or a governmental unit.

✪ The formula and method for the computation of the tax is identical to that of a U.S. tax payer with one exception: the marital deduction is not allowed the foreign person unless it was granted by treaty, or unless the surviving spouse is a U.S. citizen, or unless the property is conveyed through a qualified domestic trust. Furthermore, after making the required computations, the rates now range from eighteen to fifty-five percent of the adjusted estate.

The United States imposes estate taxes upon the estate of a nonresident alien if that alien has assets situated in the United States at the time of death. A *nonresident* for purposes of the estate and gift tax laws refers to a person who is not *domiciled* in the United States. *Domicile* is normally defined to be that place where a person intends to live permanently—the place that a person has selected as the permanent home. The question of domicile can sometimes be difficult to define precisely. In general, it has been held by the courts that a person can only have one domicile even though there may be many residences. It does not necessarily follow, however, that a person who is domiciled in the United States must be a *resident* for estate tax purposes. Though this result would generally follow, it is technically possible for persons to have a foreign residence (and passport) even though they might be domiciliaries of the United States based upon other considerations and circumstances.

The determination of *residence* for estate tax purposes is of paramount importance to a foreign person in the United States because if the person is deemed to be a resident, that is, domiciled in the United States, then the United States government may impose an estate tax on the worldwide property held by that person. If the foreign person is considered to be a nonresident alien, then the United States can only impose a federal estate tax on the assets located in the United States at the time of death. The tax rate applicable to a nonresident alien is the same as would apply to a citizen except that certain normal tax-credit devices (the marital deduction) are inapplicable. This fact could make a devastating impact on the total tax liability of a foreign person and requires careful study.

In this situation, the source rules are very important as to what constitutes U.S.-located *(situs)* property. Currency and other tangible personal property are considered to have a situs based upon physical location. Corporate stock of a U.S. corporation has a U.S. situs while corporate stock of a foreign corporation has a foreign situs, regardless of where the stock certificates are actually located.

Thus, in most situations when aliens do not intend to reside in the United States for extended periods of time, it is not advisable to hold even residential property or even *casual property* (condominium, apartment, raw land, etc.) in the United States in their own name.

It is better to have U.S. real property owned by a foreign corporation or a U.S. subsidiary corporation owned by a foreign corporation, since under these circumstances the property will not be deemed as situated in the United States. Of course, this suggestion must be balanced with the foreign person's other tax interests to ensure that there are no other income tax or other problems created by this device. In general, though, the above is a preferred way of holding property in the United States by a nonresident person. However, before a commitment is made, it is advisable to discuss the tax and other economic consequences of these purchases with a trained professional. This is one of those instances where an hour or two of consultation before taking what may be irrevocable steps can be worth much money and much peace of mind.

Investment Reporting Requirements

The federal government maintains various investment disclosure laws that provide for the filing of certain reports by a foreign person who owns either agricultural land or other types of business enterprises. The financial threshold for the reporting requirements of commercial business is generally $1,000,000 of cost, or the actual value of the business assets whenever less than 200 acres of real estate involved.

The U.S. Department of Commerce regulations require the reporting of a transaction when a foreign person acquires ten percent or more interest in a U.S. business (including real estate). A *Form BE-13* is filed by the U.S. business within forty-five days after the investment. If the foreign person or entity directly acquires United States real property interest, the form is filed in the name of that foreign person entity and describes the real property acquired. *Form BE-13* identifies each foreign person owning a United States business enterprise and discloses the ultimate beneficial foreign owner, that is, the person or entity in the chain of ownership that is not more than fifty percent owned by another person. Additionally, *Form BE-13* requests the name, ownership percentage, and country of location of each foreign owner.

If the ultimate beneficial owner is an individual, however, only the country of residence must be disclosed. Exemptions from filing this form include the acquisition of real estate for personal residence; acquisition of a United States business by a U.S. affiliate of a foreign person that merges the U.S. business into its business if the cost is less than $1 million and less than 200 acres of U.S. land is acquired; and, an acquisition for establishment of a United States business if its total assets are less than or equal to $1 million and it does not own 200 or more acres of United States land. Bearing in mind, then, the recent provisions for a United States investor visa as defined in this book, it is clear that upon investment of $1 million for the acquisition of a U.S. business, reporting to the Department of Commerce may be required if the business and its assets includes 200 or more acres of United States land.

Department of Commerce reports are to be used solely for analytical or statistical purposes and are confidential. However, anonymity can never be fully guaranteed. If anonymity is needed, a request for confidentiality can be made in writing to the Department of Commerce. Failure to file the above forms or to provide the information required under these forms may result in civil penalty not exceeding $10,000 or criminal penalty of a fine not exceeding $10,000, or imprisonment up to one year, or both. The reporting requirements should not be taken lightly.

The U.S. Department of Agriculture has a series of reporting requirements for the purpose of monitoring the disposition of agricultural land. *Agricultural land* is defined as land currently used or used within the past five years for agricultural, forestry, or timber production purposes unless the land is ten acres or less and the income from the products on the land amounts to less than $1,000.00 on an annual basis, or the land is for personal use. In addition, some states have their own reporting requirements, while other states may have some restrictions on the type of real estate that can be purchased by a non U.S. resident. These factors should be examined carefully beforehand by a foreign person to ensure that the purchase of certain U.S. assets will be compatible with the investor's overall business plan.

The tax regimen of the United States obviously provides for a considerable amount of disclosure of the foreign person's interest in the United States. In addition to the tax reporting requirements for acquisitions, there are also the nontax reporting requirements under the Department of Agriculture and Department of Commerce rules and regulations mentioned in the previous paragraphs.

In addition, there is a regimen of reporting requirements known as EXON-FLORIO regulations. The regimen authorizes the President of the United States to block or suspend an acquisition by a foreign entity of a United States business if it negatively affects national security. Administration of this law has been delegated to the Committee of Foreign Investment in the United States (SFIUS). Consequently, it is recommended that a foreign person making a transaction that could possibly result in the acquisition of control of a U.S. business, and possibly affect U.S. security, give notice to the SFIUS.

The reason for doing so is to eliminate within a designated time period any potential (future) action by the United States to require the foreign investor to divest itself of the transaction investment. The law gives the United States up to three years to issue a divestiture order. Therefore, it is certainly worthwhile to give a written notice in advance of the investment and force the government to reveal any interest that it may have in the transaction.

A FINAL WORD

The immigration law of the United States is not only broad and complex; it is also subject to constant modification. In addition, the economic environment of the United States is dynamic and fast-paced. The prospective foreign entrepreneur or business executive must successfully maneuver within the systems of both of these critical areas at the same time. These circumstances make it difficult for the small sized foreign business entrepreneur to attempt to manage all these issues by him or herself. A friend of mine used the analogy of attempting to learn simultaneously how to juggle crystal goblets and bounce on a trampoline to describe this endeavor.

The necessity of pre-entry planning cannot be over-emphasized, especially since the transfer of a successful enterprise will result in certain U.S. state and federal income tax consequences. The strategy of pre-entry planning is also beneficial to those individuals who seek a long-term visa to the United States based upon employment, education, or other personal interests. As an example, U.S. persons who desire to obtain a *K* visa for a *significant other* should carefully read the section in this book concerning the requirements for that visa as well as the Introduction and Preface to this book. In this manner, persons will understand the documentation requirements and the reasoning behind these requirements. Thus, the key to success for obtaining any visa entry into the United States is planning—particularly long term.

I enjoy hearing from my readers. You may contact me at my business office:

Ramon Carrion
28100 U.S. 19 N., Suite 502
Clearwater (Tampa), Florida, 33761
United States of America
http://ilw.com/carrion
E-mail: ramoncarrion@yahoo.com

Appendix A:
USCIS Offices

Following are the addresses of the USCIS Service Centers, District Offices, and Sub-offices where papers may be filed. Certain service centers and offices only handle certain types of applications so it is always best to verfiy which location you shoulud use. The USCIS website, **http://uscis.gov**, contains instructions for where to file. It is also best to verify the current address of the location you need, as they are subject to change.

USCIS SERVICE CENTERS

WESTERN U.S.

USCIS California Service Center
P.O. Box 30080
Laguna Niguel, CA 92607-0080

Overnight Delivery Address:
USCIS California Service Center
2400 Avila Road
Laguna Niguel, CA 92677

(This address should be used for people from Arizona, California, Hawaii, Nevada, Territory of Guam, or the Commonwealth of the Northern Mariana Islands.)

MIDWEST

USCIS Nebraska Service Center
P.O. Box 87400
Lincoln, NE 68501-7400

Overnight Delivery Address:
USCIS Nebraska Service Center
850 S. Street
Lincoln, NE 68508

(People from the following states will use this center: Alaska, Colorado, Idaho, Illinois, Indiana, Iowa, Kansas, Michigan, Minnesota, Missouri, Montana, Nebraska, North Dakota, Ohio, Oregon, South Dakota, Utah, Washington, Wisconsin, or Wyoming.)

MIDSOUTH

USCIS Texas Service Center
P.O. Box 851204
Mesquite, TX 75185-1204

Overnight Delivery Address:
USCIS Texas Service Center
4141 North St. Augustine
Dallas, TX 75227

(The Texas Service Center handles paperwork for the following states: Alabama, Arkansas, Florida, Georgia, Kentucky, Louisiana, Mississippi, New Mexico, North Carolina, Oklahoma, Tennessee, or Texas.)

EAST COAST

USCIS Vermont Service Center
75 Lower Weldon Street
St. Albans, VT 05479-0001

Overnight Delivery Address:
USCIS Vermont Service Center
75 Lower Weldon Street
St. Albans, VT 05479-0001

(This Service Center handles Connecticut, District of Columbia, Delaware, Maine, Maryland, Massachusetts, New Hampshire, New Jersey, New York, Pennsylvania, Rhode Island, Vermont, Virginia, West Virginia, Commonwealth of Puerto Rico, or the U.S. Virgin Islands.)

STATE-BY-STATE

Alabama:
USCIS Atlanta District
Martin Luther King Jr.
Federal Building
77 Forsyth Street SW, Room 111
Atlanta, GA 30303
404-331-0253

Alaska:
USCIS Anchorage District Office
620 East 10th Avenue, Suite 102
Anchorage, Alaska 99501
907-271-3521

Arizona:
USCIS Phoenix District Office
2035 North Central Avenue
Phoenix, AZ 85004
602-514-7799

USCIS Tucson Sub Office
South Country Club Road
Tucson, AZ 85706-5907
520-670-4624

Arkansas:
USCIS
4991 Old Greenwood Road
Fort Smith, AR 72903
501-646-4721

California:
USCIS Los Angeles District Office
300 North Los Angeles Street, Room 1001
Los Angeles, CA 90012
213-830-4940

USCIS Fresno Sub Office
865 Fulton Mall
Fresno, CA 93721
559-487-5132

USCIS Sacramento Sub Office
650 Capitol Mall
Sacramento, CA 95814
916-498-6480

USCIS
34 Civic Center Plaza
Room 520
Santa Ana, CA 92701
714-972-6600

USCIS San Diego District Office
U.S. Federal Building
880 Front Street, Suite 1234
San Diego, CA 92101
619-557-5645

USCIS San Francisco District Office
630 Sansome Street
San Francisco, CA 94111
415-844-5200

USCIS San Jose Sub Office
1887 Monterey Road
San Jose, CA 95112
408-918-4000

Colorado:
USCIS Denver District Office
4730 Paris Street
Denver, CO 80239
303-371-0986

Connecticut:
USCIS Hartford Sub Office
450 Main Street, 4th Floor
Hartford, CT 06103-3060
860-240-3050

Delaware:
USCIS
1305 McD Drive
Dover, DE 19901
302-730-9311

District of Columbia:
USCIS Washington
District Office
4420 N. Fairfax Drive
Arlington, VA 22203
202-307-1642

Florida:
Fort Lauderdale/Port Everglades Sub Office
1800 Eller Drive, Suite 1401
P.O. Box 13054
Port Everglades Station
Fort Lauderdale, FL 33316
954-356-7790

USCIS Miami District Office
7880 Biscayne Boulevard
Miami, FL 33138
305-762-3680

USCIS Jacksonville Sub Office
4121 Southpoint Boulevard
Jacksonville, FL 32216
904-232-2164

USCIS Orlando Sub Office
9403 Tradeport Drive
Orlando, FL 32827
407-855-1241

USCIS Tampa Sub Office
5524 West Cypress Street
Tampa, FL 33607-1708
813-637-3010

USCIS West Palm Beach Sub Office
301 Broadway, Suite 142
Riviera Beach, FL 33401
561-841-0498

Georgia:
USCIS Atlanta District
Martin Luther King Jr. Federal Building
77 Forsyth Street SW, Room 111
Atlanta, GA 30303
404-331-0253

Hawaii:
USCIS Honolulu District Office
595 Ala Moana Boulevard
Honolulu, HI 96813
808-532-3746

USCIS Agana Sub Office
Sirena Plaza, Suite 100
108 Hernan Cortez Avenue
Hagatna, Guam 96910
671-472-7466

Idaho:
Boise Office Location
USCIS Boise Sub Office
1185 South Vinnell Way
Boise, ID 83709

Illinois:
USCIS Chicago District Office
10 West Jackson Boulevard
Chicago, Illinois 60604
312-385-1820 or 312-385-1500

correspondence regarding
adjustment cases:
U.S.B.C.I.S.
P.O. Box 3616
Chicago, IL 60690

adjustment/work permit
applications:
U.S. B.C.I.S.
P.O. Box A3462
Chicago, IL 60690-3462

USCIS
Citizenship Office
539 S. LaSalle Street
Chicago, IL 60605
312-353-5440

Indiana:
USCIS
Indianapolis Sub Office
950 N. Meridian St., Room 400
Indianapolis, Indiana 46204

Kansas:
USCIS Wichita Satellite Office
271 West 3rd Street North, Suite 1050
Wichita, KS 67202-1212

Kentucky:
USCIS Louisville Sub Office
Gene Snyder U.S. Courthouse and Customhouse
Room 390
601 West Broadway
Louisville, KY 40202
502-582-6526

Louisiana:
U.S.DHS
USCIS
701 Loyola Avenue,
Room T-8011
New Orleans, LA 70113
504-589-6521

Maine:
USCIS Portland
Maine District Office
176 Gannett Drive
So. Portland, ME 04106
207-780-3399

Maryland:
USCIS Baltimore District
Fallon Federal Building
31 Hopkins Plaza
Baltimore, MD 21201
410-962-2010

Massachusetts:
USCIS Boston District Office
John F. Kennedy Federal Building
Government Center
Boston, MA 02203
617-565-4274

Michigan:
USCIS Detroit District Office
333 Mt. Elliot
Detroit, MI 48207
313-568-6000

Minnesota:
USCIS St. Paul District
2901 Metro Drive, Suite 100
Bloomington, MN 55425
612-313-9020

Mississippi:

USCIS Jackson Sub Office
Dr. A. H. McCoy
Federal Building
100 West Capitol Street
Suite B-8
Jackson, Mississippi 39269

Missouri:

USCIS Kansas City District
9747 Northwest Conant Avenue
Kansas City, MO 64153
816-891-7422

USCIS St. Louis Sub Office
Robert A. Young Federal Building
1222 Spruce Street, Room 1.100
St. Louis, MO 63103-2815
314-539-2516

Montana:

USCIS Helena District Office
2800 Skyway Drive
Helena, MT 59602
406-449-5220

Nebraska:

USCIS Omaha District Office
3736 South 132nd Street
Omaha, NE 68144
402-697-1129

USCIS Omaha District Office
Information Office
13824 T Plaza (Millard Plaza)
Omaha, NE 68137

Nevada:

USCIS Las Vegas Sub Office
3373 Pepper Lane

Las Vegas, NV 89120-2739
702-451-3597

USCIS Reno Sub Office
1351 Corporate Boulevard
Reno, NV 89502
775-784-5427

New Hampshire:

USCIS Manchester Office
803 Canal Street
Manchester, NH 03101
603-625-5276

New Jersey:

USCIS Newark District Office
Peter Rodino, Jr. Federal Building
970 Broad Street
Newark, NJ 07102
973-645-4421

USCIS Cherry Hill Sub Office
1886 Greentree Road
Cherry Hill, NJ 08003
609-424-7712

New Mexico:

USCIS Albuquerque Sub Office
1720 Randolph Road SE
Albuquerque, NM 87106
505-241-0450

New York:

(Mailing address:)
USCIS Buffalo District Office
Federal Center
130 Delaware Avenue
Buffalo, NY 14202
716-849-6760

USCIS Albany Sub Office
1086 Troy-Schenectady Road
Latham, New York 12110
518-220-2100

USCIS New York City
District Office
26 Federal Plaza
New York City, NY 10278
212-264-5891

USCIS Rochester Satellite Office
Federal Building
100 State Street, Room 418
Rochester, NY 14614

USCIS Syracuse Satellite Office
412 South Warren Street
Syracuse, NY 13202

North Carolina:
USCIS Charlotte Sub Office
Woodlawn Green Office Complex
210 E. Woodlawn Road
Building 6, Suite 138
Charlotte, NC 28217
704-672-6990

North Dakota:
USCIS St. Paul District
2901 Metro Drive, Suite 100
Bloomington, MN 55425
612-313-9020

Ohio:
USCIS Cleveland District
A.J.C. Federal Building
1240 East Ninth Street,
Room 1917
Cleveland, OH 44199
216-522-4766

USCIS Cincinnati Sub Office
J.W. Peck Federal Building
550 Main Street, Room 4001
Cincinnati, OH 45202
513-684-2412

USCIS Columbus Sub Office
Bureau of Citizenship and Immigration Services
50 W. Broad Street
Columbus, OH 43215
614-469-2900

Oklahoma:
USCIS Oklahoma City
Sub Office
4149 Highline Boulevard,
Suite 300
Oklahoma City, OK 73108-2081
405-231-5944

Oregon:
USCIS Portland, Oregon
District Office
511 NW Broadway
Portland, OR 97209
503-326-7585

Pennsylvania:
USCIS Philadelphia
District Office
1600 Callowhill Street
Philadelphia, PA 19130
215-656-7150

USCIS Pittsburgh Sub Office
Federal Building
1000 Liberty Avenue
Room 2130
Pittsburgh, PA 15222
412-395-4460

Puerto Rico and U.S. Virgin Islands:

(Street address:)

USCIS San Juan District Office

San Patricio Office Center

7 Tabonuco Street, Suite 100

Guaynabo, Puerto Rico 00968

787-706-2343

(Mailing address:)

USCIS San Juan District Office

P.O. Box 365068

San Juan, PR 00936

USCIS Charlotte Amalie

Sub Office

Nisky Center, Suite 1A

First Floor South

Charlotte Amalie, St. Thomas

United States Virgin Islands 00802

340-774-1390

(Street address:)

USCIS

Sunny Isle Shopping Center

Christiansted, St. Croix

United States Virgin Islands 00820

(Mailing address:)

USCIS

P.O. Box 1468

Kingshill

St. Croix, USVI 00851

340-778-6559

Rhode Island:

USCIS Providence Sub Office

200 Dyer Street

Providence, RI 02903

401-528-5528

South Carolina:

USCIS Charleston Office

170 Meeting Street, Fifth Floor

Charleston, SC 29401

843-727-4422

South Dakota:

USCIS St. Paul District

2901 Metro Drive, Suite 100

Bloomington, MN 55425

612-313-9020

Tennessee:

U.S. DHS

USCIS

701 Loyola Avenue

Room T-8011

New Orleans, LA 70113

504-589-6521

USCIS Memphis Sub Office

Suite 100

1341 Sycamore View Road

Memphis, TN 38134

901-544-0256

Texas:

U.S. USCIS

8101 North Stemmons Freeway

Dallas, TX 75247

214-905-5800

USCIS El Paso District Office

1545 Hawkins Boulevard

Suite 167

El Paso, TX 79925

915-225-1750

USCIS Harlingen District
2102 Teege Avenue
Harlingen, TX 78550
956-427-8592

Houston USCIS District Office
126 Northpoint
Houston, Texas 77060
281-774-4629

USCIS San Antonio District
8940 Fourwinds Drive
San Antonio, TX 78239
210-967-7109

Utah:
USCIS Salt Lake City Sub Office
5272 South College Drive, #100
Murray, UT 84123
801-265-0109

Vermont:
USCIS St. Albans Office
64 Gricebrook Road
St. Albans, VT 05478

Virginia:
USCIS Washington
District Office
4420 N. Fairfax Drive
Arlington, VA 22203
202-307-1642

USCIS Norfolk Sub Office
5280 Henneman Drive
Norfolk, VA 23513
757-858-7519

Washington:
USCIS Seattle District Office
815 Airport Way South
Seattle, WA 98134
206-553-1332

USCIS Spokane Sub Office
U.S. Courthouse
920 W. Riverside Room 691
Spokane, WA 99201
509-353-2761

(Street address:)
USCIS Yakima Sub Office
417 E. Chestnut
Yakima, WA 98901

(Mailing address:)
USCIS Yakima Sub Office
P.O. Box 78
Yakima, WA 98901

West Virginia:
USCIS Charleston Sub Office
210 Kanawha Blvd. West
Charleston, WV 25302

Wisconsin:
USCIS
Milwaukee Sub Office
310 E. Knapp Street
Milwaukee, WI 53202
414-297-6365

Wyoming:
USCIS Denver District Office
4730 Paris Street
Denver, CO 80239
303-371-0986

APPENDIX B:
MEMORANDUM FOR THE
CHILD STATUS
PROTECTION ACT

In August of 2002, the President approved a law known as the *Child Status Protection Act*. It protects foreign children from *ageing-out* of permanent residency eligibility. While the language of the law is somewhat complex, in general, it provides that the age of a child is generally frozen at the time a petition for permanent residency is filed.

Eligibility under this law may require an in-depth analysis of many factors and consultation with an experienced immigration attorney is highly recommended. In certain individual cases, not even the U.S. consular officials or USCIS officials, may be clear as to eligibility. It would be highly advantageous to have a well prepared legal and factual analysis to present along with the application form.

This appendix contains a current policy memorandum from the USCIS that discusses the application of this law.

U.S. Department of Justice
Immigration and Naturalization Service

HQADN 70/6.1.1

Office of the Executive Associate Commissioner   *425 I Street NW*
                                                        Washington, DC 20536

February 14, 2003

MEMORANDUM FOR REGIONAL DIRECTORS
                DEPUTY EXECUTIVE ASSOCIATE COMMISSIONER,
                   IMMIGRATION SERVICES DIVISION
                ACTING DIRECTOR,
                   OFFICE OF INTERNATIONAL AFFAIRS

FROM: Johnny N. Williams /s/
             Executive Associate Commissioner
             Office of Field Operations

SUBJECT: The Child Status Protection Act – Memorandum Number 2

Purpose

On August 6, 2002, the President signed into law the Child Status Protection Act (CSPA), Public Law 107-208, 116 Stat. 927, which amends the Immigration and Nationality Act (Act) by permitting an applicant for certain benefits to retain classification as a "child" under the Act, even if he or she has reached the age of 21. On September 20, 2002, this office issued a memorandum providing preliminary guidance to Immigration and Naturalization Service (Service) officers concerning the amendments made to the Act by the CSPA. The purpose of this memorandum is to provide additional guidance to Service officers concerning this new law. As with the previous memorandum, while this memorandum will provide examples of cases that may be affected by the CSPA, it is impossible to anticipate and address every possible scenario. This memorandum should be read in conjunction with the September 20, 2002, memorandum (attached).

CSPA Coverage

In determining whether an alien's situation is covered by the CSPA, begin the analysis by using section 8 of the CSPA. Pursuant to section 8 of the CSPA, the provisions of the CSPA took effect on the date of its enactment (August 6, 2002) and are **not** retroactive. For adjustment applications based upon a provision of section 204 of the Act, the amendments made by the CSPA to the Act benefit an alien who aged out on or after August 6, 2002.[1]

---

[1] In determining whether an alien aged out before or after August 6, 2002, officers should keep in mind the special 45-day Patriot Act rules discussed in section 424 of the USA PATRIOT Act. Under this rule, if the alien is the beneficiary of a petition filed before Sep. 11, 2001, the alien remains eligible for child status for 45 days after

If the alien aged out prior to August 6, 2002, the only exception allowed by the CSPA is if the petition for classification under section 204 of the Act was pending on or after August 6, 2002; or the petition was approved before August 6, 2002, but no final determination had been made on the beneficiary's application for an immigrant visa or adjustment of status to lawful permanent residence pursuant to such approved petition. Thus, if an alien aged out prior to August 6, 2002, the petition must have been filed on or before August 6, 2002, and either: 1) remained pending on August 6, 2002, or; 2) been approved before August 6, 2002, with an adjustment application filed on or before August 6, 2002, and no final determination made prior to August 6, 2002. "Pending" for purposes of the visa petition means agency action on the petition, including an appeal or motion to reopen filed with the Administrative Appeals Office (AAO) or the Board of Immigration Appeals, if such appeal or motion was filed and/or pending on August 6, 2002. "Final determination" for purposes of the adjustment application means agency approval or denial issued by the Service or Executive Office for Immigration Review.

Inapplicability of the CSPA

Nonimmigrant visa (e.g. K or V)[2], NACARA, HRIFA, Family Unity, and Special Immigrant Juvenile applicants and/or derivatives will not benefit from the provisions of the CSPA.

Immediate Relatives

Section 2 of the CSPA addresses eligibility for retaining classification as an immediate relative. The CSPA does not apply to an alien obtaining K2 or K4 visas or extensions. While nothing would necessarily prohibit an alien who once was a K4 from seeking to utilize the CSPA upon seeking adjustment, an alien who is a K2 cannot utilize the CSPA when seeking to adjust.

Preference Categories

Direct Beneficiaries

Section 3 of the CSPA addresses whether certain aliens will be able to adjust as a "child" of a lawful permanent resident (LPR) even if they are no longer under the age of 21. As discussed in the previous memorandum, the beneficiary's "age" is to be calculated for CSPA purposes by first determining the age of the alien on the date that a visa number becomes available. The date that a visa number becomes available is the first day of the month of the Department of State (DOS) Visa Bulletin, which indicates availability of a visa for that

---

turning 21.
[2] Under the literal language of the statute, the CSPA applies only to immigrant visa categories specified in the statute and the law does not contain a provision allowing for its application to V visa/status, K, or other nonimmigrant visa cases.

Memorandum for Regional Directors, et al.   Page 3
Subject: The Child Status Protection Act – Memorandum Number 2

preference category. Of course, if upon approval of the Form I-130, Petition for Alien Relative, a visa number is already available according to the DOS Visa Bulletin, the date that a visa number becomes available is the approval date of the Form I-130. From that age, subtract the number of days that the Form I-130 was pending, provided the beneficiary files a Form I-485, Application to Register Permanent Residence or Adjust Status, based on the subject petition, within one year of such visa availability. The "period that a petition is pending" is the date that it is properly filed (receipt date) until the date an approval is issued on the petition.

Derivative Beneficiaries – Family and Employment-Based

In addition to the direct beneficiary family-based preference category examples provided in the previous memorandum and above, section 3 of the CSPA also applies to derivative beneficiaries in both family-based and employment-based preference categories. Just as with the case of the Form I-130, with an adjustment based upon an approved Form I-140, Immigrant Petition for Alien Worker, [and other immigrant petitions filed under section 204 of the Act for classification under sections 203(a), (b), or (c) of the Act], the beneficiary's age is to be calculated by first determining the age of the alien on the date that a visa number becomes available. The date that a visa number becomes available is the approval date of the immigrant petition if, according to the DOS Visa Bulletin, a visa number was already available for that preference category on that date of approval. If, upon approval of the immigrant petition, a visa number was not available, then the date for determining age is to be the first day of the month of the DOS Visa Bulletin which indicates availability of a visa for that preference category. From that age, subtract the number of days that the petition was pending, provided the beneficiary files a Form I-485,[3] based on the subject petition, within one year of such visa availability. The "period that a petition is pending" for the Form I-140 is the date that the Form I-140 is properly filed (receipt date and *not* priority date) until the date an approval is issued on the petition.

Visa Availability Date Regression

If a visa availability date regresses, and an alien has already filed a Form I-485 based on an approved Form I-130 or Form I-140, the Service should retain the Form I-485 and note the visa availability date at the time the Form I-485 was filed. Once the visa number again becomes available for that preference category, determine whether the beneficiary is a "child" using the visa availability date marked on the Form I-485. If, however, an alien has not filed a Form I-485 prior to the visa availability date regressing, and then files a Form I-485 when the visa availability date again becomes current, the alien's "age" should be determined using the subsequent visa availability date.

---

[3] An alien may benefit from section 3 of the CSPA if the alien "sought to acquire" the status of an LPR within one year of visa number availability. The filing of the Form I-485 within one year of the immigration petition approval date (or visa becoming available subsequent to petition approval date, whichever is later) has been determined to meet that definition.

Memorandum for Regional Directors, et al.   Page 4
Subject: The Child Status Protection Act – Memorandum Number 2

Diversity Visa (DV) Applicants

Section 3 of the CSPA also applies to derivative DV applicants. Because the DV application and adjudication process differs substantially from the application and adjudication process for preference categories, the treatment of DV derivatives will also be somewhat different. For the purpose of determining the period during which the "petition is pending," Service officers should use the period between the first day of the DV mail-in application period for the program year in which the principal alien has qualified and the date on the letter notifying the principal alien that his/her application has been selected (the congratulatory letter). That period should then be subtracted from the derivative alien's age on the date the visa became available to the principal alien.

Motions to Reopen and/or Reconsider

As discussed above, if a denial had been issued on an application for adjustment of status based on a petition for classification under section 204 prior to enactment of the CSPA, then the CSPA cannot benefit such alien. As such, it appears that no motion to reopen or reconsider could be granted based solely on an allegation that the alien is now eligible for CSPA consideration. In addition, it appears that no motion to reopen or reconsider could be granted where the motion was filed prior to enactment of the CSPA alleging solely a "due process / Service delay" argument where the alien was properly denied due to not being a child under the law at the time. While such motion may have been pending on August 6, 2002, such motion could not be granted where the alien was properly denied due to not being a child under the law at the time.

Expediting of Cases

The CSPA should dramatically reduce the amount of requests for expeditious adjudication of cases due to an impending age-out. For immediate relative adjustments, as the age is locked in on the date of filing, no expediting should ever be needed. However, given that preference category adjustments retain the possibility of aging out, it is suggested that any practices regarding expedites in existence prior to enactment of the CSPA be continued for preference category cases where the CSPA will not benefit the alien.[4]

---

[4] It appears that most preference category aliens will gain significant benefits from the CSPA. However situations could arise where an alien does not meet the section 3 requirements and be on the verge of turning 21. For example, an alien on whose behalf a Form I-140 was filed and approved a year and a half ago today files a Form I-485 and will soon turn 21. Such alien does not qualify for CSPA benefits and may age-out if not adjudicated before the alien's 21st birthday.

Memorandum for Regional Directors, et al.   Page 5
Subject: The Child Status Protection Act – Memorandum Number 2

Unmarried Sons and Daughters of Naturalized Citizens

        As discussed in the September 20, 2002, memorandum, section 6 of the CSPA provides
for the automatic transfer of preference categories when the parent of an unmarried son or
daughter naturalizes, but also provides the unmarried son or daughter the ability to request that
such transfer not occur. If an unmarried son or daughter does not want such automatic transfer
of preference categories to occur upon his or her parent's naturalization, the Service shall accept
such request in the form of a letter signed by the beneficiary. If the beneficiary does make this
written request to the Service, then the beneficiary's eligibility for family-based immigration will
be determined as if his or her parent had never naturalized.

Examples

        If a Form I-140 was filed in 1998 when the derivative beneficiary was 20, the priority
date became available at that time, the Form I-140 was not adjudicated until today, and a Form I-
485 was filed one month after approval, the derivative beneficiary's "age" for CSPA purposes
would be 20 (the beneficiary is 24 today, but the Form I-140 was pending for 4 years). Thus, this
derivative beneficiary would be able to retain classification as a child.

        If a Form I-140 was filed in 1998 when the derivative beneficiary was 20, the Form I-140
was adjudicated in 2000, a visa number was available at the time of approval, and the Form I-
485 was filed today, the derivative beneficiary's "age" for CSPA purposes would be 20 (the
beneficiary was 22 at the time the visa number became available, and the Form I-140 was
pending for 2 years). This beneficiary, however, could <u>not</u> benefit from the provisions of the
CSPA because (s)he did not file a Form I-485 within one year of visa availability. Thus, this
derivative beneficiary would be unable to retain classification as a child.

        If a Form I-130 was filed in 1998 when the derivative beneficiary was 20, the priority
date became available at that time, the Form I-130 was not adjudicated until today, and a Form I-
485 was filed nine months after petition approval, the derivative beneficiary's "age" for CSPA
purposes would be 20 (the beneficiary is 24 today, but the Form I-130 was pending for 4 years).
Thus, this beneficiary would be eligible to retain classification as a child.

        If a Form I-130 was filed in 1998 when the derivative beneficiary was 20, the Form I-130
was approved one year later, but the priority date did not become available until 2003, the
derivative beneficiary's "age" for CSPA purposes would be 24 (the beneficiary will be 25 at the
time of visa availability, but the Form I-130 was pending for 1 year). Thus, this beneficiary
would be unable to retain classification as a child.

        If a Form I-140 was filed and denied in 1998 when the derivative beneficiary was 20; the
petitioner filed a timely appeal with the AAO which, in 2003, sustains the appeal, remands the
matter, and approves the petition (on grounds other than the new availability of the CSPA); the

alien files a Form I-485 six months later, then the derivative beneficiary's "age" for CSPA purposes would be 20 (the beneficiary is 24 today, but the Form I-140 was pending for 4 years). Thus this beneficiary would be eligible to retain classification as a child.

If a Form I-130 was filed and denied in 1998 when the beneficiary was 20; the petitioner filed a timely motion to reopen; today the motion to reopen is granted (on grounds other than the new availability of the CSPA) and the petition is approved; the alien files a Form I-485 nine months later, then the beneficiary's "age" for CSPA purposes would be 20 (the beneficiary is 24 today, but the Form I-130 was pending for 4 years). Thus, this beneficiary would be eligible to retain classification as a child.

APPENDIX C: MEMORANDUM FOR THE CONTINUING VALIDITY OF FORM I-140

The *American Competitiveness in the 21st Century Act* acknowledges foreign workers' critical role in the United States' economy and contains provisions regarding changes relating to the labor certification process.

The purpose of the memorandum contained in this appendix is to provide field offices of the USCIS with guidance regarding the processing of *Form I-485, Application to Register Permanent Residence or Adjust Status*, when the beneficiary of an approved I-140, *Petition for Immigrant Worker*, is eligible to change employers under the Act. Understanding the procedures that the field offices follow will help as you go through the application process.

U.S. Department of Homeland Security
Bureau of Citizenship and Immigration Services

HQBCIS 70/6.2.8 - P

425 I Street NW
Washington, DC 20536

August 4, 2003

MEMORANDUM FOR   SERVICE CENTER DIRECTORS, BCIS
REGIONAL DIRECTORS, BCIS

FROM: William R. Yates /s/ Janis Sposato
Acting Associate Director for Operations
Bureau of Citizenship and Immigration Services
Department of Homeland Security

SUBJECT: Continuing Validity of Form I-140 Petition in accordance with Section 106(c) of
the American Competitiveness in the Twenty-First Century Act of 2000 (AC21)
<u>(AD03-16)</u>

The purpose of this memorandum is to provide field offices with guidance on processing
Form I-485, Application to Register Permanent Residence or Adjust Status, when the beneficiary
of an approved Form I-140, Petition for Immigrant Worker, is eligible to change employers
under §106(c) of AC21.

On January 29, 2001, the legacy Immigration and Naturalization Service's (Service)
Office of Field Operations issued a memorandum entitled "*Interim Guidance for Processing
H-1B Applications for Admission as Affected by the American Competitiveness in the
Twenty-First Century Act of 2002, Public Law 106-313.*" On June 19, 2001, the Office of
Programs issued a follow-up memorandum entitled "*Initial Guidance for Processing H-1B
Petitions as Affected by the American Competitiveness in the Twenty-First Century Act (Public
Law 106-313) and Related Legislation (Public Law 106-311) and (Public Law 106-396).*" On
February 28, 2003, Immigration Services Division issued a memorandum entitled "*Procedures
for concurrently filed family-based or employment-based Form I-485 when the underlying visa
petition is denied.*" These memoranda remain in effect. On July 31, 2002, the Service published
an interim rule allowing, in certain circumstances, the concurrent filing of Form I-140 and Form
I-485. Previous Service regulations required an alien worker to first obtain approval of the
underlying Form I-140 before applying for permanent resident status on the Form I-485.
Institution of the concurrent filing process, and other issues relating to revocation of approval of
Form I-140 petitions, have resulted in questions on how to process adjustment applications when
the alien beneficiary claims eligibility benefits under §106(c) of AC21 due to a change in his or
her employment.

A. Approved Form I-140 Visa Petitions and Form I-485 Applications

The AC21 §106(c) states:

A petition under subsection (a)(1)(D) [since re-designated section 204(a)(1)(F) of the Act] for an individual whose application for adjustment of status pursuant to section 245 has been filed and remained unadjudicated for 180 days or more shall remain valid with respect to a new job if the individual changes jobs or employers if the new job is in the same or a similar occupational classification as the job for which the petition was filed.

Accordingly, guidance in the June 19, 2001, memorandum provides that the labor certification or approval of a Form I-140 employment-based (EB) immigrant petition shall remain valid when an alien changes jobs, if:

(a)   A Form I-485, Application to Adjust Status, on the basis of the EB immigrant petition has been filed and remained unadjudicated for 180 days or more; and

(b)   The new job is in the same or similar occupational classification as the job for which the certification or approval was initially made.

This policy is still in effect and has not changed as a result of implementation of the concurrent filing process.

If the Form I-140 ("immigrant petition") has been approved and the Form I-485 ("adjustment application") has been filed and remained unadjudicated for 180 days or more (as measured from the Form I-485 receipt date), the approved Form I-140 will remain valid even if the alien changes jobs or employers as long as the new offer of employment is in the same or similar occupation.[1] If the Form I-485 has been pending for less than 180 days, then the approved Form I-140 shall not remain valid with respect to a new offer of employment.

B. Provisions in Cases of Revocation of the Approved Form I-140

---

[1]AC21 also provides that any underlying labor certification also remains valid if the conditions of §106(c) are satisfied.

Memorandum for Regional Directors, et. al.   Page 3
Subject: <u>Guidance for Processing Form I-485 in Accordance with Section 106(c) of AC21</u>

As discussed above, if an alien is the beneficiary of an approved Form I-140 and is also the beneficiary of a Form I-485 that has been pending 180 days or longer, then the approved Form I-140 remains valid with respect to a new offer of employment under the flexibility provisions of §106(c) of AC21.

Accordingly, if the employer withdraws the approved Form I-140 on or after the date that the Form I-485 has been pending 180 days, the approved Form I-140 shall remain valid under the provisions of §106(c) of AC21. It is expected that the alien will have submitted evidence to the office having jurisdiction over the pending Form I-485 that the new offer of employment is in the same or similar occupational classification as the offer of employment for which the petition was filed. Accordingly, if the underlying approved Form I-140 is withdrawn, and the alien has not submitted evidence of a new qualifying offer of employment, the adjudicating officer must issue a Notice of Intent to Deny the pending Form I-485. *See* 8 CFR 103.2(b)(16)(i). If the evidence of a new qualifying offer of employment submitted in response to the Notice of Intent to Deny is timely filed and it appears that the alien has a new offer of employment in the same or similar occupation, the BCIS may consider the approved Form I-140 to remain valid with respect to the new offer of employment and may continue regular processing of the Form I-485. If the applicant responds to the Notice of Intent to Deny, but has not established that the new offer of employment is in the same or similar occupation, the adjudicating officer may immediately deny the Form I-485. If the alien does not respond or fails to timely respond to the Notice of Intent to Deny, the adjudicating officer may immediately deny the Form I-485.

If approval of the Form I-140 is revoked or the Form I-140 is withdrawn before the alien's Form I-485 has been pending 180 days, the approved Form I-140 is no longer valid with respect to a new offer of employment and the Form I-485 may be denied. If at any time the BCIS revokes approval of the Form I-140 based on fraud, the alien will not be eligible for the job flexibility provisions of §106(c) of AC21 and the adjudicating officer may, in his or her discretion, deny the attached Form I-485 immediately. In all cases an offer of employment must have been bona fide, and the employer must have had the intent, at the time the Form I-140 was approved, to employ the beneficiary upon adjustment. It should be noted that there is no requirement in statute or regulations that a beneficiary of a Form I-140 actually be in the underlying employment until permanent residence is authorized. Therefore, it is possible for an alien to qualify for the provisions of §106(c) of AC21 even if he or she has never been employed by the prior petitioning employer or the subsequent employer under section 204(j) of the Act.

Questions regarding this memorandum may be directed via e-mail through appropriate channels to Joe Holliday at Service Center Operations or to Mari Johnson in Program and Regulation Development.

Accordingly, the *Adjudicator's Field Manual (AFM)* is revised as follows:

1. Chapter 20.2 of the AFM is revised by adding a new paragraph (c) to read as follows:

Memorandum for Regional Directors, et. al.   Page 4
Subject: <u>Guidance for Processing Form I-485 in Accordance with Section 106(c) of AC21</u>

20.2 Petition Validity.

(c) <u>Validity after Revocation or Withdrawal</u>. Pursuant to the provisions of section 106(c) of the American Competitiveness in the Twenty-First Century Act (AC21), Public Law 106-313, the approval of a Form I-140 employment-based (EB) immigrant petition shall remain valid when an alien changes jobs, if:

$ A Form I-485, Application to Adjust Status, on the basis of the EB immigrant petition has been filed and remained unadjudicated for 180 days or more; and

$ The new job is in the same or similar occupational classification as the job for which the certification or approval was initially made.

If the Form I-140 has been approved and the Form I-485 has been filed and remained unadjudicated for 180 days or more (as measured from the form I-485 receipt date), the approved Form I-140 will remain valid even if the alien changes jobs or employers as long as the new offer of employment is in the same or similar occupation. If the Form I-485 has been pending for less than 180 days, then the approved Form I-140 shall not remain valid with respect to a new offer of employment.

Accordingly, if the employer withdraws the approved Form I-140 on or after the date that the Form I-485 has been pending 180 days, the approved Form I-140 shall remain valid under the provisions of §106(c) of AC21. It is expected that the alien will have submitted evidence to the office having jurisdiction over the pending Form I-485 that the new offer of employment is in the same or similar occupational classification as the offer of employment for which the petition was filed. Accordingly, if the underlying approved Form I-140 is withdrawn, and the alien has not submitted evidence of a new qualifying offer of employment, the adjudicating officer must issue a Notice of Intent to Deny the pending Form I-485.   See 8 CFR 103.2(b)(16)(i). If the evidence of a new qualifying offer of employment submitted in response to the Notice of Intent to Deny is timely filed and it appears that the alien has a new offer of employment in the same or similar occupation, the BCIS may consider the approved Form I-140 to remain valid with respect to the new offer of employment and may continue regular processing of the Form I-485. If the applicant responds to the Notice of Intent to Deny, but has not established that the new offer of employment is in the same or similar occupation, the adjudicating officer may immediately deny the Form I-485. If the alien does not respond or fails to timely respond to the Notice of Intent to Deny, the adjudicating officer may immediately deny the Form I-485.

If approval of the Form I-140 is revoked or the Form I-140 is withdrawn before the alien's Form I-485 has been pending 180 days, the approved Form I-140 is no longer valid with respect to a new offer of employment and the Form I-485 may be

Memorandum for Regional Directors, et. al.   Page 5
Subject: <u>Guidance for Processing Form I-485 in Accordance with Section 106(c) of AC21</u>

denied. If at any time the BCIS revokes approval of the Form I-140 based on fraud, the alien will not be eligible for the job flexibility provisions of §106(c) of AC21 and the adjudicating officer may, in his or her discretion, deny the attached Form I-485 immediately. In all cases an offer of employment must have been bona fide, and the employer must have had the intent, at the time the Form I-140 was approved, to employ the beneficiary upon adjustment. It should be noted that there is no requirement in statute or regulations that a beneficiary of a Form I-140 actually be in the underlying employment until permanent residence is authorized. Therefore, it is possible for an alien to qualify for the provisions of §106(c) of AC21 even if he or she has never been employed by the prior petitioning employer or the subsequent employer under section 204(j) of the Act.

2. The *AFM* **Transmittal Memoranda** button is revised by adding the following entry:

AD 03-16 [INSERT SIGNATURE DATE OF MEMO]	Chapter 20.2(c)	Provides guidance on the validity of immigrant petitions under section 106(c) of AC21 (Public Law 106-313

INDEX

U

V

W

ABOUT THE AUTHOR

Ramon Carrion is a graduate of Rutgers University (NCAS) from which he graduated with honors in Political Science and Rutgers Law School. He has practiced U.S. immigration and international commercial law since 1976. He has assisted hundreds of individual and corporate clients from around the world with their U.S. immigration requirements. He has been certified by the Florida Bar as a specialist in Immigration and Nationality Law and served on the Certification Committee for Immigration and Nationality Law of the Florida Bar from 1998 through 2004. He is also a member of the American Immigration Lawyers Association (AILA) and past president of AILA's Central Florida Chapter.

Mr. Carrion lives and works in the Clearwater, Florida area, where in addition to a busy law practice, he is a sought-after lecturer on related immigration, business, and foreign investment topics.

Your #1 Source for Real World Legal Information...

SPHINX® PUBLISHING
An Imprint of Sourcebooks, Inc.®

• Written by lawyers
• Simple English explanation of the law
• Forms and instructions included

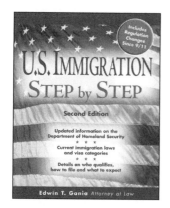

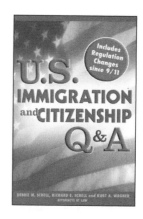

U.S. Immigration Step by Step, 2nd ed.

This book is designed to help you through the complicated and often confusing immigration process. From understanding eligibility requirements to accurate documentation, this guide provides the information you need to successfully make an application for a visa.

336 pages; $24.95;
ISBN 1-57248-387-3

Legal Research Made Easy, 3rd ed.

Simplify the process of doing your own legal research in law libraries and on computers. This book explains how to research statutes, case law, databases, law reports, and more. Learn how to access your state's statutes on the Internet. Save enormous amounts of time and money by handling your own legal research.

224 pages; $21.95;
ISBN 1-57248-223-0

U.S. Immigration and Citizenship Q&A

This book provides easy-to-understand answers to many, if not all, of your immigration and citizenship questions. It will take you from the beginning of the immigration process through naturalization.

384 pages; $16.95;
ISBN 1-57248-362-8

See the following order form for books written specifically for California, the District of Columbia, Florida, Georgia, Illinois, Maryland, Massachusetts, Michigan, Minnesota, New Jersey, New York, North Carolina, Ohio, Pennsylvania, Texas, and Virginia!

What our customers say about our books:

"It couldn't be more clear for the lay person." —R.D.

"I want you to know I really appreciate your book. It has saved me a lot of time and money." —L.T.

"Your real estate contracts book has saved me nearly $12,000.00 in closing costs over the past year." —A.B.

"...many of the legal questions that I have had over the years were answered clearly and concisely through your plain English interpretation of the law." —C.E.H.

"If there weren't people out there like you I'd be lost. You have the best books of this type out there." —S.B.

"...your forms and directions are easy to follow." —C.V.M.

Sphinx Publishing's Legal Survival Guides
are directly available from Sourcebooks, Inc., or from your local bookstores.

For credit card orders call 1–800–432–7444, write P.O. Box 4410, Naperville, IL 60567-4410,
or fax 630-961-2168

Find more legal information at: **www.SphinxLegal.com**

Sphinx® Publishing's National Titles
Valid in All 50 States

LEGAL SURVIVAL IN BUSINESS

The Complete Book of Corporate Forms	$24.95
The Complete Patent Book	$26.95
Employees' Rights	$18.95
Employer's Rights	$24.95
The Entrepreneur's Internet Handbook	$21.95
The Entrepreneur's Legal Guide	$26.95
How to Form a Limited Liability Company (2E)	$24.95
How to Form a Nonprofit Corporation (2E)	$24.95
How to Form Your Own Corporation (4E)	$26.95
How to Form Your Own Partnership (2E)	$24.95
How to Register Your Own Copyright (4E)	$24.95
How to Register Your Own Trademark (3E)	$21.95
Incorporate in Delaware from Any State	$24.95
Incorporate in Nevada from Any State	$24.95
Most Valuable Business Legal Forms You'll Ever Need (3E)	$21.95
Profit from Intellectual Property	$28.95
Protect Your Patent	$24.95
The Small Business Owner's Guide to Bankruptcy	$21.95
Tax Smarts for Small Business	$21.95

LEGAL SURVIVAL IN COURT

Attorney Responsibilities & Client Rights	$19.95
Crime Victim's Guide to Justice (2E)	$21.95
Grandparents' Rights (3E)	$24.95
Help Your Lawyer Win Your Case (2E)	$14.95
Jurors' Rights (2E)	$12.95
Legal Research Made Easy (3E)	$21.95
Winning Your Personal Injury Claim (2E)	$24.95
Your Rights When You Owe Too Much	$16.95

LEGAL SURVIVAL IN REAL ESTATE

The Complete Kit to Selling Your Own Home	$18.95
Essential Guide to Real Estate Contracts (2E)	$18.95
Essential Guide to Real Estate Leases	$18.95
Homeowner's Rights	$19.95
How to Buy a Condominium or Townhome (2E)	$19.95
How to Buy Your First Home	$18.95
Working with Your Homeowners Association	$19.95

LEGAL SURVIVAL IN SPANISH

Cómo Hacer su Propio Testamento	$16.95
Cómo Restablecer su propio Crédito y Renegociar sus Deudas	$21.95
Cómo Solicitar su Propio Divorcio	$24.95
Guía de Inmigración a Estados Unidos (3E)	$24.95
Guía de Justicia para Víctimas del Crimen	$21.95
Guía Esencial para los Contratos de Arrendamiento de Bienes Raices	$22.95
Inmigración a los EE. UU. Paso a Paso	$22.95
Manual de Beneficios para el Seguro Social	$18.95
El Seguro Social Preguntas y Respuestas	$14.95

LEGAL SURVIVAL IN PERSONAL AFFAIRS

101 Complaint Letters That Get Results	$18.95
The 529 College Savings Plan (2E)	$18.95
The Antique and Art Collector's Legal Guide	$24.95
The Complete Legal Guide to Senior Care	$21.95
Credit Smart	$18.95
Family Limited Partnership	$26.95
Gay & Lesbian Rights	$26.95
How to File Your Own Bankruptcy (5E)	$21.95
How to File Your Own Divorce (5E)	$26.95
How to Make Your Own Simple Will (3E)	$18.95
How to Write Your Own Living Will (3E)	$18.95
How to Write Your Own Premarital Agreement (3E)	$24.95
Living Trusts and Other Ways to Avoid Probate (3E)	$24.95
Mastering the MBE	$16.95
Most Valuable Personal Legal Forms You'll Ever Need (2E)	$26.95
Neighbor v. Neighbor (2E)	$16.95
The Nanny and Domestic Help Legal Kit	$22.95
The Power of Attorney Handbook (4E)	$19.95
Repair Your Own Credit and Deal with Debt (2E)	$18.95
Sexual Harassment:Your Guide to Legal Action	$18.95
The Social Security Benefits Handbook (3E)	$18.95
Social Security Q&A	$12.95
Teen Rights	$22.95
Traveler's Rights	$21.95
Unmarried Parents' Rights (2E)	$19.95
U.S. Immigration and Citizenship Q&A	$16.95
U.S. Immigration Step by Step (2E)	$24.95
U.S.A. Immigration Guide (5E)	$26.95
The Visitation Handbook	$18.95
The Wills, Estate Planning and Trusts Legal Kit	$26.95
Win Your Unemployment Compensation Claim (2E)	$21.95
Your Right to Child Custody, Visitation and Support (2E)	$24.95

SPHINX® PUBLISHING ORDER FORM

BILL TO:		SHIP TO:	
Phone #	Terms	F.O.B. Chicago, IL	Ship Date

Charge my: ☐ VISA   ☐ MasterCard   ☐ American Express

☐ **Money Order or Personal Check**

Credit Card Number

Expiration Date

Qty	ISBN	Title	Retail	Ext.	Qty	ISBN	Title	Retail	Ext.
		SPHINX PUBLISHING NATIONAL TITLES			___	1-57248-165-X	Living Trusts and Other Ways to Avoid Probate (3E)	$24.95	
___	1-57248-363-6	101 Complaint Letters That Get Results	$18.95	___		1-57248-186-2	Manual de Beneficios para el Seguro Social	$18.95	___
___	1-57248-361-X	The 529 College Savings Plan (2E)	$18.95	___		1-57248-220-6	Mastering the MBE	$16.95	___
___	1-57248-349-0	The Antique and Art Collector's Legal Guide	$24.95	___		1-57248-167-6	Most Val. Business Legal Forms You'll Ever Need (3E)	$21.95	
___	1-57248-347-4	Attroney Responsibilities & Client Rights	$19.95	___		1-57248-360-1	Most Val. Personal Legal Forms You'll Ever Need (2E)	$26.95	
___	1-57248-148-X	Cómo Hacer su Propio Testamento	$16.95	___	___	1-57248-098-X	The Nanny and Domestic Help Legal Kit	$22.95	___
___	1-57248-226-5	Cómo Restablecer su propio Crédito y Renegociar sus Deudas	$21.95	___	___	1-57248-089-0	Neighbor v. Neighbor (2E)	$16.95	___
___	1-57248-147-1	Cómo Solicitar su Propio Divorcio	$24.95	___	___	1-57248-169-2	The Power of Attorney Handbook (4E)	$19.95	___
___	1-57248-166-8	The Complete Book of Corporate Forms	$24.95	___	___	1-57248-332-6	Profit from Intellectual Property	$28.95	___
___	1-57248-353-9	The Complete Kit to Sellng Your Own Home	$18.95	___	___	1-57248-329-6	Protect Your Patent	$24.95	___
___	1-57248-229-X	The Complete Legal Guide to Senior Care	$21.95	___	___	1-57248-344-X	Repair Your Own Credit and Deal with Debt (2E)	$18.95	___
___	1-57248-201-X	The Complete Patent Book	$26.95	___	___	1-57248-350-4	El Seguro Social Preguntas y Respuestas	$14.95	___
___	1-57248-369-5	Credit Smart	$18.95	___	___	1-57248-217-6	Sexual Harassment: Your Guide to Legal Action	$18.95	___
___	1-57248-163-3	Crime Victim's Guide to Justice (2E)	$21.95	___	___	1-57248-219-2	The Small Business Owner's Guide to Bankruptcy	$21.95	___
___	1-57248-367-9	Employees' Rights	$18.95	___	___	1-57248-168-4	The Social Security Benefits Handbook (3E)	$18.95	___
___	1-57248-365-2	Employer's Rights	$24.95	___	___	1-57248-216-8	Social Security Q&A	$12.95	___
___	1-57248-251-6	The Entrepreneur's Internet Handbook	$21.95	___	___	1-57248-221-4	Teen RIghts	$22.95	___
___	1-57248-235-4	The Entrepreneur's Legal Guide	$26.95	___	___	1-57248-366-0	Tax Smarts for Small Business	$21.95	___
___	1-57248-346-6	Essential Guide to Real Estate Contracts (2E)	$18.95	___	___	1-57248-335-0	Traveler's Rights	$21.95	___
___	1-57248-160-9	Essential Guide to Real Estate Leases	$18.95	___	___	1-57248-236-2	Unmarried Parents' Rights (2E)	$19.95	___
___	1-57248-254-0	Family Limited Partnership	$26.95	___	___	1-57248-362-8	U.S. Immigration and Citizenship Q&A	$16.95	___
___	1-57248-331-8	Gay & Lesbian Rights	$26.95	___	___	1-57248-387-3	U.S. Immigration Step by Step (2E)	$24.95	___
___	1-57248-139-0	Grandparents' Rights (3E)	$24.95	___	___	1-57248-392-X	U.S.A. Immigration Guide (5E)	$26.95	___
___	1-57248-188-9	Guía de Inmigración a Estados Unidos (3E)	$24.95	___	___	1-57248-192-7	The Visitation Handbook	$18.95	___
___	1-57248-187-0	Guía de Justicia para Víctimas del Crimen	$21.95	___	___	1-57248-225-7	Win Your Unemployment Compensation Claim (2E)	$21.95	
___	1-57248-253-2	Guía Esencial para los Contratos de Arrendamiento de Bienes Raices	$22.95		___	1-57248-330-X	The Wills, Estate Planning and Trusts Legal Kit	&26.95	___
___	1-57248-103-X	Help Your Lawyer Win Your Case (2E)	$14.95	___	___	1-57248-138-2	Winning Your Personal Injury Claim (2E)	$24.95	___
___	1-57248-334-2	Homeowner's Rights	$21.95	___	___	1-57248-333-4	Working with Your Homeowners Association	$19.95	___
___	1-57248-164-1	How to Buy a Condominium or Townhome (2E)	$19.95	___	___	1-57248-162-5	Your Right to Child Custody, Visitation and Support (2E)	$24.95	___
___	1-57248-328-8	How to Buy Your First Home	$18.95	___	___	1-57248-157-9	Your Rights When You Owe Too Much	$16.95	___
___	1-57248-191-9	How to File Your Own Bankruptcy (5E)	$21.95	___			**CALIFORNIA TITLES**		
___	1-57248-343-1	How to File Your Own Divorce (5E)	$26.95	___	___	1-57248-150-1	CA Power of Attorney Handbook (2E)	$18.95	___
1-57248-222-2		How to Form a Limited Liability Company (2E)	$24.95	___	___	1-57248-337-7	How to File for Divorce in CA (4E)	$26.95	___
___	1-57248-231-1	How to Form a Nonprofit Corporation (2E)	$24.95	___	___	1-57248-145-5	How to Probate and Settle an Estate in CA	$26.95	___
___	1-57248-345-8	How to Form Your Own Corporation (4E)	$26.95	___	___	1-57248-336-9	How to Start a Business in CA (2E)	$21.95	___
___	1-57248-224-9	How to Form Your Own Partnership (2E)	$24.95	___	___	1-57248-194-3	How to Win in Small Claims Court in CA (2E)	$18.95	___
___	1-57248-232-X	How to Make Your Own Simple Will (3E)	$18.95	___	___	1-57248-246-X	Make Your Own CA Will	$18.95	___
___	1-57248-200-1	How to Register Your Own Copyright (4E)	$24.95	___	___	1-57248-196-X	The Landlord's Legal Guide in CA	$24.95	___
___	1-57248-104-8	How to Register Your Own Trademark (3E)	$21.95	___	___	1-57248-241-9	Tenants' Rights in CA	$21.95	___
___	1-57248-233-8	How to Write Your Own Living Will (3E)	$18.95	___			**FLORIDA TITLES**		
___	1-57248-156-0	How to Write Your Own Premarital Agreement (3E)	$24.95		___	1-57071-363-4	Florida Power of Attorney Handbook (2E)	$16.95	___
___	1-57248-230-3	Incorporate in Delaware from Any State	$26.95	___	___	1-57248-176-5	How to File for Divorce in FL (7E)	$26.95	___
___	1-57248-158-7	Incorporate in Nevada from Any State	$24.95	___	___	1-57248-356-3	How to Form a Corporation in FL (6E)	$24.95	___
___	1-57248-250-8	Inmigración a los EE.UU. Paso a Paso	$22.95	___	___	**Form Continued on Following Page**		**SubTotal**	___
___	1-57071-333-2	Jurors' Rights (2E)	$12.95	___					
___	1-57248-223-0	Legal Research Made Easy (3E)	$21.95						

To order, call Sourcebooks at 1-800-432-7444 or FAX (630) 961-2168 (Bookstores, libraries, wholesalers—please call for discount)

Prices are subject to change without notice.

Find more legal information at: **www.SphinxLegal.com**

SPHINX® PUBLISHING ORDER FORM

Qty	ISBN	Title	Retail	Ext.
___	1-57248-203-6	How to Form a Limited Liability Co. in FL (2E)	$24.95	___
___	1-57071-401-0	How to Form a Partnership in FL	$22.95	___
___	1-57248-113-7	How to Make a FL Will (6E)	$16.95	___
___	1-57248-088-2	How to Modify Your FL Divorce Judgment (4E)	$24.95	___
___	1-57248-354-7	How to Probate and Settle an Estate in FL (5E)	$26.95	___
___	1-57248-339-3	How to Start a Business in FL (7E)	$21.95	___
___	1-57248-204-4	How to Win in Small Claims Court in FL (7E)	$18.95	___
___	1-57248-381-4	Land Trusts in Florida (7E)	$29.95	___
___	1-57248-338-5	Landlords' Rights and Duties in FL (9E)	$22.95	___

GEORGIA TITLES

Qty	ISBN	Title	Retail	Ext.
___	1-57248-340-7	How to File for Divorce in GA (5E)	$21.95	___
___	1-57248-180-3	How to Make a GA Will (4E)	$21.95	___
___	1-57248-341-5	How to Start a Business in Georgia (3E)	$21.95	___

ILLINOIS TITLES

Qty	ISBN	Title	Retail	Ext.
___	1-57248-244-3	Child Custody, Visitation, and Support in IL	$24.95	___
___	1-57248-206-0	How to File for Divorce in IL (3E)	$24.95	___
___	1-57248-170-6	How to Make an IL Will (3E)	$16.95	___
___	1-57248-247-8	How to Start a Business in IL (3E)	$21.95	___
___	1-57248-252-4	The Landlord's Legal Guide in IL	$24.95	___

MARYLAND, VIRGINIA AND THE DISTRICT OF COLUMBIA

Qty	ISBN	Title	Retail	Ext.
___	1-57248-240-0	How to File for Divorce in MD, VA and DC	$28.95	___
___	1-57248-359-8	How to Start a Business in MD, VA or DC	$21.95	___

MASSACHUSETTS TITLES

Qty	ISBN	Title	Retail	Ext.
___	1-57248-128-5	How to File for Divorce in MA (3E)	$24.95	___
___	1-57248-115-3	How to Form a Corporation in MA	$24.95	___
___	1-57248-108-0	How to Make a MA Will (2E)	$16.95	___
___	1-57248-248-6	How to Start a Business in MA (3E)	$21.95	___
___	1-57248-209-5	The Landlord's Legal Guide in MA	$24.95	___

MICHIGAN TITLES

Qty	ISBN	Title	Retail	Ext.
___	1-57248-215-X	How to File for Divorce in MI (3E)	$24.95	___
___	1-57248-182-X	How to Make a MI Will (3E)	$16.95	___
___	1-57248-183-8	How to Start a Business in MI (3E)	$18.95	___

MINNESOTA TITLES

Qty	ISBN	Title	Retail	Ext.
___	1-57248-142-0	How to File for Divorce in MN	$21.95	___
___	1-57248-179-X	How to Form a Corporation in MN	$24.95	___
___	1-57248-178-1	How to Make a MN Will (2E)	$16.95	___

NEW JERSEY TITLES

Qty	ISBN	Title	Retail	Ext.
___	1-57248-239-7	How to File for Divorce in NJ	$24.95	___

NEW YORK TITLES

Qty	ISBN	Title	Retail	Ext.
___	1-57248-193-5	Child Custody, Visitation and Support in NY	$26.95	___
___	1-57248-351-2	File for Divorce in NY	$26.95	___
___	1-57248-249-4	How to Form a Corporation in NY (2E)	$24.95	___
___	1-57248-095-5	How to Make a NY Will (2E)	$16.95	___
___	1-57248-199-4	How to Start a Business in NY (2E)	$18.95	___
___	1-57248-198-6	How to Win in Small Claims Court in NY (2E)	$18.95	___
___	1-57248-197-8	Landlords' Legal Guide in NY	$24.95	___
___	1-57071-188-7	New York Power of Attorney Handbook	$19.95	___
___	1-57248-122-6	Tenants' Rights in NY	$21.95	___

NORTH CAROLINA TITLES

Qty	ISBN	Title	Retail	Ext.
___	1-57248-185-4	How to File for Divorce in NC (3E)	$22.95	___
___	1-57248-129-3	How to Make a NC Will (3E)	$16.95	___
___	1-57248-184-6	How to Start a Business in NC (3E)	$18.95	___
___	1-57248-091-2	Landlords' Rights & Duties in NC	$21.95	___

NORTH CAROLINA AND SOUTH CAROLINA TITLES

Qty	ISBN	Title	Retail	Ext.
___	1-57248-371-7	How to Start a Business in NC or SC	$24.95	___

OHIO TITLES

Qty	ISBN	Title	Retail	Ext.
___	1-57248-190-0	How to File for Divorce in OH (2E)	$24.95	___
___	1-57248-174-9	How to Form a Corporation in OH	$24.95	___
___	1-57248-173-0	How to Make an OH Will	$16.95	___

PENNSYLVANIA TITLES

Qty	ISBN	Title	Retail	Ext.
___	1-57248-242-7	Child Custody, Visitation and Support in PA	$26.95	___
___	1-57248-211-7	How to File for Divorce in PA (3E)	$26.95	___
___	1-57248-358-X	How to Form a Croporation in PA	$24.95	___
___	1-57248-094-7	How to Make a PA Will (2E)	$16.95	___
___	1-57248-357-1	How to Start a Business in PA (3E)	$21.95	___
___	1-57248-245-1	The Landlord's Legal Guide in PA	$24.95	___

TEXAS TITLES

Qty	ISBN	Title	Retail	Ext.
___	1-57248-171-4	Child Custody, Visitation, and Support in TX	$22.95	___
___	1-57248-172-2	How to File for Divorce in TX (3E)	$24.95	___
___	1-57248-114-5	How to Form a Corporation in TX (2E)	$24.95	___
___	1-57248-255-9	How to Make a TX Will (3E)	$16.95	___
___	1-57248-214-1	How to Probate and Settle an Estate in TX (3E)	$26.95	___
___	1-57248-228-1	How to Start a Business in TX (3E)	$18.95	___
___	1-57248-111-0	How to Win in Small Claims Court in TX (2E)	$16.95	___
___	1-57248-355-5	The Landlord's Legal Guide in TX	$24.95	___

SubTotal This page ___

SubTotal previous page ___

Shipping— $5.00 for 1st book, $1.00 each additional ___

Illinois residents add 6.75% sales tax ___

Connecticut residents add 6.00% sales tax ___

_Total ___

To order, call Sourcebooks at 1-800-432-7444 or FAX (630) 961-2168 (Bookstores, libraries, wholesalers—please call for discount)

Prices are subject to change without notice.

Find more legal information at: **www.SphinxLegal.com**